ODDS

a compilation of fantastic yet true pioneer tales

& ENDS

ODDS & ENDS

a compilation of fantastic yet true pioneer tales

SHIRLEY
BAHLMANN

CFI
AN IMPRINT OF CEDAR FORT, INC.
SPRINGVILLE, UTAH

Publisher's Note

The stories in *Odds and Ends* were first published in Shirley Bahlmann's *Against All Odds*, *Isn't That Odd*, and *Odd People.* We are now pleased to bring you these stories in a brand new compilation.

Disclaimer

The author has made every effort to report the facts correctly as far as her research allowed. It is interesting to note that even in different accounts of the same incident, the "facts" are sometimes reported differently, depending on the point of view of the person telling the story.

Sometimes several stories are combined into one for a richer reading experience, and because they fit so well together.

Most of these stories were researched from the "Saga of the Sanpitch" publications. Some are oral histories told to the author.

The author anticipates that people of both genders and all ages will enjoy these unusual tales. It is hoped that anyone who might be related to the people in these stories will find them to be very close to the traditions that have been passed down from generation to generation.

ISBN 13: 978-1-4621-1234-0

Published by CFI, an imprint of Cedar Fort, Inc.
2373 W. 700 S., Springville, UT 84663
Distributed by Cedar Fort, Inc., www.cedarfort.com

Library of Congress Cataloging-in-Publication data on file

Cover design by Shawnda T. Craig
Cover design © 2013 by Lyle Mortimer

Printed in the United States of America

10 9 8 7 6 5 4 3 2 1

CONTENTS

AUTHOR'S NOTE

I have made every effort to portray the events herein as accurately as possible within the framework of first-person narrative, adding details that I felt would enhance the story and convey its message with maximum impact. I used various historical documents, various family histories, out-of-print books, and oral accounts to compile this collection of stories. It is my wish that all who read these accounts, whether they're familiar with the stories or not, will find value in them and use the life lessons they teach to better their own lives and the lives of others.

—Shirley Bahlmann

PART I
AGAINST ALL ODDS

STRANGE BEDFELLOWS

They always came in the dark, like nightmares. Through the window, I saw their painted faces, flickering like demons in the torchlight. The shadows danced and crawled across their angry features as if they had lives of their own.

Trembling, I slid down under the window and covered my eyes. But I could still hear them. Their voices were low and muffled, a threatening buzzing sound, like bees upset from their hive.

I could smell the smoke from their torches, implements of torture that they used to start houses and sometimes people on fire.

Any second now they would reach the front door. They would pound it, smash the wood, break it down. They would swarm through the house, breaking dishes, tearing books, throwing bedcovers off to look underneath, ripping out clothes to search wardrobes. They would find me. They would grab me by the hair and drag me outside, thumping my body down the bare wooden steps, laughing at my pain. They would beat me, unless I could escape.

My eyes snapped open as fear yanked me awake and pushed me upright. My heart hammered painfully, my breathing was fast. My legs were twitching to run until I caught sight of my mother bending over a cooking fire at the mouth of the dugout. I could smell the lingering torch smoke, but it came from the cooking fire, not the mob. The hated mob was gone.

When I saw that I was safe, the fear leaked out of my muscles and I fell back onto my bed of blankets, trembling.

The mobs with their smoking torches, guns, knives, sickening burning hot tar and feathers were a thousand miles away in Illinois and Missouri. They were too cowardly to follow us across the wilderness to Utah, to this place called Manti. They would never find me in this dugout, those evil, shrivel hearted people, who hated us Mormons for no reason.

We had done nothing to them, yet they burned our homes, beat us, stole from us, and drove us out. I had seen them strip people, scorch their screaming bodies with burning hot tar that stuck like a second skin, then stick feathers to the tar for further humiliation. When the tar was eventually peeled off the victim by loving friends and family, skin usually came off, too.

Those mobs were worse than the Indians. Even though both groups painted their faces, took prisoners, and were cruel to their enemies, the Indians were more honorable than those hated mobs. If the Ute Indians attacked, you knew it was them, and they didn't pretend it wasn't. They did not deny it. Fighting was their way of life.

The mobs disguised themselves so that after their night of evil acts, they could go to church the next day. They would smile, greet their neighbors, and entertain in their parlors. If they heard about the burnings and killings, those horrid hypocrites would act surprised, as though they knew nothing about it.

I thought of Papa, and then angrily rubbed my stinging eyes. Crying wouldn't bring him back no matter how much I missed him. It still twisted my insides in knots and made me feel sick when I remembered his gentle face contorted with fear as the mob dragged him out of our house and out of my life forever.

At Papa's funeral, Bishop Whitmer said we should forgive our enemies. He said Papa was joyfully serving our Lord and Savior, and was far from the pain, sorrow, and toil of this life. I could not get past my own misery to feel joy for my father. I could not wait to leave that hellish place and those vicious people.

I smiled a hard little smile to myself as I remembered overhearing Sister Siddons say to Mama, "That Annie of yours works like a boy!" I knew I had worked long and tirelessly to get our handcart ready. I did it because I had to get out of that place of evil. Mama had never been the same since Papa was taken from us. She couldn't seem to decide what to do unless I told her. It wasn't that she was weak-minded. She was just scared. I don't think she would have gone on the trek to Utah if I hadn't insisted. She followed me across the rivers, plains, and through the mountain passes.

Any time I felt hot, tired, hungry, dirty, itchy, sick, or scared while walking and walking and walking to get to Salt Lake City, I repeated to myself, "We're going to a better place. We're going to a better place." It helped me to make it. I felt like I could do anything. Being a girl could not stop me. Being thirteen years old could not stop me. Being hungry and cold could not stop me.

When we got to Salt Lake City, there wasn't much there. I was happy to dig in and help, for when I was working hard, I didn't have time to re-live my horrible memories.

Then a Ute Indian chief named Walkara, or Walker as some settlers called him, came to Salt Lake City and told Brigham Young he wanted him to send some settlers to San Pitch, in central Utah. He said he would welcome the white man to this valley, to teach his people farming and the white man's ways. When President Young decided to send settlers, he asked for volunteers. I convinced Mama that we should go. It's hard to explain, but it seemed to me that if I could get to a brand new place, where no one had settled before, I could finally feel safe.

It was cold November when we got to the barren valley. Mama and I settled in a dugout on the south side of a hill. Bishop Morley said the hill would be used for building a temple. Most of the other families made dugouts, too. It was hard work to get our dugouts large enough to live in. The Coxes wanted us to move into theirs, but I said no. I'd had enough of people being able to watch me walk, eat, sleep, scratch myself, blow my nose, and do my private business on the trek. Now I wanted walls. I needed walls. It didn't matter if they were wood, brick, rock or dirt—just so they were walls.

Mama helped dig out the dirt to enlarge our primitive little home. She stopped when she was tired. I kept working. Some of the men helped us, which was fine with me, but I didn't ask them for their help. We finally had our own place, Mama and me.

A few other families simply tipped their wagons over and put a tarp over the top keep out the snow. It was easier than digging, but I secretly thought the dugout was better. There were no drafts at the back, and when the sun was out it shone right into our place, warming things up and lifting my spirits.

As the cold, bitter winter of 1849–50 wore on, the wagon tippers realized what poor shelters they had against the elements, and many of them moved into dugouts, too.

Now that the winter was almost over, I was thankful the past two weeks had been steadily warming up. It felt like spring was finally, really and truly, coming to this wild valley. I was filled with a renewed determination to get started on a cabin for my mother and me. I'd never built a house before, but I told myself I could do it.

After our meager breakfast, I went out to the spot where Mama's and my house would be. I had borrowed a shovel. I wasn't sure whose it was, but it didn't really matter, because we all shared pretty much everything.

I struggled through the sticky mud, which sucked and pulled at my high-buttoned shoes. I traced a shallow trench for what I thought was a pretty good house. It was not too big because Mama and me didn't need much. I imagined where the kitchen would be, and in my mind I put a bed in the farthest corner, on the east side where the sun would wake us up in the morning.

I felt better when I was done, as I always did when carrying out a plan. That night I went to bed with a light heart.

I woke up to an eerie gray stillness. A sense of unease and foreboding had replaced my earlier optimism. Although this morning was the warmest one yet, I thought that if I built a fire, it might shake off the bad feeling I had. Just doing something normal and routine should help me feel better. I got up quietly so as not to wake Mama, built a tinder pile in the cooking pit, and then reached for a smooth stick that I could see out of the corner of my eye. When I grabbed it, it moved. I yanked my hand back and screamed. I stared at the "stick," horrified as it coiled up and raised its head. It was a snake!

Mama sat up from her blanket pile. "What is it?" she asked.

"Snake!" I squealed. When I heard the panic in my voice, I was embarrassed. I told myself to calm down, that I had been through much worse in my life than a snake.

I noticed my mother's blanket moving, and thought she was getting up to help me. Then I realized that she was sitting stock-still, staring down in silent, horror-stricken fascination at a crawling, twisting pile of snakes writhing on her lap.

An urgent need to protect my mother prompted me to action. I grabbed the bottom edge of her quilt and pulled it off of her, then dragged it out of the cave opening, rolling it down the hill with a swift kick of my foot.

"Rattlesnakes," Mama said, standing up in her nightgown and nightcap. "They're poisonous." She looked frail and childlike, standing there, wringing her hands, and biting her lip to keep from crying.

I was angry. We had been through enough. I grabbed the shovel I'd used the day before, and I hit the snake lying beside the cooking pit over and over again until I was sure that it was dead. Then I scooped it up and threw it out of the dugout.

As I turned to go back inside, a snake plopped down on the ground next to me. I cringed and looked up. Squirming out of the cracks in the ledge above our dugout were more rattlesnakes. Some of them dripped down the sides of the rocks like pus out of an infected wound. Some dropped to the ground where they landed in the dugout doorway forming a writhing, twisted pile. They were too cold to move fast, but they were moving.

I thought of the plagues of Egypt from the Bible. What had we done so wrong? Hadn't we suffered enough? What did God want from us? My jaw clenched. My muscles tightened. I was too angry to cry or even to feel scared. I lifted my shovel again, and beat at the pile of snakes. I hit the ones on the rocks until they fell to the ground. I hardly thought about what I was doing. I just knew I had to protect my mother, and that nothing must happen to her. I needed her.

I heard some screams, and almost told Mama that it was all right, we'd be all right, we had to be all right, when I realized the screams were coming from the other dugouts. There was shouting, and banging. Mama stepped cautiously to the mouth of the dugout, shuddering at the snake bodies spread on the ground.

"There are more of them," she said almost hopelessly. "They're everywhere." I didn't have to guess what "they" were. It could only be snakes.

The first onslaught of snakes was killed in a couple of hours. Other people in the settlement were piling them up outside of their dugouts, too. Throughout that day, snakes would slither out of a crack, a partially-opened dresser drawer, or out from under a blanket. We were constantly vigilant and did not relax, even when the sun started to go down.

The Indians had been watching our unusual behavior from their camp. Chief Walkara, along with some braves and squaws, came over to see what new and strange activity these pale-faced people were doing.

His dark face fascinated me as I watched him approach the hill. When he caught sight of the snake piles, his eyes lit up and shone like black stars.

"You have many great snakes," he complimented Isaac Morley, our settlement leader and bishop who was often fondly addressed as "Father Morley."

"Yes, too many snakes," replied Father Morley.

"You no want, we take," Walkara said eagerly.

"You want these snakes? What for?"

"Plenty good. We eat, use skins, much good snakes."

Father Morley spread his hands toward the snakes. "They're yours," he smiled.

The chief gave a curt order to his Indians in their language. His underlings gathered the dead snakes onto hides with sticks, then folded up the corners of the hides and carried them away. I found out later that even dead snakes can bite. It's a reflex action, but it's just as poisonous as if they're alive.

I hate to admit that my Plagues of Egypt complaint was unjustified.

No one was bitten by the three hundred snakes that were killed that day. When the infestation was over, about five hundred snakes were dead. They had been found everywhere, in people's beds, clothing, even cooking pots.

It was a blessing that everyone survived the spring awakening of hundreds of poisonous serpents, but another benefit was the Indians. Getting a feast of snakes from us put the Indians in such a good mood that they helped us with our spring planting.

I repented of my anger toward God. I finally understood what "blessing in disguise" meant.

The first settlers to Manti arrived in November and built dugouts in what is now Temple Hill to shelter them for the winter. In the spring, rattlesnakes coming out of winter hibernation crawled through the dugouts. The pioneers killed about 500 snakes, and the Indians were glad to receive them as gifts.

BUFFALO TAG

"Wake up, Sloppy Joe," I said as I poked my finger into my twin brother's ear. He jerked his head away and flailed his arms as though to ward off a whole swarm of horseflies. I laughed as he opened his eyes, sat up, and glared at me.

"Why should I, Miss Maggie Messy?" he said testily.

"Because if you don't, all the soda bread will be gone, and you won't get any breakfast."

Joe moaned and fell back onto his blanket. "If I have to eat any more soda bread, I think I will die," he groaned.

"You'll definitely die if you don't eat," I retorted.

"I'll eat something else," Joe said in a small, hopeful voice.

"Help yourself," I said smugly. "There's plenty of grass growing here beside the trail. I'm sure the horses and oxen won't mind sharing."

Joe covered up his face with his blanket, and I got up and walked over to the fire where Ma was patting the mixture of flour, water, baking soda, and a little salt—if Ma remembered, into flat little discs. As much as I teased Joe about the soda bread that we had to eat since our supplies were running dangerously low, I didn't relish the thought of eating it any more than he did. I just had to pretend I didn't care because then it bothered him more.

Ma was never careful about getting all the bugs out of the flour. The resulting hard, flat cakes were often speckled with insect parts. They were hard to chew and had a tang from the soda that left a bad aftertaste. The only thing that kept me from despair was that the mountains were in sight. We were almost to Zion.

"Margaret, please get me some water," Ma said as she plunked a piece of soda dough into the hot pan supported over the fire on a couple of flat rocks. She pushed her hair back off her forehead with the back of her hand. Even though it was a moderately cool morning, Ma's face was red and sweating from working beside the fire. Ma looked up at me and smiled hopefully. "Don't you think you're old enough to start pinning your hair up?"

I shook my head hard, enjoying the feel of the braid that danced down my back. I could also feel the loose hair that had pulled out of the braid, which tickled my face and neck as I slept. I imagined that I did look rather messy. But I also felt free. If I had my way, I'd never be old enough for stiff corsets and hard pins to scrape my head in the effort to create ridiculous, elaborate hairdos.

I took pity on my mother and picked up the wooden pail that sat beside our handcart, then made my way over to the stream beside our camp. The water rolled and chuckled in the early morning light, and I took the liberty of sticking my feet into it. I gasped at the cold, but relished the clean feeling of the water running over my dusty bare feet, swirling in between my tired toes and washing away all the fatigue that was left over from spending another night sleeping on the ground. Once we reached the promised land, the Zion of Salt Lake City, I would have a bed to sleep on again.

I sighed as the smell of scorched soda bread reached my nose, and lowered the bucket into the water, careful to dip it upstream from my dirty feet, and lugged it over to our campfire. Joe was sitting by Ma, forlornly picking at his portion of soda bread. Just as I let the bucket thud to the ground, I heard shouting.

"Buffalo!"

"Buffalo! C'mon, men!"

"Get your rifles!"

The camp jumped to life as several of the men grabbed their guns and jumped on their horses. I was amazed to see them ride toward a herd of buffalo that was leisurely grazing out from behind a hill on the opposite stream bank. I had just been sitting there and hadn't noticed them.

The nearest bison raised their dark, shaggy heads and looked curiously at the hunters as they splashed across the stream. They seemed interested, but not particularly alarmed.

Joe appeared at my side, looking triumphant. "There's your answer to this old soda bread!" he said, waving his scorched brown bread disc under my nose.

"Don't count your buffalo before they're skinned," I said.

"Aw, what do you know?" Joe said impatiently. "I could throw a rock and hit one from here!"

"You only wish you could," I said.

"Well, I'm not going to prove it to you. I might mess up the hunt," Joe said stoutly.

Then, seeing the scowl on his face and feeling sorry that I'd spoken unkindly, I said, "Let's go closer."

We walked together to the edge of the stream and watched the hunters approach the herd. If the buffalo didn't spook and run, we would be able to see the whole hunt from where we stood. I felt my mouth water and my stomach rumble at the thought of fresh meat roasting on our fire. One of those huge buffalo would feed the whole camp. Two would probably get us to Salt Lake City.

I jumped as Henry Shomaker's rifle suddenly exploded a bullet from its barrel, then saw the buffalo that was his target, the biggest one in the herd. I also saw a puff of dust kick up on the ground just beyond the big, shaggy bull. My heart sank with disappointment. Brother Shomaker had missed!

Then, faster than I would have thought an animal as big and heavy as that one could move, the old bull took off running at Brother Shomaker, its head lowered as it pointed its heavy black horns directly at horse and rider. I clutched Joe's sleeve and pointed.

"Turn the horse, turn the horse, turn the horse," Joe advised rapidly under his breath as Brother Shomaker hesitated. It seemed a long time, although it was really only a couple of seconds, before Brother Shomaker finally twisted on his saddle in a desperate turn, and the horse followed his lead, needing no urging to gallop as fast as she could away from the shaggy black menace that was chasing her with appallingly sharp horns.

Brother Shomaker kept glancing back over his shoulder at the buffalo that was hot on his trail. I was close enough to see the fear on his face, his mouth open in mute disbelief, his eyes wide as they cast behind him, then darted forward as though desperately seeking an escape route that hadn't been there the last time he looked.

The bull seemed to be closing in. What his wickedly pointed horns and sheer weight could do to a person, I didn't even want to imagine. Still holding onto Joe's shirt, I clasped my hands together for a brief, desperate prayer, "Oh, please help him," I breathed.

"Amen," said Joe, his eyes glued to the terrified rider.

Then I screamed. It was a short scream that just sort of squeezed out of me when I saw Brother Shomaker vault off his horse and land in a rolling heap on the hard prairie floor. He tumbled along until he hit into a large clump of grass, then he collapsed and lay still. I held my breath as the buffalo approached the fallen man. Then I let it out again in a big whoosh of relief as the huge beast thundered past Brother Shomaker, his eye and his aim on the unfortunate horse.

I didn't know if Brother Shomaker was dead, but I saw a couple of the mounted men riding toward him. I knew there was nothing I could do for him, so I let my eyes follow the horse.

Mouth open, hooves pounding, mane twisting in the artificial wind created by her speed, the horse tried vainly to outrun the angry buffalo. As soon as the big bull drew close enough, he stabbed his lowered horns into the horse's backside and gave a mighty toss of his massive head. The horse flipped up and over in a perfect somersault.

His attackers dispatched, the bull turned and trotted back to the center of the herd, seemingly satisfied that he had done a good day's work.

The horse struggled pitifully and finally got up, limping her way as fast as she could toward camp and the companionship of the other riderless horses. Brother Shomaker was brought in on the back of Brother Dayton's horse. He was bruised, scraped, and shaken up, but not broken.

His horse was worse off. She had deep cuts where the buffalo horns had gouged her flanks. She was bruised and skittish. Her wounds were doctored, and she eventually recovered. She had to be led riderless along the trail when we finally took up our journey again.

We had a slight delay as we cut up buffalo meat and smoked it on our campfires. The smell alone was almost enough to sustain me for the rest of the trek to Salt Lake City.

I did learn one thing. Never tease a buffalo. They have no sense of humor. Just like some people I know.

When charged by a buffalo on the prairie, a hunter leaped off his galloping horse in an effort to escape. The horse got flipped in a somersault when the buffalo tossed it with his horns. The horse and rider both survived.

BLOODY FINGER

I tried to work the sliver out with my fingernails, but it was in too deep. My finger was really starting to hurt.

I had felt the sliver go in when I hurried to grab up the firewood for the cook stove earlier that morning, but ignored it. It had seemed more important to get away to my friend Ann Olsen's than to get out a little sliver. Being the oldest of five children, and a girl at that, made me the most likely to get more chores if Mama thought of any before I left. I had to hurry!

Mama had let me deliver diaper flannel to the Olsen's, and I was happy to do it so I could visit Ann. Now the mile home was growing longer than the mile I'd walked to Olsen's. I trudged down the dusty trail in my long, hot skirt, shaking my head at the flies that buzzed around my sweaty face. I could have borrowed the Olsen's needle to dig out the sliver, if they still had one. Needles were precious and easy to lose. But I hadn't even thought to ask.

My miserable reverie was broken by the sound of pounding feet and a strange gagging sound. Startled, I twisted around to look behind me, my heart jumping, until I saw that it was just Will Jorgensen lumbering along the track toward me. He was running a wobbly course, and he kept swiping his hand at his eyes as he ran. He didn't seem to be able to see very well, for he would occasionally crash his big leg through a gray-green sagebrush by the side of the trail. It did not even slow him down.

Alarmed by his behavior, I wondered whether he was being attacked by bees or if he had been bitten by a rattlesnake and was going crazy from the poison. I didn't know much about rattlesnakes except that the first people that settled San Pitch Valley had killed a whole pile of them after they arrived.

Will was a big bully. I had seen him mimicking lame old Brother Hancock's crooked walk. I thought it was tragic that Brother Hancock had to have part of his frozen feet cut off at Winter Quarters. Will was mean to me, too, calling me names when no adults were around. He pushed little kids who got in his way. I had seen him throw rocks at dogs, even though President Brigham Young had told us to be kind to animals.

It surprised me to see big, mean Will run past me with what looked like tears running down his face! The gagging noise sounded more and more like crying. He didn't even seem to see me, which was unusual since I was the only other person in sight on the sagebrush flat. I had never seen Will act like this. My slivered finger forgotten, I walked faster, but still couldn't catch up to Will. I wanted to tell my mother what had happened.

Mama was a small, smiling, busy woman. I took after Papa, and had already grown taller than her. Her good nature was contagious. Even after crossing the plains with her six children, doing her best to provide for us from the supplies in a small handcart, and suffering the heartbreak of our baby brother Martin dying along the way, she still had a joy for living. I wondered what she would say about Will.

As soon as I got home, I reached for the latchstring that was supposed to be threaded through the small hole in the door. The string was attached to a crossbar that held the door closed on the inside. But the latchstring, which was really a strand of leather, wasn't there, so I couldn't pull the crossbar out of the metal bracket to get the door open. As I stared at the empty hole, which was about as big around as a finger, I felt a flash of irritation. Ned or Sam was playing tricks on me again.

"Let me in!" I called through the hole as I pounded on the door. After a few seconds, Ned pulled the door open. One look at his pale, somber face changed my mind about yelling at him. I couldn't remember the last time he had been so scared. I felt uneasy as I glanced around the room and saw our mother sitting on a chair, looking at the floor.

"What's wrong?" I asked fearfully, my stomach tightening as I imagined little Rosalie deathly ill, or Samuel having fallen down the well and broken an important bone. "Oh, Carrie," she whispered, "Indians."

I was confused. The Indians had originally welcomed us. I still wasn't used to them, even though they occasionally came to our homes, especially on baking day. They really liked our bread.

Mama followed Brigham Young's advice and would give them bread or old clothes if she had any. I wondered if the Indians had come and taken all our food while I was gone to the Olsen's.

"Indians?" I said stupidly.

"They killed some men who were working in the fields this morning," Mother put her hands up to cover her eyes.

"Who?" I asked, my heart squeezing painfully in a sudden spasm, "Not . . . ?"

"No, not your father," Mother quickly replied. "It was Brother Meade and young Simon Jorgensen."

I sank to the floor, my knees weak with relief and dread, and wondered just how it had happened. I imagined thin, old, dour-looking Mr. Meade out working in the fields in his faded brown hat, and Simon Jorgensen, eighteen years old, with a square, pleasant face and a wry humor, who'd only come to our settlement last winter.

I couldn't help wondering about the details. Were the two men hoeing? Changing irrigation water? Did the Indians sneak up, or did they charge down on their horses, hollering? Were the men scared? Why did the Indians do it? Did they want to steal something? Was it revenge for something we didn't even know we did wrong? Were they in a bad mood? Would they attack again? Would they come to my house?

My whirling thoughts settled on the fact that Simon had moved here to live with his older brother, Lars, who was Will's father. Simon was Will's uncle. Being so close to Will's age, though, he'd been more like a big brother to him. Now Will's behavior this morning made sense! Poor Will. I never thought I'd feel sorry for that bully.

Perhaps my slumped posture, or the look on my face triggered some resolve inside my mother, for she got up briskly and, although shorter than me, put out a hand to help me to my feet. I winced as she squeezed the slivered finger. After a brief examination, she went to fetch the needle. I hardly felt it as she dug the offending bit of wood out. Some things in life were worse than a sliver.

Just about everyone from town was at the funeral the next morning. The men stood around the outer edges of the gathering with their rifles in their hands, although I personally doubted whether the Indians would interrupt a funeral. I'd heard that they were very particular about not desecrating burial places, even those of their enemies.

I sneaked a glance at Will, who was standing close to his mother, his head bowed. He looked oddly like a small child in a too-large body, and seemed to want to hide behind his mother's dress. He kept swiping his hands at his eyes in an irritated, almost angry way.

Bishop Allred talked about Angus Meade and Simon Jorgensen going together like missionaries into the next life, and having work to do there. He said that Heavenly Father needed them more than we did, and that they were happy and wanted us to be happy, too. By the time he was done speaking, I did believe that Brother Meade and Simon were in a better place, but I still felt sorry for their families left behind.

I looked at my father, so much taller than Mother that she barely reached his shoulder, and I imagined that it could have been him killed.

I did not feel happy, even when we sang "Come, Come, Ye Saints," one of my favorite songs.

After the brief funeral, Papa said he was going to work in the fields. Mother looked at him in alarm.

"Today? Oh, Joseph!" she exclaimed.

"The fields must be tended and watered," he replied. "We must do our part, and the Lord will protect me or take me, whatever His will is. I could die standing right here, if it were His will. Remember, the Lord has a plan, and He is in charge. We need to go on with life as usual."

Mother embraced him, clasping his waist with her strong, slender arms. "You're not going alone?" she asked.

"No, the brethren decided that we should work in groups, with our guns at our sides," Father replied.

Mother wouldn't let any of us go outside, and eight-year-old Thelma didn't want to. Petite like our mother, she was quite a homebody. But unlike Mother, Thelma was timid and did not seek people out. She was content to sit at the table by the front door, peeling potatoes so Mother could make a fresh batch of sourdough starter out of potato water. Sam had accidentally thrown the last batch of sourdough start out the door, thinking it was sour mush. He decided that if he got rid of it, he wouldn't have to eat it. The starter was used like yeast to make bread rise light and airy before it was baked.

Some of the potatoes would also go into a venison stew for dinner with enough extra to take to the Meade and Jorgensen families after Papa got home.

Mother wouldn't even let Sam go out to the outhouse and told him to use the chamber pot in the cabin corner. The little ones got restless, whining and pulling hair and crying. I also felt trapped in our small adobe house. The two windows seemed very small. They were covered with oiled paper, which was much cheaper than glass, but you couldn't see through it.

I felt as though I needed air, and offered to take the children outside for a few minutes. Mother looked up at me with intense, searching eyes, and finally consented after I agreed to stay right by the house. I gratefully pulled up the latch and opened the door.

The summer heat hit my face as I led the children into the yard. Our adobe house stayed cool even in the summer, because the thick walls of dried mud kept out most of the heat. Rosalie burst out into the sunshine, her two-year-old legs running to the shade of the young Russian Olive tree by our house and plopping down in the dirt. Sam pulled out the stick horse Father had helped him make from a tree branch with some dried grass for a mane and tail. He began galloping around the house, but not for long because it was a hot afternoon. I was glad that Pettyville almost always cooled off at night from an evening breeze that wound its way down the canyon, blowing a cool breath across the valley.

We sat peacefully for a while, a few buzzing flies disturbing the quiet, until Sam stood up and pointed. "Horses!" he yelled excitedly. I wondered who was coming to visit. We didn't have a lot of horses. Most of us had arrived here by handcart, but there were some work horses and a few buggy pullers. I looked toward the veil of dust that was rapidly growing larger. It made me uneasy. It was coming from the mountains, not the fields or the direction of other houses in the settlement.

I suddenly called to Sam and ran over to snatch up Rosalie. Sam was reluctant to leave the yard, because he wanted to see the horses, which he loved. Ned opened the door before I could grab the latchstring. "Indians!" I almost sobbed at Ned's startled face. Mama overheard me. Her mouth a grim, straight line, she took Rosalie out of my arms and laid her on the big bed. Mama smiled at her and said, "You and Sam can play ships!" Sam bounded onto the bed and announced that he was captain. That was fine with Rosalie, who was perfectly content to be crew, passengers, or even a fish if that's what Sam wanted her to be.

Mama called me to help her move the washtub in front of the door. It was a meager effort to block the door, since even I could have pushed it aside if I had wanted to. As Mama straightened from pulling the washtub into place, I saw her lips moving, and guessed that she was praying. Her eyes lit on the latch bar, and the leather string that snaked out of the small hole. She reached out and pulled the string to the inside, leaving the bar resting in its iron arm, securely blocking the wooden door. She walked quickly around the single room, pausing in front of each window to fasten the wooden shutters and listen. The house darkened, but a little light still leaked through the windows. "Get under the bed," she said suddenly. Sam and Rosalie thought this was a fine new game. Ned helped by saying, "Let's pretend we're in a cave!" Thelma was much less enthusiastic, but tucked herself in under the headboard, obedient as usual.

By then, there was not enough room for me. We could distinctly hear the hoofbeats drawing rapidly closer. My heart began to pound. This was real. We were not pretending. The Indians had killed two men yesterday, and now they were here, at our house.

"Hide!" Mother commanded me, in an unusually high-pitched voice. I ducked under the kitchen table next to the front door. The horses stopped their rhythmic hoofbeats and began stepping quietly around in front of our house. I heard softer footfalls approaching, and listened as they circled the cabin, pausing at the windows.

Mother had flattened herself against the wall by the door, and jumped when the door suddenly vibrated with powerful hammering. Loud, heavy voices yelled something I could not understand.

I could hardly breathe and covered my ears with my hands and squeezed my knees between my elbows, but I couldn't stop staring at the door. I felt tight and scared inside. It seemed to me that by watching the door, I could somehow will it to stay closed and keep the danger outside.

The pounding stopped and the footfalls made their way around the cabin again, pausing at the windows as before. I could hear what sounded like arguing. The footsteps made their way to the front door again. I found myself praying that they would just go away and not hurt us. *Please go away. Papa, come home!*

Then I thought I heard laughter. It startled me. I did not see anything funny about our situation. It was strange to hear someone laughing when the fear I felt made me sick inside. I looked at the door, then almost choked on my fear. A dark, brown finger was poking through the latchstring hole and was feeling its way along the wooden bar where the string was attached. If that probing finger found the latchstring, it could pull it back through the hole and open the door!

I was so fixed on the horrifying sight that I didn't notice what my mother was doing until I saw her raise a large knife in her hands and bring it down on the finger with such force that it was completely severed from the hand in one blow. A loud scream from outside pierced my reserve, and I screamed, too, and began to shake. I heard screaming and crying from under the bed. Staring at the bloody brown finger on the floor, I started to cry.

The horses galloped away. As the sound of their hoof beats faded in the distance, I crawled out from under the table and found my mother leaning against the wall with her eyes closed and tears running down her cheeks. I grabbed her in a desperate hug, and it seemed to break whatever spell she was under.

She moved to the window, listened intently, then walked over to the bed and called the children out from under it. She fell down onto the comforter. Rosalie scrambled up to snuggle by Mother's side, Thelma climbed up and stroked her hand. Sam and Ned stared at the finger on the floor. "Mother, you are so brave!" Ned exclaimed in awe.

As Mother held her daughters, Ned used the stove poker to push the finger to the edge of the door. He quickly opened it, shoved the finger out, and slammed the door again. He led Sam by the hand to join us on the bed.

It was nearly dark when Papa got home from the fields. He listened to garbled accounts of the incident from several voices at once, then understood what had happened. He inspected the bloody stain on the floor, then scrubbed it with ashes and lye. He scraped and scrubbed until he got the stain out for Mama. His grave face looked around at each one of us, and he had us all kneel down and say a prayer of gratitude for our safety.

The next day, Papa didn't go to the fields. He began making adobes for an addition to the cabin. Ned and I helped set out the wooden block forms, mix the clay-like mud with straw to help hold the finished bricks together, and then added water from the well. We shoveled the mixture into the molds with satisfying plops. When they were all filled, we had to stop to let the bricks dry before we took the wooden frames off. That could take a week or more, depending on the weather.

Papa moved over to the dried logs he'd dragged down to the house from the river bottom and began cutting firewood. Ned and I hauled the cut wood to the woodpile.

Thelma came around the house and called to us to come and eat, then made a little choking sound. We looked up, wondering if she was all right. She was staring at the mountains. As I turned to follow her gaze, I felt my stomach clench. A dust cloud was working its way toward us. It looked just like the dust cloud from the day before. I momentarily felt courage that Papa was there, but then I realized that though he was big and strong, he could be killed just like Brother Meade and Simon Johansen.

"In the house," Papa said tersely. I was already on my way. I could only imagine what the Indians would do to us in revenge for cutting off one of their fingers. They couldn't set our adobe house on fire, because adobe wouldn't burn, but our front door was made of wood. I just hoped Papa knew what to do. He was right behind me as I quickly followed Ned through the door. "Lord help us," I heard him mutter.

Just like a nightmare, I heard the horse's hooves draw closer to our house until they stopped. My heart was squeezed so tight in fear, I wondered if it would hurt any worse to have an Indian arrow shot into it.

I crouched on the floor with Sam and Ned on either side, Rosalie on my lap. Thelma sat by Ned, clutching his arm and hiding her face in his shoulder.

Mama stood in front of us, the knife held firmly in her hand. The stiffness in her back reflected the look of grim determination she wore on her face. A small measure of comfort filled me knowing that she would defend us to the death. I bit my lip to keep from crying out loud. I did not want my mother dead!

Papa stood by the door, his rifle in his hands.

The footsteps did not go around the cabin like the day before. They walked up to the front door and then a knock sounded. There was no imperative hammering on the wood. I figured it could be a trick. Papa looked back at us, his eyes intense but unafraid. Then he turned back to the door.

I wanted to call out, "No!" when I saw Papa reach for the latch, but before my dry throat could form a sound, he'd opened the door wide enough that he could see out. I heard a guttural voice that spoke halting English say, "Where brave woman, cut off Indian finger?"

"What do you want with her?" Papa demanded.

"See brave woman. Good medicine," was the reply.

There was a long moment of silence. Then Papa opened the door all the way and called, "Elizabeth." Mother walked over and stood by him.

As he moved aside to make room for her in the doorway, I saw a dark brown face just outside the opening, with long black hair hanging down either side. There was a feather cocked sideways, sticking out from behind his head. His chest was bare, his mouth was held in a firm, straight line, but his dark eyes looked admiringly at my mother and took a lively interest in the knife she still clutched in her hand.

"Heap brave," he said respectfully as he held out his hand, which had some kind of wrapping that looked like leather with brown mossy packing sticking out the sides. Only three fingers and a thumb poked out from the primitive bandage.

His gesture was similar to what he'd seen white men do when they shake hands, but with the palm up. Mama glanced up at Papa, who nodded encouragingly at her. With the knife-free hand, Mother reached out and touched the Indian's upturned palm, below the bandage. He seemed satisfied, as though it were good medicine just to have her touch him. He moved aside, and another Indian appeared in the doorway, slightly shorter, a bit heavier, but also with a feather in his greasy black hair, and saying, "Heap brave," as he extended his hand toward Mother.

So it went, until every Indian in the raiding party of the day before had complimented Mother on her bravery and had a chance to touch her hand. Then they all got on their horses and I heard them ride away.

I got up with all the children and we embraced our parents. Papa had us kneel down right then and there, and offer up a prayer of thanks for our safety.

The Indians never bothered us again. There were times when they were in a bad mood, or angry, and attacked people, but not anyone at our house. The other mothers in the settlement would bring their children to our house for safety if they heard that the Indians were on the warpath. Their children were always safe in the home of "Heap brave woman."

A woman alone at home with her children in Pettyville (now a ghost town) cut off the finger of an Indian who was part of a raiding party when he tried to lift the door latch through the latch string hole. The next day the Indians returned to the house and praised the woman for her bravery, each one wanting to touch her for "good medicine." When they felt the need, other pioneer mothers brought their children to her house for safety because the Indians never bothered her or her household again.

SAVAGE SAMARITAN

I blew on my fingers to try to warm them up, but even my breath felt cold. I hunkered down by the small campfire.

"John!" I jumped up and whirled guiltily. My grandfather's icy blue eyes were fixed on me. "We need to make another wood run!" he snapped impatiently. As I left the only spot of warmth I had in the whole world, resentment seeped into my heart like cold into my clothes. I resented my father who had forced me to go on this adventure with a grandfather I barely knew.

Salt Canyon, east of Fort Nephi, had become my whole world since the supply wagons had gotten stuck in the blizzard. The snow was clear up past the wagon boxes and deeper than the wheels. It was frozen so hard, it would take a team of twenty horses to pull the wagons out.

Grandfather had thought of making shelters by digging a doorway out of the snow from under each of the wagons, leaving the rest of the snow around the sides, making windproof dugouts. Grandfather and I shared one, and Daniel Henrie and his young wife Amanda shared the other.

I dragged along behind my grandfather as we searched for wood. We'd burned all the fuel close to the wagons days before. I was so miserable I wasn't watching where we were going nor was I looking for wood as I was supposed to. I walked with my head down and followed the fresh footprints made by my grandfather who was breaking trail ahead of me.

I did not want to get to know this gruff man who was my dead mother's father. I did not like him. He was impatient and ornery. From the little I knew about him already, I could understand why Mother and Grandmother had stayed in the east when my restless Grandfather had come west. He'd been a mountain man for awhile, then settled down to a small ranch. He kept writing to Grandmother, trying to persuade her to join him, but she never did. And then she'd died.

My father had gone to college in New York, met my mother, and married her. After I was born, we had a perfectly happy little family, until the missionaries came. My mother and father joined The Church of Jesus Christ of Latter-day Saints and headed west for Zion, for a perfect life, for peace and happiness. My mother died on the trek. That took away my happiness. If I had even had a testimony before then, it died with my mother.

I was startled out of my miserable thoughts when I bumped into the back of my grandfather. I quickly stepped back, and he threw a disgusted look over his shoulder at me. Instead of speaking, he pointed, like I was some kind of dog that couldn't understand speech. I followed the direction of his rough, bony finger and saw a fallen tree lying on the south-facing hillside of the canyon. A skiff of snow still clung to the bark, but the biggest part of the frozen white powder had been blown away by the canyon breeze and melted off by the infrequent sun. Although my grandfather considered me "citified," even I could see that the tree was dead, and I knew what finding a whole tree of dead wood meant to our small encampment. Warmth. "That looks too big for us to pull," I said doubtfully.

"Of course it's too big! We're goin' back to get the horses."

We slipped and scrambled our way back to camp faster than we'd left. This time I was glad to keep my head up and look around as we stomped and slid through the frozen landscape. The snow actually appeared smooth, clean and pristine this morning. I was glad to be alive.

Amanda Henrie looked out from under her wagon when she heard us approach. In the early morning light, the jagged pink scar on her cheek stood out like a fresh brand on cattle. She had been living in Salt Lake when her husband's feisty black stallion had reared up and struck Amanda in the face with his front hoof, even though she had been standing on the other side of the fence. The horse did not live another day, as Dan Henrie had shot it.

Amanda Henrie was on her way to Manti to visit her parents as well as to help deliver the desperately-needed supplies to the new settlement. Although she was much younger than my own mother and had no children of her own, I had secretly begun to think of her as my substitute mother.

"You two look like you just found a hot spring!" she said. We grinned at her like two schoolboys. When she turned her head the other way and the scar didn't show, she was exceptionally pretty.

"We found us some wood," said Grandfather.

"Well, that is a good thing, we could always use more wood!" she smiled.

"It's a whole tree!" I gushed, then stopped, realizing I sounded like a little boy.

"Well, you just get that tree on over here and I'll cook you some breakfast!" Amanda said, and started mixing biscuits. At least we ate well, since we had two wagon loads of supplies intended for a settlement of over two hundred people.

Dan Henrie showed up from around the back of the wagons, walking a team of horses toward us. "I heard you talking," he said. "I'll gladly give you a hand to get that tree closer to the fire."

We guided the horses to the tree, hitched them up to the trunk, and "yee-hawed" them back to the camp. The team pulled the dry wood easily along the hillside that was blown almost barren of snow. They seemed happy to exercise their legs.

As we got closer to the campsite at the bottom of the canyon, the horses began to lunge and pull through the deep, frozen snow collected in the shadowy places and tucked down out of reach of the canyon breeze. Hooves slipped, and breath blew out in clouds as the horses scrabbled for solid footing. The stiff, wide branches of the tree swept out a broad pathway in the snow as the team fought to pull it back to our shelters. An occasional sagebrush or rock poked its way up in the wake of our tree plow.

Blowing and snorting, the horses finally made it to the campsite. Dan Henrie spoke to them in soothing tones, "That's a boy, Patch, good job, good job. You did it, Major, good boy, good job." His deep voice rumbled continual praise to the two animals as he unhitched them and led them around to the back of the wagons.

It had taken us longer than we thought to accomplish our task, so we had cold biscuits for breakfast. Amanda had collected snow into a pan and boiled it into water. When she saw us approaching, she'd dropped in a handful of the strangely jointed green stems that grew wild in Utah and boiled up into "Mormon Tea." We had plenty of sugar to sweeten it. I felt much more optimistic after drinking a cup of the hot, sweet liquid.

After breakfast, we all helped clear more snow away from the pasture where the horses were digging and scraping with their hooves to find food. We uncovered some sparse brown grass and the horses eagerly bent their heads to eat.

There wasn't much to do now that we were set up with wood and the horses had been provided for the best we could. When Grandfather went off with his rifle to hunt for fresh meat, I crawled under our wagon and allowed some time to feel sorry for myself.

I wanted to go back to New York, where Father and I belonged. We could be good Latter-day Saints there. Why did we have to live in this wilderness to worship God? Lots of people in the eastern states went to church. Even as I argued with myself, I knew Father was only trying to do what was right. He said we were needed here. He said Grandfather needed us, since we were the only family he had. He said we should be good examples, so Grandfather would want to join the church. I didn't think Grandfather even wanted us around. I fell asleep wishing that my mother could come back and make everything all better.

Some time later, I heard snow crunching outside the wagon. Looking out, I saw that Grandfather was empty-handed. I crawled out of the shelter, hoping it was almost time for dinner. As I stood, I noticed a movement far down along the wide swath we'd made with our firewood tree.

"Grandfather, look!"

"Shush, Boy, are ya tryin' to scare it away?"

Stung by the rebuke, I fell silent for a few moments. Watching the halting progress of the brown object became more engrossing than my self-pity, so I spoke again, more quietly, "It doesn't look like a deer."

"How would you know what a deer looks like?" Grandfather squinted into the sights on his rifle. I suspected that his eyesight was failing him, but he didn't want to admit it.

The object moved sporadically, like it was wounded. I wondered if Grandfather had shot something earlier and wounded it, and now he could finish the job. I kept waiting for the bang. Suddenly I reached up and grabbed the rifle barrel.

"It's a man!" I yelled.

"How could it be?" Grandfather snapped, but he lowered his rifle and concentrated more intently on the staggering figure.

Daniel Henrie came up behind us and also watched the unusual progress of the man. "I think he's hurt," he said. Almost as if he'd heard the words, the figure fell into the snow and lay still. Dan started out along the tree drug path to investigate. "It's a trick!" said Grandfather. Daniel Henrie put his hand out toward Grandfather, motioning him to stay back and be still. Curious, I took a couple of steps toward the fallen man. "Get back!" Grandfather barked at me.

We watched Dan reach the dark lump in the snow, bend, then stagger upright, the man supported on his right side. As he made his way toward us, he called out for help. I hurried toward him. My grandfather said something, but I wasn't sure what he said and pretended I didn't hear. I only hesitated for a second when I saw that what Dan was struggling to support was a bloody Indian. I got on the other side of the drooping figure and put my arm around his cold, stiff buckskin clothes. Together we walked him to the fire. As we laid him down, Grandfather said, "You'd best leave him die."

"I can't do that," replied Dan.

"Might be sorry later, if he gets well."

"I'll concern myself with that later."

Amanda Henrie seemed glad of something to do besides cooking, and set about tearing bandages and boiling water to clean the deep cuts that crisscrossed the Indian's muscled legs. She also found a deep wound in his side, and some smaller cuts on his hands. The Indian was bandaged and covered with blankets. Dan Henrie forced some Mormon Tea into his mouth. Although he didn't seem to be awake, the Indian swallowed.

Dan built a lean-to shelter close to the fire out of evergreen branches. More branches were spread on the ground, then a blanket, then the Indian was laid on the make shift bed with more blankets and a fur robe on top of him. Dan said he would get up every two or three hours to stoke the fire.

Grandfather had dire predictions for me that night as we bedded down in our shelter. I tried not to listen as he mumbled about being murdered in our beds and "can't expect no honor from savages."

After a couple of days, the Indian woke up. He spoke some pidgin English, and Dan Henrie spoke some Indian words, so they were able to communicate. I was fascinated by the exchange, and listened intently when Dan told us what had been said.

The Indian's name was Tabinaw, and he'd been on a raiding party to an enemy Indian camp. He'd been wounded while fighting from astride his horse. A spear had struck him in the side, almost unseating him. He'd been able to gallop out of the camp with his fellow raiders. After a few miles he was so weak, he could no longer sit on his horse. When his fellows saw his weakened condition, they took the horse and left him behind.

"Oh, how awful!" gasped Amanda Henrie, her eyes troubled as she watched the wounded man.

Tabinaw understood, and looked at the white woman calmly. "It is our way," he answered.

Two days later, Tabinaw could get around. He saw our horses struggling for food and us struggling to feed them. He told us to get some branches down and let them chew on the bark and eat the smaller tips off the end to supplement their diet of dead, frozen grass. He showed me how to fashion a spear, although Grandfather grumbled about him having a knife within reach. He told fascinating stories about Indian life and customs. It was hard for me to understand it all, but I did my best and managed to learn a few Indian words along the way.

The days were no longer endless and empty. I got up eagerly each morning. The cold was in the back of my mind now, instead of being the main focus of my thoughts. Learning and doing things with Tabinaw kept me in good spirits.

One afternoon, I noticed dark shapes moving through the trees and brush toward our camp. I studied them for a few moments, and decided they were men on horses. We're found! We're rescued! Then I realized it was more likely to be Indians.

"Dan!" I called. Tabinaw looked up when he heard the urgency in my voice. Grandfather followed Dan out to where I stood. I pointed. Dan looked grim. "Looks like a war party."

The Indians broke out of the brush and into our tree-drug swath of scraped snow. They had weapons, and their faces were painted. They did not raise a hand or call a friendly greeting. They advanced on us with deadly purpose.

I watched their approach with a dread fascination, conscious of my heart beating heavily against my ribs. I gave a gasp of surprise as Grandfather took hold of me and put me behind his tough and bony frame. His rifle was clutched in his hands, although it seemed small protection against the large war party.

One of the advancing Indians began whooping, and they all pushed their mounts to greater speed, raising their weapons as they drew nearer. Dan Henrie took hold of Amanda and pushed her toward the shelter, speaking rapidly and urgently. Grandfather muttered, "I knew it, I knew it."

Tabinaw stepped out in front of us and raised up his arms toward the menacing war party. They slowed, lowered their weapons, and then stopped, staring at Tabinaw with wonder. He began speaking rapidly to them in their own language. I couldn't understand any words, he spoke too fast. The war party dismounted. Tabinaw turned toward us and said, "These my friends."

Amanda hesitated at the doorway of the shelter. "The ones who left you?" she asked.

Tabinaw gave one nod of his head. "You safe. They no harm."

Dan whispered in Amanda's ear and she began preparing food for the visitors. They stood or sat around our fire and talked to Tabinaw, gesturing and laughing. I had never associated Indians and laughter in my mind. Before now, they'd seemed so serious and savage to me.

Their painted faces and primitive weapons were a feast for my eyes. Grandfather stood silently beside me. The war party seemed to enjoy our food. They wanted more sugar, and took turns eating it plain.

When they were satisfied, they made preparations to leave. Tabinaw told Dan Henrie that he would go to the Manti settlement and tell them where we were and that we needed help. Tabinaw grinned at me, mounted a horse, and rode off with his tribesmen. I crawled inside my shelter to get the spear Tabinaw had helped me make. I heard my grandfather outside speaking to Dan. "I was wrong," he said simply. I had not thought my grandfather was capable of apologizing. Hearing the gruff apology that I never thought could come out of his mouth made me think that I didn't know my grandfather very well. There just might be something in him worth getting to know.

Amanda had fixed a grand dinner, and we ate with a satisfaction we hadn't felt since we'd been stranded. Help was on the way. It was only a matter of a few more days before we were rescued and could take the remaining supplies to the settlers. I imagined the people without food, feeling desperate, cold and hungry. I was bringing them food and news from Salt Lake City. I could speak a few words of the Indian language, and I knew how to make a spear. I felt a purpose to my life that hadn't been there before. I thought maybe New York didn't need me as much as Utah Territory did.

After our nightly group prayer, just before we separated to our shelters, Amanda looked me in the eyes. "It looks as though we won't be here much longer. I wanted to be sure you knew, John, that you'll always be special to me. Wherever we go, know that I'll always be there for you, thinking fondly of you, and will help if ever you need me." She pulled me into a brief, warm hug.

I felt a strange sensation as though my mother had spoken the same words I had just heard come out of Amanda's mouth, as though they had both spoken together. I knew my mother was all right, and I knew then that I would be, too.

Daniel and Amanda Henrie became snow bound in Salt Creek Canyon east of Nephi while delivering supplies to the settlements. They found a seriously wounded Indian named Tabinaw, who was a brother to Chief Walkara. They nursed him back to health. When an Indian war party threatened them, Tabinaw stopped the attack then rejoined the Indians as they went to Manti to get help for the stranded supply wagons.

IRON LADY

"Mama! Indians! Two lady ones, and no kids!" I called out. I liked to give a lot of information, and get a lot of information, too. In her cross moments, Mama sometimes called me "Tattletale Tess." But I knew she relied on me.

The lady ones weren't so scary, but the men were. But they all looked strange—Indian men, women, or kids. Their skin was so dark, and even the boys had long black hair! They wore thick, stiff clothes made out of animal skin. Sometimes I saw Indians wearing cloth clothes they had gotten from the pioneers. Even then, they still walked different and still talked and looked different. It wasn't just the clothes.

Sometimes the kids didn't even wear any clothes. Big kids, almost my size, would run around naked in the summertime. Mama said it was disgraceful. I thought it was interesting. The Indians all smelled funny, too. Men, women, big or little, they smelled kind of greasy, smoky and earthy.

Mama came out just as I recognized one of the Indian ladies on the road as Anoet. "It's Anoet and another Indian lady I don't know," I said to Mama.

Anoet had been to our house before. She smiled broadly with her gap-toothed grin. "Miektagovan!" she called out her Indian greeting.

"Hello," Mama replied.

"This my da-ter, Kimeat," said Anoet. Kimeat looked down at the ground as Mama said hello. I looked at her suspiciously. She was as big as Anoet, although she wasn't as wrinkled up. How could she be her daughter? Daughters were supposed to be little, and mothers were big. I looked up doubtfully at my mother as she invited them in. I thought something was fishy. Anoet didn't waste time. She said, "Kimeat need dress. You have dress?"

"I'll go see," Mama replied, and went into the next room. I stared politely, smiling, at the two visitors for a few moments. They weren't doing anything interesting, so I walked over to the kitchen table and lifted the cloth that was thrown over the big wooden bowl. I sniffed the yummy smell of rising bread dough. Even though baking day made the house hot, I loved it! Mama's bread was the best! As I poked at the springy dough with my finger, Anoet and Kimeat talked together in a mishmash way. There were no words I could understand. It was a very boring conversation.

Mama came back with a faded blue dress folded over her arm. I recognized it as one she had worn to work in the fields last summer. Kimeat's eyes got big. She smiled for the first time. She took the dress and hugged it to her. "Toe-ak," she whispered, "Toe-ak!" I knew that meant "thank you."

"Now," Anoet turned to Mama with her big, gappy smile, "You have ham?"

"No, sorry, we're out of ham until we butcher again this fall."

Mama must be getting forgetful. I knew I wasn't! But to be respectful, I wrinkled up my forehead in a question. "Mama," I asked, "Don't we have a hambone left in the smokehouse?"

Mama smiled a very small smile, "It's just a bone, Tess. Anoet doesn't want just a bone."

" It has some ham on it," I said helpfully.

"Not much," Mama said as though her throat were getting sore. "Just enough to flavor one little batch of beans."

Anoet smiled, "It is good, I take!" she announced.

Mama gave me a look that made me feel smaller than I already was. She left and got the ham bone. When she came back and offered it to Anoet, she didn't hold it out very far. "It's just an old dried up bone with shreds on it," she said.

Anoet grabbed it eagerly and tucked it under her arm. "Toe-ak!" she said cheerfully.

Mama sighed and then smiled. "I must get back to work," she said as she pulled open the front door to let the Indian ladies out. I opened my mouth to tell them that Mama's work was baking bread, but Mama looked at me before I could say any words, and I closed my mouth.

After Mama put the bread in the oven, I saw three braves coming down the trail. They had on the strange, stiff kind of clothes. Their long black hair was shiny with grease. One of them carried a bow, with a leather skin full of arrows hanging down his back. Another one had a knife in a sheath at his waist. I did not like the look of them. "Mama! Indians! Three man ones!" I shrieked. These were a scary kind of Indian.

They stopped at our house. The one without any weapons pointed his face up and sniffed the air noisily. "Mmmmmm!" he said, rubbing his stomach. His friends laughed and rubbed their stomachs, too.

"We have bread," said the one with the knife. I wasn't sure if he was asking or telling. I sure didn't like the looks of them. I looked down the road hopefully. I would feel better if some lady Indians came along, too.

"The bread is not quite ready," Mama said. "You may come in and sit down and wait if you want to."

Mama turned to go into the house. I saw those three Indians look at each other with raised up eyebrows and grinning like the boys at church who took a frog in one of their pockets. Mama didn't see them. I knew I had to go in the house to keep an eye on them. They were up to no good, I thought.

They each sat on a chair in the kitchen side of the room by the table. They were talking the mishmash talk that I couldn't understand. I tried to make sense of it so I'd know what they were up to, but nothing sounded like anything I knew. I decided I'd better ask one of those Indian kids to teach me their language, clothes or no clothes.

Mama picked up her hot pads, opened the oven door, and bent over to check the bread. I could not believe what I saw next! The Indian with the bow leaned forward and put the tip of his bow under the back of my mother's skirt! My mouth opened and I pointed, but no sound would come out! I even tried to make my feet move, but they felt like they were stuck to the floor! That Indian started lifting the bow up. I could see my Mama's boots, and then her stockings! Those Indians were grinning like monkeys.

When Mama's skirt got up to her knees, she suddenly whirled around and conked that Indian right on top of his head with her frying pan! The other two Indians held as still as statues while he tipped over sideways and slid to the floor. I was scared that the Indian with the knife might jump up and stab my Mama. She still had hold of the frying pan, though, in both hands. "Get him out!" she yelled.

The two friends jumped up and grabbed the limp Indian by his arms and dragged him out the door. They didn't seem to care that his legs and feet were dragging and thumping down the front porch stairs.

Mama's face was red and her eyebrows were angry. My feet and mouth got unstuck and I ran toward her. "Mama?" I asked fearfully. Mama looked at me, put down her frying pan, and her forehead smoothed out. "I'm not angry at you, Tess!" She pulled me into her arms. Right then I wasn't scared of any Indians, men, ladies or naked kids. I knew I was safe.

It wasn't until almost dark that any more Indians came toward our house. There were two of them, and they approached slowly. It wasn't until they got to the porch that I recognized Anoet and Kimeat. Kimeat was wearing the blue dress and walking carefully. Anoet's eyes were big with wonder when she saw my mother. "You Iron Lady!" she announced.

Mama started to laugh. "Oh, is that what they're calling me now?" she said.

Anoet smiled a small, respectful smile. "They no bother you no more," she said. And they never did.

Indians had a real taste for pioneer bread and ham, and a curiosity about white man's clothes. An Indian man lifted the skirt of a pioneer woman with his bow while she was checking on the bread baking in her oven. She knocked him out with her frying pan, and his friends dragged him from the house. From that day on, she was known as "Iron Lady" among the Indians.

HORSE RAID

Lying back against a woolly buffalo hide, I took hold of the tough deer meat venison with my teeth. It resisted until my strong jaws wrenched a piece off. Old toothless Wambayot could never do that. He could only sip the broth from a pot of boiled meat.

As I chewed, I felt proud of my new manhood, and idly wondered whether or not we'd soon need to go hunting again. I noticed some movement at the east end of camp. No one acted alarmed, so it wasn't an enemy raid. Curious, I sat up and watched the moving bodies, deciding if it was worth the effort to walk over there to see what was happening.

When I caught sight of Chief Walkara on a tall brown horse, I was on my feet and heading toward him in an instant. He was one of the six brothers that sometimes fought for control of the Ute tribes of central Utah. When he got down off his horse, his head was still above that of any Indians in our camp.

The chief received a bowl of boiled meat as he seated himself on the ground. Tribesmen gathered around him as he ate.

Finished, he tossed the bowl aside and spread his hands out to us. "My brothers," he said, "I have had a dream that there are fine horses many day's ride south, in the land called Mexico. Those who go with me will return as rich men. Who will go?"

I hesitated only a moment. The journey would go through the southern desert, where water holes could dry up. Poisonous snakes and scorpions liked to crawl into your sleeping blankets with you to feel the warmth of your skin. There were hostile tribes, and even the Mexicans would kill us if they caught us taking their horses. Horses were valuable. He who owned many horses was wealthy, and much respected.

The people who had moved into our valley and had to wear hats to keep their pale faces from turning red told us that it was not good to take horses. They called it "stealing," and said it made God angry. My people believed if you need something, you take it. If the one you took from needs it, he takes it back. My tribesman Senniga had taken an ax from a settlement. Axes were useful, much needed in our tribe. Senniga's ax was dull, and did not cut so good. He went to town, to a blacksmith, and said, "You sharpen ax."

Blacksmith say, "I can't sharpen. Is worn out. There no steel there."

Senniga say, "It all steel! Me steal it last night!"

Paleface settlers did not understand our ways. It was a fact of our life that a man without horses was nothing. A horse raid was a measure of manhood, and he who successfully took horses from another was looked upon as noble, and was respected. Owning horses made it so you could live a good life, and have many wives and children. Taking horses was good.

Walkara had been to California on a horse raid a few summers ago, and had come back with many fine horses. He and his brother Tabinaw, and all the braves who went with them, were very rich. On the way home, Walkara and Tabinaw had disagreed about which horses each one would get. They raised their voices louder and louder. Finally in his anger, Walkara pulled out his gun and shot Tabinaw's horse. Tabinaw mounted another horse and shot Walkara's horse. They kept shooting the horses the other brother mounted until they only had the horses they were riding to return home.

I knew Walkara could get many horses home, if he stayed master of his temper. I was ready to be a rich brave. All I had was a swaybacked old horse that had been taken from a wagon train in Wyoming. No one had ever tried to steal him.

When we set off for Mexico, there were almost as many of us as there are fingers on two hands. We rode many days, and crossed the Green River, the horses easily swimming the width of the mild current. We found enough water along the way for horses and men. It took many long, hot days to make it to the hills of Mexico. I was doubting Walkara's dream of fine horses as we traveled through cactus and sagebrush desert between brown hills.

The next day, we crossed between more hills and suddenly came upon a broad, green valley, dotted with many fine horses! I stopped and looked and looked. My heart flew like a bird. I had never seen so many horses in one place! Walkara had a shine in his eyes. "My dream is true!" he said.

That night when it was very dark, we rode slowly into the valley, our horses walking. When we drew close to the valley horses, our mounts made soft noises to them. The valley horses were curious, and made soft noises back. I was afraid that the horse noises would wake the Mexicans, and they would kill us. My legs wanted to kick my old horse and gallop after our new treasure, running away with them from the danger I felt all around me.

Walkara had said that moving slowly kept the new horses from being startled or running away. I held my fear inside me and kept my legs tight around the old sway back as we walked our horses into a big, curved line behind the horses in the valley. We rode slowly back toward the hills, our newly acquired wealth walking and sometimes trotting ahead of us, tossing their heads and looking back with curious eyes. We kept moving steadily toward the stars shaped like a big bear in the sky.

When we made it out of the valley and up into the hills, I turned and looked behind us. There were no lights, no sign of us being followed.

I knew that by morning, there would be armed Mexicans after us. If we were seen, we would be shot. If we were captured alive, we would probably be tortured before being killed. I had been taught to say, "It is a good day to die," when I saw that death was close at hand, but I did not want to die. I wanted to live as a rich brave, and enjoy these fine horses. My new wealth would allow me to marry some wives to take care of my teepee, and I would have many strong sons and beautiful daughters.

Walkara set a faster pace. As dawn broke, he was riding in front of the herd, letting the new horses follow his horse, as it showed them which way to go. The rest of us were riding behind to keep the horses together.

I looked back on the ground, and saw the tracks that more than two hundred horses left in the dirt, and knew that even a paleface could follow our trail. Our pursuers would not be far behind us. I imagined at any moment hearing shouts of discovery and bullets thudding into my skin. I urged my horse to go faster. We only stopped for water and ate dried venison as we rode.

When we got into familiar surroundings Walkara sent scouts to see whether the Mexicans had turned back, as he suspected they had. The scouts returned quickly, saying they were still following. Walkara picked up the pace again, and the tired horses loped along after him, heads hanging.

I did not recognize the Green River when we came to it. It was no longer a calm river. It was fast and wide. Large logs and rocks were rolling along with the strong current. The rain had fallen in the mountains while we were gone, and it had run down all the mountain gullies and valleys and gathered together in force in the river. Our tired horses refused to get in the water to swim across. Even if they had tried, in their tired state and with the fast water, they would have been swept away and drowned, or killed with the rocks and logs. I felt heavy with hopelessness, and pained with fear.

The scouts who had seen the Mexicans following us urged Walkara to abandon the horses and ride for his life. They already had their horses pointed upriver to find a narrower crossing.

Chief Walkara looked at them with a sneer. "Are you women?" he asked sarcastically. "Are you children, that you cry and run when you are scared?" I felt a pang of shame that I had thought the same thing. Walkara turned to the rest of us, pointedly ignoring the scouts. "I need some of you brave men to guard the horses, and some of you go with me to meet the Mexicans."

"But they will kill you!" said Walkara's brother, Arropine.

"They have never seen me," was Walkara's reply, "They won't know it is me." He looked at Arropine and me. "You come with me," he said. My heart felt like it would hammer out of my chest. I did not want to go back to see the Mexicans, but I did not want to tell Walkara that.

I followed his directions to cut certain horses out from the herd. They were not the best horses. Some I could tell were old, and some were not well formed. It did not take long. The horses were now used to us, and they were tired, so did not run away.

We pushed the small, scrawny horse herd ahead of us as we began back down the trail we'd just traveled. Walkara said only one thing to us, "I chose you for your closed mouths."

It didn't take us as long as I had hoped before we saw many men in large hats approaching us along the trail. They had rifles at their sides. When they spotted us, some men pulled their rifles out. I did not like the looks of this. I wished I had stayed back in camp and never gone to get horses. Better a poor man with one old horse, than a dead man in the desert. I let none of my feelings show on my face. I kept it still and straight.

Walkara raised his hand to the approaching Mexicans and called out, "There you are! I thought we'd never find you! We have had a long journey to return your horses to you!"

The Mexican in the lead, a broad faced, squinty-eyed man, said angrily, "These are not all of our horses!"

Walkara put on a sad face. "No, they aren't. Chief Walkara went crazy. He started shooting the braves who were with him. He said he wanted all the horses for himself. He even shot some of the horses! He was possessed by evil spirits! We were lucky to escape with our lives! Many of our friends are dead." If I hadn't already made my face stiff, I think my jaw would have fallen down at the story I heard Walkara tell.

Then Walkara put on a friendly face. "We brought you as many horses as we could. We did not want them in the hands of that crazy man. They should go to their rightful owners."

The Mexicans listened to what Walkara said, then talked angrily among themselves. I did not understand all of what they said. The squinty-eyed man finally turned back to us and said, "We will catch Walkara, and kill him, and get the rest of our horses back! Show us where he went, and we will avenge your friends."

Fear ran painful cactus prickles through my body. I let none of it show on my face. I kept my face still as death. If they rode ahead, they would surely find the fine horse herd by the side of the Green River, and kill us all very slowly for making fools out of them.

Walkara lowered his head and shook it side to side. "Walkara is many days ahead of you. We rode for two days to get back here. He is in the strongholds of the mountains where he lives now, and we will never catch up to him." He looked directly at the Mexican and said with such hate in his voice that even I believed he meant what he said, "Walkara is a devil! We hope to never cross his path again!"

The Mexicans spoke some more, looked over at the small herd we had brought with us, and seemed to slump in their saddles. "Alright," said the Mexican, "We thank you for the horses you brought back to us. We will rest and eat before we go home. You may eat with us."

"Thank you," said Walkara humbly.

While eating with the Mexicans, Walkara spoke again of the terror of being around evil, crazy Walkara, the sacrifice of losing his friends, and the hardship of traveling so far to bring the horses back. By the time we parted company, the Mexicans had paid him in gold coins for his trouble.

We watched them depart southward. Walkara spoke to us as they rode away, saying things like, "Now where shall we go? I don't want to go back to live with Walkara, so shall we go west? Maybe we will travel east? What do you say?"

When the Mexicans were out of sight, Walkara headed north and we rode back to the bank of the Green River. There we rested and waited until the river went down enough for the horses to cross.

We returned to our tribe in triumph. I was much admired for my strong, beautiful horses. I had been to Mexico. I had proved my bravery. Life was good.

Chief Walkara was an accomplished horse thief. He took a band of Indians to Mexico, stole hundreds of horses, and was keeping ahead of the angry owners in pursuit until his horse herd reached a flooded river. He cut the poorest horses out and took them back to meet his pursuers. He pretended to be an enemy to Walkara. The vigilantes paid him for his trouble, and returned to Mexico.

THE BROKEN MAN

"Thanks, Ma," I said as I got up from the table. My younger brothers Andrew and Erastus kept on eating.

"Do you guys have hollow legs, or are you just trying to put off your chores?" I said. They both looked at me and grinned around their mouthfuls of food.

Little Hannah, blonde and blue-eyed, looked up at me and said hopefully, "Can I come with you?"

"No, Hannah, I've got to go to work." Disappointment clouded my sister's face. I couldn't just leave her like that. Her sad eyes tugged at my heart, so I bent, gave her a hug, and said, "I'll play with you tonight after work." Hannah brightened, smiled and nodded eagerly.

We were all missing Pa, who had gone to Salt Lake City for supplies. I tried to do my best to fill in for him, to help Ma out, but my brothers didn't always think they had to mind me. I looked forward to Pa being back within the week.

Stepping out into the brisk autumn morning, I paused to admire the tall mountains speckled with bright yellow aspens and flaming red maples. Starting down the road at a brisk walk, I checked my pockets to be sure that the thick gloves needed for work were there. The thought of handling timber without their protection was a painful one. Slivers, torn skin, and bleeding blisters were all possible consequences. Little did I know that by the end of the day, those injuries would be counted as nothing.

I was fifteen and strong from working lumber with Brother Mickel all summer. We had recently been sawing logs into boards. It was a difficult process that required coordination and precision. I hoped that by now we had sawn enough boards so I could make a delivery. I was ready to do something different.

The San Pitch valley was growing in population, and lumber was needed for building projects. I was most curious about the talk of a temple that was supposed to be built on a hill in Manti that Brigham Young had dedicated. So far nothing had been done on the building. I wondered if it would be built after the style of the Nauvoo Temple.

"Hello, Lewis!" Brother Mickel greeted me. A large, red-faced man with a perpetual smile on his face—my employer—already had the wagon in position, the pile of rough-sawn lumber that we had been working on rising behind it like a miniature mountain.

"Are you feeling strong today?" Brother Mickel asked.

"As a bear," I answered. I pulled on my gloves and positioned myself at the opposite end of the lumber stack from my employer. Working together in practiced rhythm, it wasn't long before we had the wagon piled high with the fragrant wood. As I tied the load down with rope, Brother Mickel hitched up the horses. I had driven these horses before, and they were a good team.

"If you get back in time, we'll load up one more for tomorrow," Brother Mickel said with a smile.

"I'll be sure to drive slowly," I answered. I heard Brother Mickel chuckling to himself just before I slapped the reins on the horses to get them moving.

We rolled along uneventfully for a couple of miles, and then I topped a rise on the dirt road and started down the other side. To help the horses keep ahead of the wagon that was now propelling itself down the hill, I pushed on the brake. The wagon did not slow down. I pushed harder. There was a scraping sound, and a screech. I felt the brake trying to grab the wheel.

"C'mon, c'mon," I muttered as the wagon crowded the trotting team. The horses were tossing their heads high, turning their eyes back for quick, worried glances at the wagon that was fast on their heels. I pushed the brake with all my might, but it wasn't enough. The wagon bucked a little, as if trying to comply with my demand, but the brake must have been worn out. It wouldn't slow the wagon down, even when I stood up and put my full weight on it.

I'll never know if it would have been better for me to have been sitting down when the traces broke. The wagon tongue suddenly fell as the connection to the horses snapped. It jammed into the road, acting as a brake which abruptly brought the wagon up short. The sudden, unexpected halt made me lose my balance and fall forward. The reins fell from my hands as I spread them to try to save myself. There was nothing I could do to stop my fall. One minute I was standing on top of the wagon, the next, I was falling. There was nothing to hold onto, nothing to grab to keep myself from hitting hard onto the dirt-packed road. I landed with a bone-cracking jolt that forced the air out of my lungs.

That would have been bad enough, but my ordeal was not yet over. The jolt that forced the wagon to a sudden stop only served to channel the forward momentum into a rolling tumble that flipped the wagon over. The heavy load I had tied down so securely just a short time ago snapped the ropes as easily as if it was thread. Before I could catch my breath and make any effort to escape, I realized with a sense of horror that I was being buried under an avalanche of wood. Like a terrifying nightmare that I couldn't wake up from, I felt the heavy timbers pelt me mercilessly, punishing my body, bruising me, crushing me, burying me alive.

I don't know how long I lay there. I felt like I was in a hazy fog. Sound and motion seemed to come from a long distance away. I felt the weight lifted off my face. I knew it was my face, but it didn't seem like it was still attached to my body. I could feel the sun on my cheek, but my eyes wouldn't open. A faraway voice was calling, sobbing, "Lewis!" It sounded like Brother Mickel. I felt bad that he was so worried. I didn't want him to be upset, so I tried to tell him I was sorry about the wagon. I tried to explain about the worn brake, but my mouth wouldn't move. Why couldn't I move? It felt like my body was as stiff and unresponsive as the wood that had buried me. Then, without warning, such an intense pain ripped through my being that when it reached my head, I mercifully blacked out.

When I woke up, instead of a dusty road under me and a heavy pile of lumber on top of me, I was lying on a real bed with a blanket for a covering. Had I dreamed the horrible accident? My eyes opened and recognized my house. My head hurt. I tried to raise my hand to explore the sore spot. My right arm wouldn't move. Panicked, I looked down and saw a large splint of boards fastened securely to my right arm, making it look like a huge homely rag doll. I raised my left arm, which moved according to my command, but it felt tender, sore and bruised. The motion caused an agony of sensation that shot so sharply through my chest and stomach that I cried out.

My mother appeared at the side of the bed, her bright smile warm and soothing in spite of the tears I could see in her eyes. Beside her was Doctor Jacobs. I could see the faces of Andrew and Erastus staring solemnly at me.

"Is he dead?" Hannah asked, her little face as grave as a mourner's.

"No, of course not," Ma said in a falsely bright voice. "See? He blinked his eyes."

"Can he play with me now?" Hannah asked hopefully.

"No, Sweetheart, he got hurt. You go play with Andrew and Erastus."

"I want to play with Lewis."

"Later. Run along," Ma said, "Lewis needs to sleep so he can get better." The children reluctantly left the room.

I made several attempts before I could get any sound out of my mouth. "Ma," I said, and the effort of speaking caused pain to jab through my jaw and neck. "What happened?"

Ma sat on a chair that was beside the bed. She took my left hand in hers and held it gently. "You had an accident, Lewis. Mr. Mickel knew something was wrong when he saw his team of horses heading back to his place, dragging their broken traces. So he went down the road and found you. He brought you here." Her voice broke, "He thought you were dead."

"I don't remember," I said drowsily, then closed my eyes against the pain that seemed to be invading every corner of my body. "What's wrong with my arm?"

Dr. Jacobs answered me. "It's broken. Your leg is also broken, in at least two places. You broke your collarbone, too."

I swallowed and my throat hurt. "Inside hurts real bad."

"Well, Son, that load of lumber was heavy. To put it bluntly, you're pretty mashed up inside. I've done all I can for you now. I'll check back tomorrow."

As he turned to leave, a tear squeezed out the corner of my eye. I hurt so much. My mother laid my hand down gently. "I'll get you some broth I steeped with willow bark for the pain."

After I took a few mouthfuls of the weak broth, I fell asleep again. It was just too much work to swallow.

Brother Mickel's stern voice woke me up. "Lewis Anderson!" I opened my eyes and stared with consternation at the unsmiling face of Brother Mickel. I had never seen him look so serious.

"Of all the ways to get out of working, I've never known a man to play dead before!" Then he smiled.

I swallowed carefully, exploring the pain level. I tried to smile back, but it didn't work. "Honestly, sometimes it hurts so bad I wish I was dead," I murmured.

"Would you like a blessing?" Brother Mickel said.

"Yes." I didn't nod my head because it would hurt too much.

Dr. Jacobs was there, checking up on me again. He assisted Brother Mickel. They laid their hands gently on my head, taking care not to touch the wounds that were bandaged. A calmness and comfort coursed through me, and I relaxed and fell asleep before they finished.

When Pa got home, I felt ashamed that I still couldn't get up, even to use the outhouse. I knew Pa needed me, that he depended on me to help him in this new land that we were settling. Pa was upset, but it wasn't at me. He was upset that the accident had happened at all. He gave me a blessing, too.

I watched my family struggle to prepare for winter. On more than one occasion I heard someone chopping wood outside and longed to go out and take over for them, to feel the axe handle in my hands, my two strong arms hefting it up, then swinging it down with a satisfying "crack," splitting the firewood with one chop. I imagined my two whole legs, muscled and unbroken, bending to get an armful of the split wood. Then I would walk it over to the woodpile by the house for Ma to use in cooking. I had never before appreciated the blessing of a strong, healthy body.

By the time the snow was deep and the bitter cold winter had set in, Doctor Jacobs pronounced my bones healed and took off the splints. When I tried to get up to test my legs, intense pain tore through my insides. I fell back onto the bed, disgusted and disappointed, tears of frustration running into my ears.

Although they never complained, I felt like a terrible burden to my family. I ate the food that they had harvested and stored, wore the clothes that Ma mended and washed for me, and laid in the biggest bed in the house. I wasn't doing anything useful or contributing to the family upkeep. My loved ones might be better off if I had died. Then at least there would be one less mouth to feed, and they'd have more room in the house for the members of the family that were doing their share to earn their food and sleeping space.

I forced myself to stand a little bit every day. The bones had healed, but in my opinion I wasn't getting well fast enough.

As the winter wore on, cold and chill, my heart began to feel shrunken and hard, like a chunk of ice. I began to hope that if Father in Heaven wasn't going to heal me, he would take me home to Him and bless my family with the release of my burdensome care.

The winter was dragging on, reluctant to let go of its icy hold on the world. I ate as little as I possibly could, and spent most of my time sleeping or staring out the window. I felt so bad about myself I didn't want to play with Andrew or Erastus or even Hannah, who puckered up her face with worry whenever I caught her looking at me. I didn't want to listen to Ma read to me or have Pa play his mouth organ. It was just no good.

My family usually left when I wouldn't respond to their entreaties to do something cheery, telling themselves I must just be tired, that was all. Thus I was alone one soggy spring day, staring out the window at the dirty piles of snow that were melting into mud.

My habitual dour thoughts were chasing each other around in my head like flies buzzing around a rotten carcass, when they suddenly stopped short. I stared at the window, my mouth dropping open in amazement. Where I had just been gazing at the puny struggle that spring was making to come to the valley, I now saw a beautiful white building, with arched windows and two towers, the whole edifice shining steadily before my eyes as though cupped reverently in some invisible, eternal hands. My whole body felt warm and light, the darkness of my mind lifting at the beautiful sight. My heart began to pound with joy and a zest for living that had been sorely lacking for a long time. I gazed at the radiant building until my heart was full of it, until it was impressed on my mind and had filled my soul with hope and wonder. Then it gradually faded away.

After that glorious experience, it seemed as though my body recovered at a much faster rate. I began to focus on things I could do instead of what I couldn't. By the time new grass was forcing its way up through the thick brown mud, I was walking with a cane, Hannah keeping a close vigil at my side, matching her little feet to my halting steps, smiling up at me and telling me what a good boy I was. I insisted on hauling water whenever I could get to the bucket before Andrew. I challenged Erastus to race to the woodpile, his face beaming as he handily beat his big brother. My mother cautioned me. My father encouraged me. Brother Mickel confided to me that Doctor Jacobs had told my mother the first day he examined me that I would probably be dead the next day. "It's a good thing he set your bones straight anyway!" Brother Mickel laughed.

Ironically, I stayed in the lumber industry and was called a few years after my accident to work at the temple sawmill in Canal Creek Canyon above Spring City. I worked with Bishop Amasa Tucker as he oversaw the selection of lumber for use in building the temple at Manti. Although I never actually visited the building site, I did deliver lumber out of the canyon periodically. It became a firm habit to check the brakes on any wagon before driving it.

The temple was still four years away from being completed when I was called on consecutive missions to Wisconsin, Minnesota, and Illinois.

Upon my return home, I was pleased to be called as temple recorder. I eagerly traveled to Manti for the temple dedication and my first look at the new House of the Lord. As the magnificent building came into view, my breath caught in wonder. Staring at the Manti Temple, I recognized it as the building I had seen in the vision that pulled me out of my deep depression years before. My eyes filled with tears as warmth filled my body. "There is the building I saw as a boy," I whispered.

The temple continued to be a significant part of my life, and thirty eight years later I was called as the temple president. I served gladly until the end of my days, which was twenty seven more years, in the sacred building that brought such meaning and joy to my earthly existence. I really was home.

Lewis Anderson was crushed under a load of lumber when the brakes on the wagon he was driving failed. He was presumed dead. He became despondent during his long recovery, until one day he saw a vision of the temple. When he recovered, he helped cut lumber for the temple but never saw the building until he returned from his lengthy proselyting mission. When he saw the Manti Temple for the first time, he recognized it as the building from his vision. He served as temple president from 1906 until his death in 1933.

HOSTAGE BABY

"Simeon, you're choking me!" I coughed, crawling on my hands and knees as my two-year-old cousin grabbed my neck to keep from sliding off my back. Either I wasn't a very good horsey or he wasn't a very good rider.

Aunt Hannah came in and plucked Simeon off of me. "What are you doing to Matthew?" she scolded him gently.

"Aw, it's all right," I mumbled as I stood up, accidentally kicking a corner of the braided rug into a big fold. As I hurried to smooth it, I said, "He was just playing with me. It's too cold and wet to play outside. I'm sorry if we disturbed you." I was disappointed that my apology didn't keep Aunt Hannah from carrying Simeon into the kitchen with her. His big blue eyes stared at me over her shoulder until he disappeared into the other room. I had done it again! Even when I apologized and tried to make it right, everything went wrong!

It was all Dan's fault. I hadn't wanted Ma to go and marry Dan, but she had anyway. If that wasn't bad enough, she went and had Aaron! A messy, smelly, noisy baby who got her attention every time he bawled. I hated my life. It had been much better before Dan and Aaron came; even with Pa dead, it was better than it was now.

I had decided to confront Ma when Dan was nowhere in sight. She had been in the parlor, holding her new baby, as usual. I went in and sat by her. "Ma, are you happy?"

"Why, yes, Matthew, most of the time." She smiled at me absently, "Are you?"

"No!" I blurted, surprising myself when I felt all my resentment spilling out of my mouth like a burst dam. "Why'd you have to go and marry Dan? He's not anything like Pa! And why'd you have Aaron?" Ma instinctively tightened her hold on the infant. That just added fuel to the fire I felt inside me. I plowed on, unable to stop myself, "What do you need me for? You have another husband, another son! I'm just in the way. I should die like Pa!"

Ma looked as though I had struck her. "Matthew!" Dan snapped at me from the doorway, "Don't talk to your mother that way!"

I turned on him. "She's my mother, you can't tell me how to talk to her, because you're not my father!" I yelled. Dan's face went red, and

I thought he might try to grab me, so I ran outside. The sound of my mother's crying ripped at my heart as I ran. I hated Dan. I wished with all my might that he would go back where he came from and leave us alone. I decided I hated Pa, too. Why did he go and die on us? He made this problem! And Ma. She could have left well enough alone! Why didn't she love me anymore? I felt guilty about hurting her feelings. I felt mean. I knew Pa would have been terribly disappointed in me.

I roughly wiped the tears that I didn't remember crying off my face. I wasn't going to cry like a baby. I walked and walked and walked. I finally decided if Ma didn't need me, I didn't need her. I whirled and stalked toward home. On the way, I decided that, just for good measure, I hated babies, too, and would stay as far away from them as I could. The closer I got to home, the colder my heart felt.

Ma greeted me calmly, " Matthew, sit down." Dan and Aaron were nowhere in sight. My heart jolted with hope as the sudden thought crossed my mind that Ma had sent them away for good. "You know I love you very much," she continued as she touched my arm. My mean resolve started to melt. I opened my mouth, but she put up her hand. "Let me finish, my dear. Since I love you so much, I'm concerned that you seem very unhappy here. I think you should go to Manti and visit my sister Hannah. Come back for planting. We'll need you, and I'll be missing you so desperately, you'll have to come home anyway." Ma smiled hopefully at me. I made my face hard, like my heart. Ma continued, "It would be an adventure for you! Matthew, I think it's for the best, so I want you to go."

Then Ma reached over and hugged me. I didn't want her to let go. I couldn't look at her. She said she loved me, but she was sending me away.

I felt like I was made of wood as I prepared to leave. It hurt inside when I left my mother behind in Salt Lake City, but I squashed the hurt with the hardness.

Now I was in Manti, with Aunt Hannah, who wasn't much like my mother. She was so proper I didn't know how to act around her. It didn't help that my arms and legs were growing faster than I could keep up with them. I felt clumsy even when I was sitting still. One good thing about being here was that Uncle Isaac Morley was famous in Manti. Being his nephew made me feel kind of famous, too. I admired how he could be tough, but kind. He was fair. He was the one Brigham Young appointed to lead the settlers to Sanpete in 1849.

After my resentment at being here had worn off some, I had to admit it was kind of exciting, living so close to Indians. We had Indians come into Salt Lake City, but they came into town. Here, they were so close, it was almost like living with them. I had even seen their camps of teepees, dogs, cooking fires, and hanging fleshed hides.

Besides the Indians, I had found a friend in Jim, who was a few years older than me. He was still unmarried, so he still knew how to have fun. I had gone out with him one evening and he'd pulled a long piece of twine from his pocket. When he produced a large nail and grinned at me, I was baffled. He tied the nail to the end of the twine, shushed me, and led the way over to the woodpile at Anderson's house.

Jim threw the twine over the roof and we bent down behind the pile of wood. When Jim gave the twine several gentle tugs, I heard a faint "tick-tick-tick" from the other side of the house. Next I heard movement and voices from inside. After a few more minutes of Jim tapping the nail against the window, Brother Anderson appeared from around the corner of the house and ran on past us, his white nightshirt flapping in the moonlight, his breath making little clouds in the nippy air every time he exhaled.

We could hear childish laughter coming from inside the house. I felt a tug of jealousy as I imagined those little Anderson kids watching their Pa run around the house in his nightshirt, delighting in his strength and trusting him to protect them from whatever was making that tick-tick-ticking noise.

It ended up that Brother Anderson found the nail, and pulled on the string so hard that it yanked right out of Jim's hand. We burst out of the woodpile and ran off into the darkness, followed by Brother Shoemaker's good-natured yell, "Go home and get some sleep, you scalawags!"

If it hadn't been for Jim and the Indians, Manti would have been too boring to tolerate. Well, Jim, the Indians, and my baby cousin Simeon. It surprised me to admit that I really was fond of the little boy.

I turned as I heard a commotion and a babble of voices outside. I opened the door. The freezing cold hail and sleet from earlier that day had melted into a slushy, muddy street. Two men on horses were arguing with four or five men on the ground. Uncle Isaac approached the group.

"Shut the door, Matthew, it's cold out there," Aunt Hannah said. I hadn't heard her walk up behind me. Quickly I shut the door on my foot. It bounced open and hit the wall. Flustered, I caught it again and shut it more slowly, fumbling with the latch. Aunt Hannah turned and went back into the kitchen.

My face hot with embarrassment, I looked out the window at the scene in the street. Uncle Isaac's posture was droopy. He was listening to the men on the horses, and then he shook his head sadly. He put his hand up as if to ward off any further words. He headed toward me, the mud oozing up around his boots with every step. He opened the door, and sat down to take off his boots. I was anxious to find out what had happened, but I didn't want to sound overly eager. I stood silently waiting. When Uncle Isaac looked up and saw me, his face brightened. "Hello, Matthew," he said warmly.

I wouldn't admit it to anyone, but I was secretly ashamed that after five years I couldn't recall the details of my father's face. I did remember his smile, though. I remembered the way he said my name. I figured that Uncle Isaac was about the next best thing to my own father. At least I felt like he wanted me here. When he headed for the kitchen, I followed.

"There's Papa!" Aunt Hannah said, smiling, as she handed little Simeon to Uncle Isaac. When she saw his expression, her smile disappeared. "What's wrong?" she asked.

Uncle Isaac sank down wearily into a chair. He held Simeon to his chest. "Those two new settlers, the ones from back east." Simeon squirmed to get down. Uncle Isaac kissed his son, set him on his two sturdy legs, and managed one pat on the curly blonde head just before Simeon ran away.

"What about them?" asked Aunt Hannah impatiently, scooping flour into the bowl she was mixing batter in. She stirred vigorously.

"They were up in the mountains to cut wood this morning. The hailstorm came up unexpectedly. They went to the lean-to cabin in North Fork for shelter. There were two young Indian boys in there, already taking shelter." Uncle Isaac sounded like he couldn't believe what he was saying. "They used whips and drove those two Indian boys out into the freezing sleet and hail. They beat them, and left them." He stared down at the floor, his face a mask of sorrow.

Aunt Hannah stood still. "Oh, those poor boys. Are they...?"

"I don't know if they survived," Uncle Isaac said. "I don't know." By the sound of his voice, I guessed that he feared they had not.

The next morning, when word came to our house that an Indian was approaching, Uncle Isaac registered no surprise. He stood, put on his coat and walked out into the street. The cold night had frozen the muddy street into hard lumps. I leaned over the windowsill to see who was coming. I knew some of the Indians by sight.

In my eagerness, I bumped into Aunt Hannah's favorite black vase with little pink roses painted on it. It had been her grandmother's, and survived the trip from England. As it tipped, I strained to catch it, but it slipped through my fingers. All those years and perilous travels it had been kept safe, and now it was in danger because of one clumsy boy. I was relieved to see that my effort to catch it did manage to slow its fall.

After it clattered to the floor, I picked it up and examined it anxiously. I could only find a small chip off one edge of the rim. It was hardly noticeable.

I set it back with the chipped part toward the wall and hung onto it with one hand as I looked outside again. I recognized Chief Sowiett on a paint horse making his way down the lumpy dirt street. His face was as still as an old oak tree trunk.

He dismounted slowly and came into our house. "Please, Chief, sit down," Aunt Hannah offered him a chair. He sat down awkwardly, then fixed his eyes on little Simeon in Aunt Hannah's arms. Aunt Hannah seemed nervous. "Let me go get you some bread and milk," she offered, and hurried out to the kitchen.

Uncle Isaac smiled pleasantly at the chief and spoke some words I couldn't understand. Chief Sowiett gave a long answer back. As he spoke, Uncle Isaac's smile faded and his face became grave. He shook his head sadly, then put his hand up to his eyes. Sowiett reached forward and touched Uncle Isaac's arm, speaking earnestly. Uncle Isaac nodded and managed a weak smile. I was almost wriggling out of my chair. What was going on? What were they saying? What had happened? A guy needs to know things.

Aunt Hannah brought out a bowl filled with chunks of homemade bread with milk poured over it. On the top was a drizzle of molasses. She handed it to Chief Sowiett with a spoon. He smiled in gratitude, and began to eat. He held the spoon awkwardly. It looked like he had to concentrate to balance the bread on his spoon to get it from the bowl to his mouth.

I watched intently as he took the first bite. My stomach growled loudly, and I quickly crossed my arms and pressed them into my mid-section. My mouth was watering, and I wondered if there was any more bread and milk in the kitchen. "Excuse me, Chief Sowiett," said Uncle Isaac in English. The chief nodded and continued eating.

I followed Uncle Isaac and Aunt Hannah out to the kitchen. I sliced some bread as I listened.

"It's bad," said Uncle Isaac solemnly. "One of those Indian boys from yesterday was Chief Sowiett's son. The chief says he was about twelve winters, so he was twelve years old. He and his friend died in the night."

Aunt Hannah put her hand to her mouth and her eyes filled with tears. "What will we do? And what will he do?" She sounded both sorry and afraid. I dripped some molasses on the floor. "Chief Sowiett is sad, he says his spirit within him is wounded, but he will not exact revenge. He is a peaceful person. He does not fault our settlement for the actions of those two men."

"Thank the Lord," Aunt Hannah sighed.

We all walked back to the parlor. Chief Sowiett was gone. His bowl and spoon were placed neatly on his chair.

Later that afternoon, the message again came that Indians were approaching the settlement. Uncle Isaac looked surprised, then concerned, and again went out into the street to meet them. Approaching this time was Chief Walkara, Sowiett's brother. He was taller than Sowiett, and younger. He had other braves with him. He looked down at Uncle Isaac from astride his horse. He began speaking in loud, angry phrases, again in that language I couldn't understand. It was driving me crazy! I was going to have to learn this Indian language so I could know what was going on!

Now Uncle Isaac was speaking earnestly to Chief Walkara, putting his hands up toward him in a pleading gesture. Chief Walkara pointed toward Uncle Isaac's house, and Uncle Isaac's head sunk down on his chest.

Will Potter, an old Mormon mountain man who told the best stories I ever heard, came from out of the small crowd of people assembled to watch the drama. He spoke loud, urgent words to the chief, gesturing toward the Morley house, and then pointing to himself. Chief Walkara shook his head. Potter spoke more loudly, his words running together. Chief Walkara shook his head again and got down off his horse, heading toward the Morley's. Uncle Isaac walked ahead of him, and called to Aunt Hannah from the doorway. She came into view, holding little Simeon, her face a question. Uncle Isaac spoke urgently to her and then took hold of Simeon and pulled him from Aunt Hannah's arms. She let out a wail as Uncle Isaac handed my cousin to Chief Walkara! I could not believe my eyes!

Chief Walkara's expression was savage satisfaction as he carried the pale, blonde, whimpering baby against his dark chest. He handed the boy to one of his braves and mounted his horse. Then he reached out and took Simeon back. Simeon seemed fascinated by the horse's mane, and stretched out his fat little hand to grab it as Chief Walkara turned his horse and rode out of Manti.

Heartbreaking wails reverberated through the street. They could have been coming from my own heart. Simeon was gone. I couldn't believe what I had seen. My Uncle Isaac had given his son to the savage Indians. It was as though my uncle had suddenly turned into a heartless beast! How could I ever have thought he was anything like my father? He wasn't! He wasn't even like a human being! My eyes were hot, my breath was fast, my body was aching. I felt shaky. I felt confused. I was angry, and I was scared.

I stumbled to the barn and curled up in a corner. I could still hear intermittent wails coming through the walls of the Morley house. As soon as Uncle Isaac had callously handed his son over to the chief, he had pulled my hysterical aunt inside. She hadn't watched her son ride away. But the impossible image was burned forever into my mind. Every time it re-rolled across my memory, I shuddered with fresh horror. I cried so hard, I felt like a baby myself. But I didn't care.

I decided to run away back to Salt Lake City the next morning. I would leave before anyone saw me and could try to stop me. I couldn't stay with a man who acted more savage than the Indians!

I woke up in the dark. I was cold inside and out, but made my way to the now silent house. I slipped inside the back door and stepped quietly and carefully along the rough wooden floorboards. Heading for the loft, my head turned involuntarily toward a disturbing glow in the parlor that faintly illuminated the kitchen, like ghost light. I saw Aunt Hannah kneeling beside a chair in the light of an oil lamp. She was talking, but I knew it was not to herself. She was praying. I crawled silently into my small, cold bed.

I slept late the next day. No one woke me up to help with chores. There were no smells of food cooking. The house was too quiet. Since people were already up and moving about, I re-thought my plan and decided to leave late that night. I didn't want anyone to stop me. I didn't want to have to try to explain. Even the thought of speaking my feelings closed my throat up tight.

I felt restless. I caught myself looking for Simeon to tickle, and throw up into the air. When I remembered, I felt a sharp pain clear into my soul. It scared me to realize how much I loved my little cousin.

I couldn't stand being in the house any more. I escaped outside so I wouldn't be surrounded and suffocated by memories of Simeon and the sorrow of my own heart. "Hey, Matthew," called Jim.

"Hey," I replied without looking up.

"What do you think about that Will Potter? That was sure something when he talked to Walkara yesterday!"

It felt like something broke inside of me, and anger spilled out. "I don't think anything," I shouted, "I don't know what anyone said, and I don't know why Uncle Isaac gave Simeon away! And to savages! He didn't fight for his own son! He didn't even try! He just gave him away! How could he do that? How could he do something as cruel as that?" I swiped at my eyes angrily. Jim put his hand on my back.

"I didn't know you hadn't heard," he said gently. "Walkara came to demand satisfaction for his nephew being killed."

"That's stupid!" I yelled, "Chief Sowiett didn't want any kind of revenge, and it was his son that was killed! Not Walkara's!"

"True. But Walkara still demanded satisfaction for his sorrow, for the loss of his nephew. He demanded blankets, flour, and sugar. We don't have as much as he wanted. Father Morley told him he'd have to send to Salt Lake City for the supplies.

Walkara said that to ensure his ransom would be delivered, he wanted Father Morley's son as hostage. Father Morley pleaded, but Walkara's heart is hard as stone. Then, what Will Potter was telling Walkara, was that if he would take him in the child's place, he would be Walkara's slave! He said the baby couldn't work, or be any help to the great chief. Walkara refused. Father Morley knows that there are more Indians than us. The entire settlement was in danger. If Walkara was offended and declared war, Simeon could be killed anyway. So all he could do was give the boy up and trust in God."

"What kind of God?" I said bitterly, feeling shocked inside myself as the words came out of my mouth. I thought Jim would turn away and call me a blasphemer. Instead, he slid his arm over my shoulder and tightened it into a hug. I felt my hard heart soften. A silent cry rose inside my soul for God to please watch over that curly haired baby that liked to about choke me to death! I let out a loud sob, and, embarrassed that Jim had heard me, headed back to the Morley house. Jim watched me trip and almost fall, but he didn't approach me or follow me.

At the Morley house, no one smiled. No one spoke, except Aunt Hannah, to pray. No food was fixed—not that I wanted any. Everything was so unnatural and depressed so that I felt like I was sitting inside a grave.

About an hour before dark, a great shout went up in the street. My heart constricted. What now? I didn't want any more adventures of any kind. I just wanted to go home to my mother.

There was a pounding on the door. My aunt stared at it, white-faced. It was Uncle Isaac who opened it. A man I didn't know very well stood in the doorway, his face red, his eyes wide. "He's coming!" he yelled.

Uncle Isaac stepped outside. Aunt Hannah put her hand to her throat and followed him. I was right behind her, and accidentally stepped on her dress, but she didn't seem to notice. Her eyes were focused on the little procession that was coming down the street. When I saw what was approaching, my mouth fell open. I could have fit a whole wagon load of hogs into it.

The Indians from the day before were back, tall Chief Walkara riding proudly behind a little white pony with blonde Simeon Morley sitting on it. He was dressed in a miniature set of Indian buckskins, and his skin was brown. I later learned that walnut juice had been rubbed on his skin to stain it. His round blue eyes caught sight of his parents and he burst into smiles. "Mama!" he called. I don't think even a grizzly bear could have stopped Aunt Hannah. She gave a strangled sound and ran to meet her baby son, snatched him off the horse, and raced for the house. After she slammed the door, I heard the click of the bolt sliding into place.

Chief Walkara wore a smug look on his dark features. Uncle Isaac said something to him. His voice broke. Chief Walkara replied in a stately voice. Uncle Isaac put his hand out toward the chief, who still sat astride his horse. Chief Walkara took it stiffly. I could tell he wasn't used to shaking hands. After the white man's handshake, the chief raised his hand to Uncle Isaac, palm forward, then turned his horse and led his entourage back to the Indian camp, leaving the little white horse behind. I was all smiles. "Jim! Jim! Tell me what happened!" Jim was smiling, too. Every face I saw was smiling. The whole world was smiling.

"He told your uncle that since he had trusted Chief Walkara with his own son, the chief knew that he could trust Father Morley to deliver the blankets and flour and sugar. He said he didn't need to keep Simeon any more, he knew 'Chief Morley' would keep his word."

"Thanks, Jim!" I said, as though he had personally delivered Simeon back to the settlement. He grinned at me. It felt like the hard, icy lump inside me had melted down to my toes. I felt warmth and respect for Uncle Isaac instead of the intense anger and hate I had felt for him earlier. A prayer of thankfulness welled up in my heart and burst out of my mouth in a quiet "thank you!" which I imagined floating up to the Heavens.

I longed to see my mother. I was ready to go back to Salt Lake City, apologize to her with all my soul, and make friends with my own baby brother.

In my joyous, soft hearted state, I could even admit that I hadn't been fair to Dan. I'd never tried to get to know him. I knew he never would replace my father, but that didn't mean we couldn't get along. Maybe I would be a man, take the first step, and break the ice. After all, I had a whopper of a story to tell!

Chief Sowiette's son was killed by white men. He wanted no revenge. Chief Walker demanded payment of goods, and took two-year-old Simeon Morley from his father Isaac as hostage until the goods were delivered. Will Potter offered to go in the baby's place. Hannah prayed all night long. Simeon was returned the next day on his own pony with his own set of buckskins and his skin dyed brown.

KILLER IN THE HEN HOUSE

I didn't mean to kill the chicken. Honest. I only threw my corncob to the hens because they like to peck on them even after all the kernels are eaten off. After dinner it was almost all dark, so I threw it as hard as I could to be sure to get it over the fence. One of the hens said, "BA-KAW!" so loud and cheerful, I said, "You're welcome!" as I walked back to my house.

The next morning I answered a knock on the door. Our neighbor, Addie, was standing there. She was as old as my granny, with whom I lived because I didn't have a mother or father alive. In one hand Addie dangled a dead chicken upside down by the feet. In her other hand she held an empty corncob. I put my hands on my hips like I'd seen my Granny do. "What on earth happened to your chicken?" I asked.

"That's what I was going to ask you!" Addie said to me. Then something clicked in my head, like maybe I was in trouble, and a cold shiver ran down my backbone. I do not ever, ever like to be in trouble. I pulled my bottom lip down, then asked casually, "Is that my corncob, or yours?"

"It's not mine."

Granny came over to see who I was talking to. "Come in, Adelia!" she said and then frowned. "What on earth happened to your chicken?"

I had been studying the stiffened bird and wondering, when a sudden thought struck me. It knocked the shivery feeling clear into yesterday! This was a matter of life or death! "Was the corn poison?" I asked in horror, covering my mouth and feeling my stomach lurch.

"No. Near as I can tell, this corncob bonked this chicken on the head. It hit so hard, it killed her."

My mouth fell open. I, Cissy Sorenson, threw a corncob hard enough to kill a chicken? Wow! My heart got all warm and big in my chest. I was stronger than I thought! I rolled my shoulders experimentally inside my long sleeved gingham dress. Yes, the sleeves felt tighter than yesterday. I squeezed my arm muscles with my fingers. They felt small, but tough.

Just wait until I saw that Jacob Olsen again! Just see if he thought he could push me around anymore! I'd show him a thing or two! I got a little grin on my face thinking of what I could do to Jacob now that I was strong enough to kill a chicken with one throw!

Granny looked sharply at me. "Cecelia!" she said in a warning tone of voice. I stared up at the two big ladies. It wasn't fair that grown ups were so much bigger than kids. How would they like it if kids were bigger than them?

I switched my gaze to the slightly flattened, stiff bird in Addie's hand so I wouldn't have to look at her angry eyes, then put on my stubborn mouth so I wouldn't cry. I would never do anything mean to Addie. Even though she was old, she was my friend—or she used to be. Before the chicken. I glared at the dead hen. Stupid bird couldn't even dodge a corncob.

Addie and I both liked chickens. Her henhouse was between our houses, and I liked to watch the busy way the hens cluck-clucked to each other, scratching in the dirt and pecking on the ground. They were especially funny to watch when they chased a bug! Sometimes two of them would both get hold of a grasshopper at the same time. Then they would have a tug of war! Sometimes they'd pull the grasshopper in half!

"CECELIA!"

I jumped. In spite of my stubborn mouth, my chin quivered. "I was just feeding the chickens! I didn't mean to! I'm sorry, sorry, sorry! I'll never eat corn again!" I swiped my eyes angrily with my sleeve. I'd run away. I'd go into the mountains and live with the Indians. They didn't have any chickens.

"Cissy," Addie said in a soft voice. I looked up at her warily. Cissy is my name when I'm being good. "You may feed my chickens any time you want to. I only ask two things."

"What?" I said suspiciously.

"First, feed them more gently." Addie smiled, "And next time you kill one, do it in the daytime so we can eat it before it spoils!"

"Deal!" I said, and held out my hand to shake Addie's, but hers were still full of chicken and corn.

I watched her head for her house. Even though we lived next door, her house was about a block away.

Later that day, Granny made me go out to pick some squishy ugly squash, which is only good if it's in a pie. I saw Addie come out in her yellow apron. She wore it almost all the time. I'd first seen it as an armful of yellow cloth that spring when Addie came over to complain to Granny.

"I got this to make some pants for my boys," she had said. I thought it was odd that she called her sons "boys." Lafayette and Gideon were huge! They were old, too, seventeen or eighteen maybe even nineteen or twenty! They weren't married yet, either. I wasn't surprised about that, because they were mean! They laughed at me when I was being serious, and sometimes they flipped my braids. They called me "Cecil" or, even worse, "Sweetheart!" So I called them "Ratface" and "Ox Ears," but not so Addie could hear me. Maybe she still called them "boys" because those meanies weren't married yet.

"It was a really good bargain," Addie sighed, smoothing the yellow fabric, "But they say they won't wear one stitch of anything I make out of this."

I curled up my lip as I imagined yellow pants. "I don't blame them," I said. "It would be harder to get a girl to marry them if they wear yellow pants. If I saw a man in pants that color, I would look twice. Maybe three times. And not because I would want to marry him, either!"

"Cecilia!" Granny had said, horrified. I scowled. What was wrong with saying what I thought? I didn't want to say "sorry" because I wasn't. I didn't want to hurt Addie's feelings, either, so I went over and felt the yellow cloth between my fingers. It was thick, and had a new fabric stiff feeling. "It feels good and strong," I said in a grown-up voice.

Addie was looking thoughtful. "My husband would have been glad for me to sew him clothes out of this. He was a practical man." I never knew Addie's husband. He'd died before they ever found me in the cabbage patch. I doubted that he would have been glad for yellow pants, either. Unless he was blind.

I glanced at Granny, not saying anything, and put a sad look on my face to show sympathy. I looked at Addie to see if she was crying about her dead husband. She had a faraway, thinking look and a smile on her face! If I'd smiled about a dead person, Granny would have lectured me all day and half the night!

Addie sat up straight. "Well, I'm not going to waste this fabric. If my boys don't want new trousers, I'm going to make me an apron." Addie was a woman of action, like me. A couple of days later, she wore her new apron over to our house. It was big, and had lots of pockets. She kept turning from side to side, making sure we could see all the pockets. She showed us how it tied behind her neck and back with thin strips of yellow fabric folded over several times and sewn into strings. It was a very fine apron. I admired it greatly. It would hold lots of rocks and sticks and bugs.

Addie used her apron pockets all summer to carry picked vegetables from her garden, eggs from the henhouse and tools to work around her place. Addie did a lot of work. Her sons sometimes helped her, but not enough. Grandma said they were "soft." I said they were lazy bums.

Then, at the end of the summer, something got into Addie's henhouse and killed a chicken. I could hear her yelling, "Lafayette! Gideon!" I ran over to her place. She was pretty upset, and I didn't blame her. Chickens were useful. If you got a broody hen that hatched out some chicks, they could get eaten by hawks or dogs or snakes. Then the ones that did live were maybe roosters instead of hens. Hens were better. They laid eggs for a couple of years before they went into the stewpot. You only need one or two roosters in a regular-sized henhouse, so extra roosters were only useful for eating.

"You boys get that rifle fixed!" Addie said, "Some dog or skunk is making a meal of our chickens and I need that rifle to put a stop to it!"

A skunk! Now that was something I'd like to see! Addie kept after her boys, "I asked you before, but you never had time, or you forgot! Today you won't forget! We can't afford to lose any more hens! Now get to town as soon as your chores are done and get Brother Olsen to fix it!"

Fay and Gid looked at each other and raised their eyebrows. They were up to something. Fay saw me standing there watching. "How's my Cecil today?" he asked with a fake nice voice. I knew it was fake because he knew I hated to be called that name.

I didn't call him Ratface in front of Addie. I stuck my tongue out at him so she couldn't see. I marched home very stiff and proper so they'd know that I knew they were up to something. I heard Gid say, "'Bye, Sweetheart!" and they both started laughing. My face got hot and my teeth got tight together.

A couple of hours later, I saw Ratface and Ox Ears walking past our house toward the center of town. They had the rifle, all right, but they weren't dressed in their working clothes. They looked kind of slick. They were talking and laughing and punching each other on the shoulder. I thought they should punch each other harder. They didn't look very serious to me. They looked like they should both be wearing yellow pants.

They still weren't back when it got dark. I knew Addie had lost her chicken at night. I was wanting to see a real live skunk, so I stepped outside and looked around. A lantern moved from Addie's front door toward the henhouse. In the lantern light, it was easy to see the yellow apron. I didn't tell Granny I was going out because she would say "no." I just started walking toward the lantern. Before I could reach it, it disappeared into the henhouse. I stopped to let my eyes adjust to the dark.

There was a sliver of moon that shone weakly over the yard. I moved slowly closer to the henhouse, feeling my way with my feet. I could hear scrabbling and squawking. "Addie?" I called, but there was no reply.

I was curious as could be, but I figured I'd get in trouble if I opened the door and let any chickens out. I found a small crack in the henhouse door and put my eye to it. I could make out Addie's outline in the lantern light. She was blocking most of my view, holding still, facing the far corner of the henhouse. She stood there for a long time. I couldn't see anything happening, nor could I smell a skunk. I moved my eyes around, trying to see something besides Addie's back.

I was beginning to feel bored until Addie shifted her weight to one side. What I saw then took all my tiredness away and made my breath freeze in my chest. My wide-awake eyes stared at two shiny spots against the far wall. The spots were eyes. Those eyes were stuck in the head of a bobcat!

I wanted to scream, but I couldn't make my mouth do it. Screaming wouldn't have helped Addie, anyway. As I stared at those slitted, cruel eyes, desperately thinking of how I could help, the eyes suddenly sprang straight at Addie! Then I did scream, but so did Addie. The bobcat crashed into the lantern Addie held in her hand, then fell and went out.

I couldn't see anything! Now what should I do? Addie was alone in the dark with a wild bobcat! I strained my eye at the crack. Was she still alive? I was so scared, it felt like the mill wheel was rolling over my chest.

Then I heard Addie muttering, and I started breathing again. She wasn't dead!

She didn't sound scared, she sounded angry! I heard the snarl of an enraged bobcat, and shivered. I heard a chilling yowl, and a scrabbling sound. The yowl turned into a gurgle, and Addie grunted and gasped. Did it have her by the throat? Did I dare open the door? What if it jumped out and got me? What if Addie was dying in there? I had to do something!

My heart thumping like Indian drums, I pulled on the henhouse door and peeked in. I still couldn't see anything. "Addie?" I called fearfully. I heard heavy breathing. Was it Addie or the bobcat?

"ADDIE!" I called desperately.

"Open the door," Addie answered shakily. I pulled the door open all the way, dreading what I would see. The thin moonlight leaked into the henhouse, faintly illuminating Addie, sitting on the henhouse floor in the straw with a yellow bundle on her lap. "Oh, Addie, I thought you were dead!"

"Not yet," she said, "*It's* dead." As she stood up on trembling legs, the bundle slid off her lap. I stared in horrible fascination at the head of a bobcat sticking out of Addie's yellow apron, with the strings pulled tightly around his neck. This was way better than a skunk!

"Help me, please," Addie said, and I took her hand and led her out of the coop. After I shut the door I noticed that she was holding her arms out away from her body. "Are you all right?" I asked.

"Got scratched up a bit," she said. I took her into her house and fetched the salve and salt she told me to get. The gashes that crisscrossed her arms and chest were leaking blood.

She told me to sprinkle salt on the wounds, but when I did, she gasped and writhed in so much pain that I stopped. Addie grabbed a handful of salt out of the bag and finished the job, making the most horrible faces, with her teeth showing and her lips pulled back tight, like a skeleton head. Her eyes were so squinted up with pain, they looked closed. I thought she might scream, but she only made pained noises, then said, "liniment" through her closed teeth. I quickly smoothed some liniment over the wounds, and Addie relaxed her face. Then I found three bleeding gashes on her jaw and cheek. She was so brave. I wanted to grow up to be like Addie.

Her two "boys" burst in the door, laughing, no rifle in their hands. When they saw Addie, their laughter turned into a look of horror. "Mother!" Gid cried, "What happened?" He looked at me as though I were to blame. I squinted my eyes at that old Ox Ears so he would know I didn't like his looks.

"You two boys go take a look at the baby doll in the henhouse," Addie replied.

"Is it yours?" Fay said really rudely to me as he and Gid headed for the door. Later Granny said he was rude because he was scared for his mother, which doesn't make any sense.

When they came back in, they looked very white and shocked. "How did you do that?" they asked their mother.

"I had to," she said. "I had no rifle, no knife, no weapon but my hands and my apron. After the bobcat broke the lantern, I figured he'd go for me again. I untied my apron in the dark. The next time he sprang at me, I caught him in the cloth and wound the strings around his neck, then pulled with all my might."

"I'm so sorry about the rifle," said Gid, who looked like he might start to cry. This was interesting.

"We got it there too late to get fixed today," Fay confessed.

"You didn't go straight to the gunsmith, did you, boys?" Addie asked.

"Fay wanted to stop by the Larsens' first," Gid blurted out. I knew the Larsens, and they weren't on the way to town. Lucy Larsen was pretty, even though she was old like Addie's boys.

Addie must have noticed the interested look on my face. She said to me, "Does your Granny know you're here?"

I looked at her sideways out of my eyes. "She might."

"I thought so. Now you go on home."

I pulled my bottom lip down with my fingers. Addie said, "Cissy, I'm tired and need to go to bed. You've been the best help. What would I have done without you?"

"Maybe you would have died," I answered solemnly as I walked over to kiss her good bye. I gave Fay and Gid a haughty look, and said, "I can kill a chicken, but I think it's much better to kill a bobcat with your bare apron strings."

I wanted to stick my tongue out at Ox Ears and Ratface, but I was being mature, so I walked out the door and shut it firmly behind me.

As I began making my way home, I heard Fay and Gid still apologizing to their mother, my friend, the Bobcat Killer.

Adelia Sidwell found a bobcat in her henhouse and strangled it with her apron strings because her two sons had put off getting the broken rifle fixed. She doctored her wounds with salt and homemade liniment. Her sons came home and found their mother scratched and bleeding and the bobcat dead in the henhouse.

DON'T JUDGE A HORSE BY ITS HIDE

Ma stacked the dirty breakfast dishes and carried them to the dishpan as Pa scooted his chair back from the table and stood up. With Ma's back turned, I crammed another biscuit into my mouth. The whole thing.

Pa lifted up one corner of his mouth in a small half-smile and shook his head. The half-smile meant that he thought it was kind of funny. The shaking head was for his obligation as a parent to try to teach me some manners. That was Ma's influence.

Pa had not always been the kind of man who needed plates and silverware to eat with. Many times his cup had been the palm of his hand, his eating utensils his own fingers as he filled his calling to help pioneer travelers on their difficult and dangerous journey across the plains and mountains to find a new home in Utah.

I swallowed my biscuit and followed Pa out to the corrals. The sun was brightening the eastern mountain range. Pa leaned against the corral poles and whistled. A plain brown horse, rather on the small side, pricked up her ears and trotted over to him.

"Hello, Flapjack, old girl," Pa said.

My friend Oscar Hakanson had told me he thought Flapjack was a stupid name for a horse. "Don't blame me," I said, "I didn't name her."

It was Ma's idea. She had taken one look at the newborn colt and said how it was just the color of a golden brown flapjack. Pa was so smitten with Ma, he'd adopted the name for the little horse. Now he seemed to be nearly as smitten with the horse as he was with Ma. He said you can't judge a book by its cover. He claimed she was the smartest horse in Utah Territory.

I thought she was the most unremarkable horse in the Territory, one that I easily overlooked every time. I much preferred to ride Captain, a big bay with a handsome blaze of white streaking down his face and four white socks that lent a flash of distinction to his proud gait.

Pa walked over to the corral gate, Flapjack shadowing him along the fence. She knew what day this was. You could see it in her eager step. Pa saddled and bridled Flapjack while I fed the livestock. Ma came out of the house just then. She carried my six-year-old brother, his head resting on her shoulder.

"How are you doing, Albert?" Pa asked the little boy. Albert coughed, then held his arms out to Pa who took him and cradled him for a few minutes. At least Albert's fever was down. He still felt weak, which meant I still had to do his chores. Ma had been busy making hot, smelly mustard plasters to stick on Albert's skinny little chest as it heaved with the effort to breathe. I was glad that Albert was breathing easier now, but his cough was still hanging on. I hoped we were all done with the stinking mustard plasters.

Now I would be in charge of Pa's chores, too, while he made his scheduled mail run. Pa handed Albert back to Ma. "Be careful," Ma said as she brushed a kiss across Pa's cheek. "Watch out for Indians."

"We always do," Pa said cheerfully. Pa clapped me on the back before he stepped up into the stirrup and threw his leg over the saddle. Then he was off down the road, trotting at a steady pace. With the mail stops along the way and the distance to Fort Provo, we wouldn't see Pa again until tomorrow evening.

The next night we were eating dinner when we heard Flapjack's hooves drum into the yard. Ma began to set a place for Pa. I went out to help him take care of the horse. When Pa came in, he smiled at the sight of Albert sitting at the table

The next week, Pa began to cough. It started out mild, but quickly progressed to the deep, rasping cough that had afflicted my brother. The morning of the mail run, Pa was lying in bed, sweat shining on his forehead.

"No!" Ma said, "You can't go!"

"But they're depending on me," Pa said just before he broke into a fit of coughing.

"They'll just have to understand. Some things are more important than the mail," Ma said sternly.

"I've never missed a run yet," Pa said in a raspy voice.

"I know. You are a good man, a man of integrity, but no one expects you to make a mail run in the condition you're in." Ma patted Pa's shoulder. "I'll make you a mustard plaster." Pa groaned.

"I'll go, Pa," I said.

Pa coughed harshly. When he could finally speak, he said, "It's dangerous."

"I can do it." I wanted my Pa to see me as a young man, not a boy.

I wanted adventure, a challenge, and I wanted to get away from those smelly mustard plasters.

"If someone has to go, you might as well send Oliver. He's a good hand with horses. You tell him all the stops, give him a blessing, and we'll say a family prayer before he leaves."

That was more than I wanted to take the time to do, especially since Ma had the plaster heating on the stove, and the smell was beginning to turn my stomach. But if that was what it took, I would do it.

I sat on the edge of the bed so my father could place his hands on my head. As he gave me a father's blessing, invoking the powers of heaven for safety on my journey, I felt a warmth on my shoulders as though someone else had placed their hands there. And Pa didn't cough once as he spoke the words of protection and guidance.

Pa laid out the route for me, the places I should stop and the stretches where I should keep out a sharp watch. "Give Flapjack her head," he said.

"But she's so small," I protested, "I thought I would take Captain instead."

Pa shook his head, but couldn't speak because he had a violent fit of coughing. When he finally stopped, he said, "You take Flapjack on the mail run. And remember to give her her head."

I agreed, as it seemed the only way to get Pa's permission to go on this adventure. Did Pa think I was a baby? I knew how to handle horses.

Right after family prayer and before Pa could think of anything else, I went out the door and shut Pa's hoarse coughing and those smelly fumes behind me. Reluctantly, I saddled Flapjack. Just as I threw my leg over the saddle, Ma came out the door. I figured she was going to tell me not to go after all, but instead she handed me a small cloth bundle. The smell of bread and cheese and an apple fritter that she had wrapped up for me to eat on my journey filled my nostrils.

"Thanks, Ma," I said, and turned the horse toward the road.

Ma said, "On your way out, check with the Hakansons and see if one of their boys will look in on us tonight in case Albert and I need help with the chores."

A twinge of guilt tweaked at my heart. I was so anxious to leave, I hadn't even thought what this would do for Ma, having to doctor Pa and do the chores, too. "Yes, Ma," I said meekly.

The Hakanson's assured me that someone would check on my mother. They had a large family, enough to spare. I'd never stopped to count, but it seemed as though they had about a dozen children of all sizes running around. I read what looked like envy in Oscar's face when he found out I was making the mail run. Sitting tall in the saddle, I turned and rode away. I was a free man with an important job to do.

The stops were not hard to find, and there weren't many. Between us and Fort Provo was mostly space. The horse and I soon finished our mail collection and headed across the Sanpete valley toward the mouth of Salt Canyon.

The day had grown hot, and I noticed a pretty little stand of cottonwoods down by the San Pitch River. The silvery green leaves stirred slightly, beckoning me into their shade. Young green willows filled the gaps between the white trunks with lush, cool leaves. I angled Flapjack toward them, welcoming the thought of a respite from the sun by riding through those cool, whispering trees. I was on my own, and was master of my time. I could go where I wanted and not have to get anyone's permission or explain myself. All was right with the world.

Suddenly, Flapjack veered away from the cottonwoods, trotting more briskly than I was asking her to. Stupid horse. She was going to miss those trees by a mile.

She balked as I pulled her head around to face the trees again, but I was firm. She needed to learn who was the boss. I urged her into a walk and eased up the pressure on the reins, but she veered off track again, and headed for the hot, treeless part of the valley floor.

I gritted my teeth. Captain would have obeyed my commands. He would have gone where I told him to go. Flapjack was just spoiled. Pa probably let her do whatever she wanted to. Well, it wouldn't work that way with me.

I again forced Flapjack's head to turn toward the trees. If she didn't cooperate soon, we would miss the stand and its soothing shade altogether. A hot breeze blew past me and into the arms of the cottonwoods. The silvery green leaves whispered an invitation to me.

Even though her head was pointed toward the trees, Flapjack was sidestepping away from the cooling shade, slowly but surely headed for the open part of the valley floor where the only cover was sagebrush.

"Give her her head."

I whipped around in my saddle to see who had ridden up behind me but I couldn't see anybody. The valley was seemingly empty of people. I wondered at the voice, but didn't feel scared. Maybe it was just a memory of what Pa had told me. Well, who was I to argue with that advice? Flapjack was going to go where she wanted to anyway.

Disgusted, I quit trying to point the little brown horse the way I wanted to go. Shaking my head, I couldn't figure out why Flapjack was Pa's favorite. She wasn't anything to look at, and what good was a horse that didn't do what you wanted it to?

Flapjack was trotting briskly, moving faster than I thought she should go. Distance riding was a matter of pacing. She'd wear herself out.

I gathered the reins up, ready to pull her back to a slower pace.

"Give her her head."

I couldn't stop myself from looking behind me again, even though I knew no one was there.

As I turned back to face forward, I noticed the willows between the silvery cottonwood trunks shaking violently. There was hardly any wind. Certainly not enough to account for that much motion. What was going on?

Before my horrified eyes, five Indians riders burst from the innocent looking cover of the willows and galloped toward us, whooping and hollering.

Without any urging from me, Flapjack broke into a gallop. I hung on, my heart racing faster than the little brown horse's hoofbeats.

It wasn't long before Flapjack put a substantial distance between us and the Indians. I was amazed at her speed and endurance. The Indians soon gave up their ambush. Thanks to the plain brown horse, we had been too far away from their hiding place to be taken by surprise.

The next day, after I had recounted my adventures to my worried mother and admiring brother, my Pa said, "I've always thought that little horse can smell Indians. She's gotten me out of more than one scrape with them."

Now Pa and I were in complete agreement. Flapjack was the best horse in Utah Territory.

A father and son team in Spring City used a Morgan cross horse for their leg of the Pony Express route. They claimed the horse could smell Indians since she always avoided them wherever they lay in wait for the mail riders. The local Indians admired the wily horse so much that it became a game for them to try to ambush the horse and rider. They would rush out from their hiding place, laughing and yelling as they waved at the speedy horse. The Pony Express rider would give a friendly wave in return as the horse galloped away.

SHE LOVES ME, SHE LOVES ME NOT

I walked a carefully measured half block behind the slender figure limping along the street. I was thinking of ways I could offer to help her with the heavy burlap sack she carried, without sounding too eager. I imagined striding up and saying gallantly, "Allow me," and taking the sack from her hand. Or I could be more direct: "I'll take that now." Or I could try the flattering approach: "That's too heavy for you, let me carry it."

As I played different possibilities over in my head, my mind wandered forward to the day when lovely Mary Artemesia Lowry and I would be married. I could see us riding down the wide main street of Manti in a shiny black carriage—Mr. and Mrs. Piers Madsen. Everyone who saw us would stop and stare in admiration. Most would wave, since we were such a popular and attractive couple. It would be spring, and my lovely bride would slap my face to get the flies off it.

I jumped back as Mary pulled her hand away from my cheek. Her large blue eyes, set in a perfect oval face and framed by glossy black hair, were wide with surprise. "Oh, Piers, I'm sorry!" she said, laughing. "I was trying to work the kinks out of my back. This potato sack is heavy."

While daydreaming, I hadn't noticed Mary drop her sack, raise her arms above her head, and slowly twist from side to side. I had walked right into her perfect white hand as she was twisting toward me.

I stood staring down at her lovely flushed face. Although I was fourteen and she was seventeen, I was tall for my age. And she was perfect for hers. Three years was nothing. Once she knew the deep feelings of my heart, she would know that no one could love her like I did, and she would wait for me. She wouldn't be able to help herself.

I had us back in the buggy, heading for the sunset, when she said, "Piers, I know I'm almost home, but would you mind carrying this sack the rest of the way for me?"

I could have stomped on my own toe! Kicked myself! Put my head in a well! What a dunce! I missed a perfect opportunity to offer to carry it for her! "Of course, yes, I'll be most honored to carry it for you, from here to Ephraim if you like, that would be no problem at all!" I babbled.

I grasped the sack with both hands and swung it over my shoulder, intending to stand straight and strong as a hardwood tree. Instead, I needed to take two steps to catch my balance when that heavy sack thwacked me in the back!

Mary pretended not to notice. "Thank you, Piers," she said sweetly. When we got to her house, she opened the door. I staggered in and she showed me where the kitchen was.

Beside the kitchen doorway sat her old Granny in a rocking chair, a crocheted afghan over her knees. "Hello, Granny," Mary said cheerily and kissed her on the cheek. Her Granny didn't speak or look at Mary. She just stared straight ahead.

"Is she all right?" I asked as I lowered the sack.

"Granny? Oh, yes, of course," Mary said, pulling an apron from a peg and tying it around her small waist. "She just doesn't speak anymore. Pa says she did all her allotted talking in life, and when she'd said it all, she just stopped!" Mary smiled a darling smile at the family joke, but after a moment of silence, she continued more soberly, "Granny doesn't speak or even seem to know we're here. Still, I can't stop myself from speaking to her and giving her a kiss. Maybe she can still feel things." Mary put her small, soft hand on Granny's shoulder. "She doesn't seem to be in pain, and she's such a dear, I'll help take care of her as long as she lives." Mary looked up at me with wet eyes that melted my insides. Confiding her innermost feelings to me swelled my heart with resolve to always protect her from any harm. She smiled and brushed at her eyes with her hand. Then her eyes focused on her sleeve and she said, "Oh, no!"

"What's wrong?" I asked.

"My button is gone!" she said with a note of despair. The end of her sleeve was loose. I could see the smooth, pink, inner part of her wrist as the fabric flopped over with an empty buttonhole dangling about an inch below her arm. The sight of her soft, rosy skin made me breathe faster.

"I'll find it!" I declared as I strode for the door. I meant to retrace every step of the way until I found that button. I charged out the door and bumped into Sarah Peacock, Mary's older sister. Her gray eyes and her mouth opened wide in surprise. Her husband, Judge George Peacock, was standing behind her and grabbed her shoulders to steady her. He was a young man for a judge and had a square face and a well-groomed moustache. He said, "Hold on there now, Son!"

I felt my face grow hot. I wished I were anywhere but here, like

Salt Lake City, or Illinois, or maybe even Africa. "I'm so sorry," I said, ducking my head and then trying to turn it into a bow, which didn't work very well. "So very sorry," I mumbled as I looked up and saw Sarah's amused expression. "Excuse me, please," I said as politely as I could through clenched teeth, and I ran down the walkway.

I felt better when I started looking for that button. I was a man on a mission. I spent a lot of time looking. Buttons were scarce in the settlements, and hard to come by.

After what felt like hours of searching, I finally noticed the gray button in the dirt by the spot where Mary had stopped and stretched her arms over her head. I scooped it up like it was a precious diamond, and headed home with it. I decided I would take it to her tomorrow, when I was sure Judge Peacock and Sarah would be gone.

When I woke up the next morning, Mary's button was the first thing I thought of. I felt warm and light headed. When I walked out to the outhouse, I got dizzy. "Ah, true love," I thought to myself.

As I made my way to Mary's house, I wondered if I should put the button in a bunch of flowers, and let Mary find it in there. Would she think that was odd? Would it make her like me better? I could hide it in a piece of my mother's cake. The thought of cake made me gag, and I stopped walking. But what if Mary swallowed the button before she found it? Bad idea. I could tell by the queasiness in my stomach. I began walking again. Maybe I would pretend I hadn't been able to find it, and then pull it out of my pocket at the last minute, just to see her face light up. Maybe she would be so happy and grateful, she would throw her arms around me. Maybe she would kiss me!

Lost in enraptured thoughts, it was only when I was across the street from Mary's that I noticed a tall, old Indian cut across the grass to the Lowry's front door. I knew who he was. He was Chief Walker, the Ute Indian who had invited the settlers to come to Sanpete County many years earlier. Exceptionally tall, he walked with a long stride. I supposed he had dealings of some sort or another with Brother Lowry. But surely he would not be home at this hour. Chief Walker did not hesitate at the door of the Lowry's house. He walked right in.

I kept going, too, but instead of heading for the door, I veered around to a side window and looked in. Things around me looked sort of foggy. I felt like I was in a dream. I wiped my sweating forehead and focused on Mary standing on a chair. It looked like she had been surprised in the act of putting something away up on a high shelf. She was shaking her head and pointing toward the door. I heard Chief Walker say, "No. I come see you."

Mary stepped down from the chair and walked quickly toward the kitchen. Chief Walker followed her. I couldn't see them anymore, so I sneaked toward the back of the house.

I wasn't sure what to do. I didn't know what Chief Walker wanted. He could be nice to the settlers, or he could be nasty. It all depended on his mood. He had been baptized a member of the Church of Jesus Christ of Latter-day Saints, but he was also still taking slaves and occasionally killing rival tribal members, as well as stealing cattle and horses. He was just plain unpredictable. I had to protect Mary. I knew I was no match for a full-grown Indian who had lived a warrior life, but I had to watch over Mary. If necessary, I would die for her.

I could imagine my funeral. All the girls in the settlement would be there, crying over my coffin, and the Bishop would say, "This boy is bound for the Celestial Kingdom. Greater love hath no man than that he lay down his life for his brother . . ."

I felt a sudden jolt as my leg sank into the ground. I fleetingly wondered if I had stepped into my grave, but a painful wrench in my knee let me know I was still very much alive. The jolt left me feeling woozy. I looked around the yard through watering eyes. It looked as though I had stepped into a hole that had been dug to set a clothesline pole. I could also see that I was very near an open kitchen window. As I dragged my leg out of it's little would-be grave, I heard Chief Walker say, "And you have teepee here, in town. No go in mountains with other squaws. Give you many best furs, ermine, beads, a fine horse. You have all you want."

I pulled myself up by the window ledge and looked in just as Mary answered, "I can't marry you."

I almost lost my hold on the ledge! Chief Walker was asking her to MARRY him? This was like a very bad dream. I could see Mary standing behind her grandmother's rocking chair, alternately placing her hands on the old woman's shoulders and on the back of the chair as though she couldn't find a comfortable place to rest them.

"Why?" Chief Walker boomed in a challenging voice. It sounded like he was far away.

Mary jumped, then straightened her spine into a stiff line. "Because I'm already married," she declared.

Now I knew this was a really bad dream! Chief Walker and I must have had similar looks of disbelief and dismay on our faces as we stared at her. Chief Walker broke the silence first. "WHO?" he bellowed. He stabbed a large hunting knife into the wooden kitchen table. It stood upright, quivering, as he challenged Mary with a steely stare.

She hesitated. I held my breath. My head was pounding, and it felt like fog was moving in over my eyes. I squinted to see better. "Judge George Peacock is my husband," she said.

Walker grabbed his knife, wrenched it from the table, and stalked out of the house. I moaned in pain—pain of the body and pain of the heart. In her hour of need, she had not thought of me, she had thought of her brother-in-law! It was more than my love-burst heart could take. Everything faded into black.

When I woke up, I was at home, in my bed. At first I was relieved. It had only been a dream. A bad dream. A very bad dream. "So they've gone off to Salt Lake," I heard my Aunt Martha say. I vaguely wondered who had gone to Salt Lake.

"Well, but it was the only thing for it," my mother replied. "Brother Lowry was right"

Lowry? Mary? My heart skipped a beat. "Mother?" I called.

"Piers!" she exclaimed, and bustled over to my side. "You had me so worried! Why didn't you tell me you had a fever? You shouldn't have gone out! Didn't you feel dizzy and weak? What were you thinking about? Brother Lowry found you lying by his house and thought you were dead!"

"Lowry," I said.

"Yes," interrupted Aunt Martha, coming up beside Mother, "You were at the Lowry's." She spoke slowly, as though I were a small child.

"I know," I said impatiently, "Where's Mary?"

"Gone to Salt Lake," said Aunt Martha slowly and distinctly.

"Why?" I asked.

"Well, that's the exciting part of the story," Aunt Martha spoke faster as she warmed up to her gossip, "See, Chief Walker asked Brigham Young if he could marry a white woman. President Young said if the woman agreed, it would be all right. So the Chief had the gall to ask Mary Lowry to marry him! Imagine! I shudder at the thought. She, of course, would have nothing to do with that. Yet that clever girl knew if she turned him down, he might take offense and retaliate on the town. Who knows what atrocities would have been rained down on our heads! That brave girl thought to tell that savage that she was already married, and to Judge George Peacock, too! That sent Chief Walker back into the mountains. When Mary's father came home and she told him what happened, he said she had to marry the judge to make good on her word to Chief Walker, so they hitched up their buggy and went to Salt Lake City to get married. Isn't it romantic?"

"Oh!" I moaned. I had never minded the thought of plural marriage until this moment. It was perfectly legal for Judge Peacock to be married to Sarah and then marry Mary, too, as long as both women agreed.

I couldn't understand how Mary could be content to live without me. I carried her potato sack for her, and even found her button! But I'd never given it to her. If I had, she would have known how much I was willing to sacrifice for her happiness. Now it was too late. She was gone from me forever. All I had left was her button, which I decided I would always keep close to me. She could get a new one while she was in Salt Lake City.

I recovered slowly from my fever. In January, Chief Walker died. Some people said it was from a broken heart. I believed it.

Chief Walkara got permission from Mormon Church president Brigham Young to marry a white woman provided he found one who would agree to marry him. He proposed to young Mary Artemesia Lowry. Fearing for the safety of the town if she refused, she told him she was already married. When he stabbed his knife in the table and asked "Who?" all she could think of was her brother-in-law Judge George Peacock. Walkara left in a temper. When Mary told her father the story, he sent Mary and George to Salt Lake as quickly as possible to be married. Chief Walkara died the following January.

PART II
ISN'T THAT ODD?

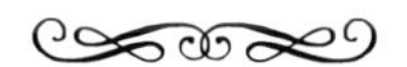

BIRDS OF A FEATHER

I grabbed the scrap pail and the egg basket and shouldered my way outside. The back door slammed behind me with a satisfying "bang."

"Ireta!" Mama called. I knew what she was going to say, so I mouthed the words along with her, but I did it so she couldn't see. "Don't slam the door!"

"Yes, Mama," I said agreeably.

As soon as Henry and the girls saw me flinging the scrap bucket onto the hard, dry ground, they came honking and waddling over. My brother Cal said they were just a noisy bunch of dumb geese, but that's because he didn't know them like I did.

Estella and Honey Bun were moving so fast, their wings were flapping like schooner sails. When they passed Nibbles, she tried to take a bite out of Estella's wing. Estella scolded her as she flapped on past. Lula Ray was, as usual, the last one to arrive.

Henry was flapping and tapping his big yellow feet back and forth, trying to guard all the choicest pieces before the girls could scoop them up. I watched as they bobbed their long necks down into a graceful curve, like a bend in a river, as they chuckled and gobbled up the scraps. Henry finally got wise and started snatching morsels off the ground as fast as he could, shoving the girls aside and asserting his position as leader of the gaggle.

I laughed and started doing a two-step around the geese. As I danced, I began to sing the song that Cal had brought home. When Mama heard him singing, she gasped, "Cal! Wherever did you learn that awful song!" So I paid especially close attention to the words.

"Take your lady by the hand, lead her like a pigeon," I sang, "Make her dance the weevily-wheat 'til she loses her religion!" Lula Ray started flapping along behind me, singing along in her deep-throated honk. Mama didn't like the song, but it was so funny to have the geese waddling and honking along behind me that I couldn't help myself. It was their favorite, so I sang it again. Before I was done, all the geese were doing their awkward goose-dance steps behind me. Henry was the last one, having to make sure there were no scraps left before he would join the parade. So there we were, laughing and chattering, skipping enough to kick up puffs of dust in the scruffy yard.

"Ireta!" Mama called. My feet stopped dancing and my shoulders slumped. Had she heard me singing the scandalous song?

"See you later, giggle gaggles," I said as I trudged toward the house. Mama didn't have her hands on her hips, so I thought maybe I was safe about the song.

"Where are the eggs?" Mama asked, looking at the empty pail and basket in my hands.

"Didn't get them yet," I mumbled.

Mama shook her head and clucked her tongue. The geese made a noise like that, too, but when Henry or one of the girls did it, it looked like they were laughing. There was no trace of humor on Mama's face.

"You need to be more serious and get your work done on time," Mama said. "Now I'll have to go to Aunt Elsie's by myself." I dropped my eyes to the floor. It's not that I really minded not going to Aunt Elsie's. She was old, smelled funny, and expected me to sit still with my hands folded in my lap. But Mama was giving me a punishment, so the least I could do was to act suitably sorry.

"When you finally get your chores done, you need to wash these plums," Mama continued, pointing to two buckets full of fat, purple fruit.

"Yes, Mama," I said in a small voice.

"And see that you do it," Mama said sternly. Then she marched out the door and was gone.

I had told Mama before that I would rather work outside with Pa than have to be inside doing the cooking and cleaning and washing. But she'd said that's what Cal was for, and I was for helping her in the house.

I swung my basket all the way to the barn. Henry and the girls were taking a dip in the pond. I watched Honey Bun do a nosedive into the water, waggling her tail in the air until her head popped back up to the surface. Nibbles bent in close to Honey Bun's face to see if she'd come up with anything good.

One thing I really liked about those geese was that they understood me. They never told me to be quiet or settle down or mind my manners. In gratitude, I adamantly refused to let anyone in the family talk about having a goose dinner. That is precisely why Cal brought it up all the time.

As Pa pointed out, the geese were very good at keeping rattlesnakes away, so Mama was more than willing to keep them in the yard and off the dinner table.

I searched for nests in the scant, musty hay. I knew Pa would be clearing this out soon to make room for the new hay that was standing in the fields.

I did a really good job hunting eggs, if I do say so myself. Maybe when Mama saw how many eggs there were, she'd let me take one down to the general store to trade for some candy.

I hurried into the house and slammed the door behind me, swinging the egg basket into the kitchen. When I saw the plums that still had to be washed, the smile melted off my face. The egg basket in my hand reminded me that maybe if I did a good job, and got it done by the time Mama got back, she'd be in such a good mood that she'd be sure to let me have an egg!

Cheered again, I set the egg basket down on the table and picked up a bucket of plums. I had to use two hands while staggering outside to the well pump. Positioning the bucket in just the right spot, I worked up a good flow of water. As it pulsed through the faucet, it spilled into the bucket, soon overflowing it and rolling a few fat plums out onto the ground in a lumpy purple waterfall.

With the water added to the plums, the bucket was now so heavy that I couldn't lift it, not even with two hands. I cocked my head to one side and looked the problem over. I hated the idea of picking each plum out of the bucket, one at a time. That would be tedious. I didn't like little picky jobs. I liked chores that were either fast or fun. The very best ones were both.

I flapped my apron up and down as I thought of what to do. If I could only get the water off the plums without dumping them out and having to pick them up again. Besides, once they'd been on the ground, I'd have to wash them again, one by one. I think I'd rather walk on rocks in my bare feet.

Then I had an idea. I could poke a hole in the bottom of the bucket. That seemed like a really good option. I started to look around for a nail or tool that would make a small hole for the water to escape, leaving the plums all together and clean, besides.

I imagined Mama coming home, smiling with delight at the whole bucket of plums, clean and shiny wet. Then, in my imagination, she dumped out the plums and discovered the hole. Her smile dissolved into a frown, and there were no eggs for me to take to the store.

At last I decided that the punishment was worse than the solution I had come up with. A hole-in-the-bucket lecture could ruin the whole rest of my day. Now I was twisting my apron in agitation, thinking so hard for another idea that was as good as the hole in the bucket.

Maybe if I left it where it was for a while, the geese would get done swimming and come over and eat the plums off the top. Then it might be light enough that I could carry it.

I looked hopefully at the geese in the pond. Estella had her head under her wing, fluffing her feathers with her busy orange beak. Henry was paddling like a fat canoe, heading for something I couldn't see on the far side of the pond. Nibbles was upside down, her orange heels breaking the surface as she searched for something as good as Honey Bun had found. Honey Bun and Lula Ray stepped out onto dry land, shaking their tail feathers in a shower of sparkly water drops.

No, I decided. Mama would notice if the bucket wasn't full when she got home.

Maybe Cal would carry it for me. But he was out with Pa in the fields. Even if he wasn't, I didn't think he would have done it anyway. Not unless I promised to do his chores for the rest of my life.

I was getting impatient. The situation was getting serious. I sighed and bent over to dump the bucket out. I guess there was no helping it. I'd have to pick the plums up off the muddy ground and re-wash them one by one. There was nothing else to do.

But as I bent over, my apron fell forward and dipped itself into the water. Annoyed, I started to bat it away, but then the perfect solution suddenly jumped into my head.

"Glory be!" I said as I pulled off my apron. I laid it over the top of the bucket and tied the strings around to hold it on. Then I tipped the bucket over and watched the purpley water push out through my bulging apron onto the ground. It worked!

I tipped the bucket back up and draped my wet, purple-spotted apron over the pump. With two hands I hauled the clean plums back into the house, and brought out the second bucket.

I was so proud of myself when at last I had two buckets of wet plums sitting side by side in the kitchen. I had done what Mama asked, and before she got home, even. Then I surprised myself and put the eggs away. She hadn't even asked me to do that.

I was waiting outside when Mama came rattling up to the house in the buggy with two baskets beside her. "What have you got?" I asked, climbing up to see.

"Aunt Elsie gave me these old preserves," Mama said, handing me a basketful of jars wrapped in rags.

"If we already got some preserves from Aunt Elsie, why do we have to make more?" I asked.

Ma climbed down from the wagon. "These are spoiled," she said, "We have to empty and wash these jars, and then we can use them for the plums."

My happy mood slumped. Washing jars was boring, and Mama was real particular about getting every little speck washed out of every single jar. The rest of the day loomed ahead of me, long and weary.

"Did you wash the plums?" Mama asked, creasing her brow as she looked at me sternly.

"Oh, yes, Mama, I washed every one!" I smiled at her, delighted that I had done my part.

We each carried our baskets full of spoiled preserves onto the porch. I was glad Mama had taken the bigger basket. I was almost dropping mine.

Mama stepped into the house as I set my basket down. "Ireta!" The tone of her voice warned me that she was displeased. What had I done this time?

I walked into the kitchen, anxiously looking for the scene of my "crime."

"Do you call these washed?" Mama asked, pointing to the plum buckets. The lovely wet shine had dried, leaving the plum skins looking dull and dusty.

"Yes!" I said earnestly, "I carried them out to the pump and filled the buckets with water, then I strained it off with my apron. I washed both buckets. I really did, Mama!"

Mama looked at me and sighed. "I meant for you to wash them one at a time and pick off the stems and leaves," Mama said.

"Oh," was all I could think of to say.

Mama was quiet for a minute. I bunched my shoulders together in case she was going to scold me.

"I'll do the plums," she said at last. My heart lifted a little. I looked up into Mama's face. Her chin was tilted down at me, her eyebrows raised, and her eyes were too serious.

"You, young lady," she said, apparently forgetting that I hate being called that, "will empty the jars and wash them out." Mama dumped a bucket of plums into the washtub. A drizzle of water followed them, pouring over the purple skins and making them shine again.

"See, Ma?" I said, pointing at the trickle. "I DID wash them!"

"Yes, you tried," Mama said, dumping the other bucket of plums onto the first. "Now dump the old preserves in these buckets. And take care not to break any jars."

I took the buckets in my hands and trudged outside, forgetting to slam the door on my way out.

As I worked the clamp wires off the hefty lids and poured the reddish-brown preserves into the buckets, I could smell a sharp, moldy smell that still held a vague scent of fruit.

I splashed water into the jars as the sun soaked my back with warmth, and the spraying water kept the insects off me. All in all, since there was no getting away from it, I was glad to be doing the outside job instead of inside sorting all those plums from the leaves and stems.

When Mama called to me, I carried the wet jars piled on top of a basket of rags. I had to make another trip for the rest of the jars and the other basket.

Ma and I sat and wiped jars. I don't know how she thought of it, but Mama started talking about her childhood. She told me how she had caught and thrown snakes at a boy that she liked. She used to tie knots in her sister's hair because it was longer than hers and she was jealous. She told me about the first time she'd made a pie, and the crust was as tough as a board and even the dog wouldn't eat it.

I was laughing so much that the jars were wiped clean before I even knew it. I was surprised when Pa and Cal came in for supper.

"What happened?" Cal asked, staring at us as though we'd told him we were going to Sunday Meeting in nothing but our shifts.

The intensity of his face was disturbing. I couldn't think what he could possibly mean, but I felt compelled to give some sort of answer. I held up a jar. "We washed jars," I said in a small voice.

"Who killed the geese?" Pa demanded, stomping up behind my brother.

The geese? My heart thudded with sudden dread as I jumped up, the jar knocking loose from my hand as it hit my chair. It crashed to the floor.

Mama didn't even look at me. "The geese are dead?" she said.

I ran out the door, and then stopped as though a rope tied to my heart had jerked me back. Henry and the girls were all lying still and silent around the water pump. I could tell right off that they weren't just sleeping. Their heads and necks were splattered with dark red blood, and they were lying much too still. And not a single beak or webbed foot so much as twitched when I yelled, "Nooooo!"

The invisible rope snapped, paining my heart as I broke free. I reached Honey Bun first and scooped her up in my arms. My eyes were so blurry from tears that I couldn't locate the wound that had done her in. But as my arms pressed around her middle, I noticed that she was fatter than she had been that morning. The pickings from the pond must have been good today. At least my Honey Bun hadn't died hungry.

With a sob, I laid her back down and checked on Estella. She was dead, too. Henry, Nibbles, and Lula Ray were all on the other side of the pump. As I headed over to them, I thumped into the old preserves bucket with my foot. It was empty. Only smears of reddish brown lined the insides.

I picked the bucket up and turned to face my wide-eyed family who had all followed me out.

"They were poisoned!" I said, my voice kind of loud in my own ears, "They ate Aunt Elsie's bad preserves and died!"

Pa took the bucket from my hands and Mama folded me into her arms. Even Cal mumbled, "Sorry, sis," as I cried and cried and cried.

When I was finally done, Pa had laid Henry and the girls out in a respectable row upon the ground.

"At least they all went together," Cal said gently. I nodded in my misery.

"Ireta," Mama said gently, "I know that you loved those geese, and you took very good care of them. Now that they're gone, I wonder if you think they would like us to have their feathers to make some pillows to remind us of them always."

"You want to pluck them?" I said doubtfully.

"Yes," Mama said. "They don't need their feathers any more, and we do." Mama took hold of both of my hands. "They were so fond of you. Don't you think they would like you to snuggle up with their feathers every night?"

As I got used to the idea, it did appeal to me. I could still have part of my friends close to me. "Yes," I said.

In the graying evening, we set to work pulling the feathers out of my former friends. When Pa stripped off Henry's thick, cloud-soft breast feathers, a muffled honk sounded from Henry's beak, no louder than a sigh.

I sat straight up. "He's alive!" I said, "Pa, did you hear that? He's still alive!"

"I'm sorry," Pa said sincerely, "It's just the gas escaping his bloated belly."

"What gas?" I asked as my heart fell into my feet.

"The rotten preserves built up gas inside their bellies, and it comes out a little bit at a time as we pull on the feathers and open their airway."

"Is that why Estella felt bigger to me?" I asked.

Pa nodded.

I sat in quiet contemplation. Pa finished with Henry and laid him in a wheelbarrow. I was bothered by the sight of my de-feathered friends. "I hope that at least they died quickly," I said, jumping up and running into the house.

I slept restlessly that night. I kept chasing geese and dancing with pigeons. The next morning I woke up to an exclamation from Mama's mouth. "Well, glory be!" she said, as though she couldn't believe it.

I sat up and looked around. There was nothing unusual in the house. But Mama was looking out the window, the curtain pulled back with one hand, her other hand resting on her heart.

"What is it?" I asked.

"Come and see," Mama said, not taking her eyes away from the window.

Rubbing my eyes, I climbed out of bed and made my way to Mama's side. What I saw made my eyes almost pop out of my head. I must still be dreaming. This couldn't be real. Five naked geese were waddling around the yard, snapping at flies and any grasshoppers that were foolish enough to cross our boundary.

I pulled open the door and rushed outside. "Henry!" I called, "You're alive!"

Henry looked expectantly at me, but didn't see any scrap bucket in my hand, so he ignored me. He waggled his few remaining tail feathers and turned his attention back to hunting insects. Lula Ray and Nibbles were working their way toward the pond.

"Pa! Pa!" I called out, "Some of the girls are headed for the pond, and without their feathers, they can't swim!"

Pa came running out behind me, his shirttail flapping, and headed the errant girls off their path of self-destruction. "Open the barn door!" he called.

I managed to find several sharp rocks with my bare feet as I hurried to the barn and swung the door open. The geese were scattering in front of Pa, seeming to be confused about what he wanted them to do. Estella seemed embarrassed by her condition and kept heading for the undergrowth at the edge of the yard.

"Take your lady by the hand," I sang, not looking at anyone but Henry, "Lead her like a pigeon." I started a little two-step with my sore feet. "Make her dance the weevily-wheat 'til she loses her religion," I finished loudly.

Mama had her hand to her mouth, but Henry and the girls were there at the barn door, looking expectantly at me. We always sang the song twice. I backed into the barn, singing the song a second time. Henry and the girls followed, Estella keeping to the shadows of the barn walls, Lula Ray dancing her awkward goose-step, which looked even funnier without any feathers on. Henry proudly waggled his few remaining tail feathers and honked politely for the scrap bucket.

At around the turn of the Twentieth Century, a gaggle of geese that lived at the house next door to Ireta Stevens gobbled up some old preserves, feasting on the sour, fermented fruit until they passed out dead drunk. Their owners thought they were really dead, and could see no reason to waste the lovely soft feathers. Ireta was there when plucking the birds caused them to make small grunts or honks, but the family figured it was just the fermented gas escaping from their bellies. Since the tragedy occurred so late in the day, the geese were laid in a wheelbarrow for disposal the next morning.

When they got up the next day, everyone was surprised to see that their "dead" geese had sobered up overnight and were now running around the yard, naked except for a few tail and head feathers! Without their feathers and natural oils to keep them afloat, the geese could easily drown, so they were locked up in a shed until their feathers grew back again.

The weevily-wheat song was sung in the 1800s and was not always approved of by sober-minded adults.

SO SHALL YE REAP

I stared in disbelief. I had never seen anything like it. "Mama, what is he doing?" I said, pointing to a man on a horse in a field.

Mama stopped on the muddy road. She was staring, too. "That's Brother Dan," she said, tipping her head one way and then the other as if to make sure, "He's riding his horse backwards."

Not only was he riding his horse backward, he was holding something under one arm. His other arm would move to whatever he was holding, then extend out over the horse's rump, then go back and out, back and out as the horse walked through the field. It looked like he was dropping rocks behind his horse, which didn't make any sense to me.

The horse turned and walked toward us. I stepped behind Mama's skirt with just my face peeking around the side to watch the strange behavior. "Why is he backward?" I said.

Mama boosted Sarah Ann up onto her hip before she said, "Those are potatoes he's planting. I would think that he's tired of waiting for the ground to dry up enough to use a shovel, so he's letting his horse make the holes. Then he's dropping the potatoes in the hoof prints."

"I don't ever want to plant potatoes," I said. The fact is, I was scared of horses. I was small enough to walk under a horse's belly, not that I'd ever want to. Their hooves were huge, and looked as hard as rocks.

Brother Dan's unusual method must have officially started the planting season, because just over a week later that I noticed men using their horses to pull long metal machines that Mama called "discs" through their fields. Mama said that we needed to get our field planted, too. I heard her ask some of the brethren to disc our field, but they were all too busy. Even after the men were done disking and planting, they were still too busy with irrigating to help us.

Finally, after several weeks, Mama took matters into her own hands. "Peter, I need you to be a big boy and help Mama plant the wheat," she told me one morning as she stirred the pot that bubbled with our breakfast porridge. My little sister, Sarah Ann, was hanging on Mama's skirts, whining to be picked up. A feeling of dread filled my stomach. "Me?" I said.

Mama burst out laughing. I felt my lip getting pouty. Mama didn't like my pouty lip, but I left it there because I didn't like her laughing at me. "You're the only Peter here," she said, "unless Sarah Ann changed her name to Peter and now I should call you Sarah Ann."

I scowled as Mama carried the pot of porridge to the table and set it down. Sarah Ann followed her, tottering along on her short little legs, her face scrunched up in a grimace as she made woeful little cries. Mama scooped Sarah Ann up and put her in her high chair.

Mama sat down in her chair facing me across the table. The extra chair and bowl for Papa were across the table from Sarah Ann. Papa was never there to eat with us, so I don't know why Mama kept setting him a place. When I asked her, she said it was because he'd always be in our hearts. I don't know what that had to do with eating. Eating was for stomachs.

I didn't know who Papa was. He'd been gone since before I could remember. Mama said he was on a mission in a country called Norway that was far across the ocean, but I didn't even know what an ocean was. It was all confusing to me, but she seemed to feel better when she told me about him, so I usually fell asleep to the sound of her voice telling me "Papa stories."

After the prayer, Sarah Ann was happily splashing her spoon up and down in her porridge. I wanted to be sure what I was getting in for, so I said to Mama, "We don't have to ride a horse backward to plant the wheat, do we?"

"No," Mama said, "Is that what you were worried about?" I nodded. Mama smiled like she might start laughing again. I wished she would quit laughing. This was serious business.

Mama didn't laugh. She pulled the corners of her mouth in tight and said, "Do you remember seeing the farmers out in their fields with their horses dragging those round metal rods with the circles on them?" I nodded again, my mouth full of mush. "Those are called discs. They disc the field, then plant the wheat in the dents made by the discs."

"Do we have a disc?" I asked Mama.

"No," Mama said, "But we have a hoe. And we will have the Lord's help."

I didn't exactly know what she meant by that, but I was interested to find out. When we went out into the field, I looked around to see if a man in a white robe and beard might be there with a disc, but he wasn't. The only adult I could see was Mama, who was carrying a hoe. She had little Sarah Ann in a sling made of fabric which she hung over her shoulder, like the Indians did with their babies. I pulled the wheat seeds along in a little wagon that Papa had made for me before he left.

At the edge of the field, Mama put the point of her hoe on the ground and started dragging it. "Peter, put the seeds in," she told me as she stepped backwards, keeping an eye on the hoe. I don't know if it was because of Sarah Ann wiggling around in the sling, or if it was because Mama wasn't very good at it, but the row I dropped the seeds in was kind of crooked. It seemed to not make any difference after Sarah Ann fell asleep. The rows still wobbled down the field, so it must have been that Mama wasn't very good at it.

We didn't get all the wheat planted in one day. The next morning Mama had to talk to me with a stern voice before I would take up the wagon handle. When we got to the field, Sarah Ann wouldn't ride in the sling any more, so Mama put her down. Sarah Ann cooed with delight and grabbed up a dirt clod. She threw it at me. It didn't hurt, but I yelled, "Hey!" just the same.

By the time we finished the planting, it was hot. Mama just collapsed into the shade of a sagebrush, and I collapsed on top of her. Sarah Ann looked at us in amazement, then she stumbled over and flung herself against us, giggling delightedly that we had gotten down where she could play with us.

"You did a man's work, Peter," Mama said. That made me glad I had helped her until the very end.

We got up to go home. This time I pulled Sarah Ann in the wagon instead of the wheat seeds. When we got to the road, Brother Brown was riding toward us on his horse. He stopped and looked down at us.

"Sister Peterson, have you planted this field all by yourself?" he asked as I got behind Mama so the horse wouldn't step on me.

"No, Brother Brown, my son helped me," Mama said firmly.

"And you used a hoe?" Brother Brown continued.

"Yes," Mama replied, "It was all that I had."

Brother Brown shook his head slowly. "I'm afraid that your seeds might be planted too deep," he said, "Unless you're very careful, a hoe drags a furrow deeper than a disc."

Mama's back went stiff. "I was very careful," she said.

"Glad to hear it," said Brother Brown. "As late as you planted, you will be fortunate if your wheat has time to ripen before the first frost." Then he clicked his tongue to his horse and rode away.

On the way home, we passed some fields that had green fuzz on them, like the fur on a kitten that's just been born, except that I've never seen a green kitten. "Mama," I asked, "Will our wheat grow?"

"Of course it will," Mama said, taking my hand firmly. I felt better.

A couple of weeks later, I found Mama sitting at the table with her head bent down on her arms that were folded in front of her. I thought she was praying, so I waited quietly until I saw her shoulders shaking.

"Mama?" I asked.

Her shoulders stopped moving and she raised her head. Then she wiped her eyes with her apron. She smiled, but it didn't look happy like a smile is supposed to. It looked strange on her red, wet face.

"What's wrong, Mama?" I asked, a scared knot tying itself in my stomach.

"Nothing, really," Mama said, "It's just taking our wheat seeds a long time to sprout. I need to be more patient."

"Maybe they're too deep, like Brother Brown told us," I said. "Maybe they won't grow."

Mama's face crumpled. "We tried so hard," she said. Then she put her head back down on her arms. I wished I hadn't said anything.

The fields around ours were filling up with tender little wheat stalks, pale green and just tall enough to wave and ripple when a breeze blew across them. Our field was brown and bare, like a scab on a head of green hair.

Then one morning just as we were finishing our porridge, I heard a lot of yelling outside. Mama rushed to the door to see what was happening. I crowded in behind her and saw bugs jumping across our yard. "Grasshoppers!" Mama gasped. She plunked Sarah Ann into the sling, grabbed a shovel, threw a burlap sack over my shoulder and grabbed me by the hand. We hurried out to the fields where men, women and children were beating on the new wheat fields with shovels and sacks. Some of the sacks were on fire, the smoke puffing upward like a distress signal with each hit to the ground.

I could hardly see the green of the wheat fields because of all the fat bugs. Our field didn't have any bugs. It didn't have any wheat, either. It sat there brown and bare, a big bruise on the land.

Mama pulled me into the field next to ours, where the tender green stalks of wheat were bending down under the weight of the insects that were chewing them to stubs. "Peter! Hit them!" Mama said, bringing her shovel down hard on a swarm of grasshoppers that were as thick as the flies on a dead lamb I'd seen by the road last week.

I swung my sack down to the ground, but the bugs I hit just crawled away when I lifted the sack off them. I swung harder, but it didn't seem like I did any damage at all. I stayed by Mama, swinging my sack as

Mama swung her shovel. Sarah Ann's eyes were big and round as she looked around at all the grown-ups beating on the ground.

After a while, I couldn't swing my sack anymore. I was too tired. I started to cry. I would have sat down, but I didn't want any of those bugs to crawl up my shirt.

Mama stopped, too. Sarah Ann was fussing. The sun was hot. "There's nothing more we can do," Mama said, taking my hand and leading me home. I had a nap with Sarah Ann for the first time since I was a baby.

When I woke up, Mama was pulling the black pot off the stove. It was just dumplings, but it smelled wonderful. Mama was sober-faced as we sat down to eat. I wondered if she was mad at me for crying in the fields.

"Mama, was I good helper to kill the bugs?" I asked.

"Yes, Peter, you did a good job," she said, "No matter what any of us could do, the grasshoppers ate all the wheat. There were just too many of them."

"Are they still out there?" I asked, afraid to look for myself.

"No. Once they ate everything here, they moved on. Like a plague."

"A what?"

"A plague is really big trouble," Mama said, "It makes problems."

"Like what will we eat?" I said, frowning at the thought of no wheat to grind into flour to make bread and cake.

"Yes," Mama said, "That is a problem."

I had a sudden thought, "Maybe Brother Dan will share his potatoes with us," I said eagerly. Mama smiled tiredly. I think she should have had a nap with Sarah Ann and me. "Perhaps he will," she said.

It was only a few days later when there was a frantic knocking at our door. I didn't pull it open because Mama had warned me about the Indians. They didn't knock if they were angry with us, but just the same, I waited for Mama to open the door.

Brother Brown was standing there, his hands lifted up toward Mama, his face twisted into an incredulous smile as he yelled, "Sister Peterson! Your wheat is sprouting!" Mama put her hand to her mouth. "All of the brethren will help you tend your crop," Brother Brown said heartily, "You don't need to worry about a thing. We'll irrigate and weed and harvest it for you! Bless you, Sister Peterson."

After Brother Brown had gone, Mama knelt down with an arm around me and one around Sarah Ann, who didn't kneel, but stood quietly for a change as Mama said a long prayer with lots of "thank

Thee's." By the time we sat down to eat, our porridge tasted better than usual. I don't know if it was because the prayer was so long that I had a chance to get really hungry, or if it was because Mama was finally smiling again. But whatever it was, I knew that the simplest food was one of the greatest blessings, and even though the Lord didn't help us plant the wheat like Mama said he would, he did hide the wheat stalks until the grasshoppers left town.

In 1855, Sarah Peterson was the last one to plant her wheat field. With her husband Canute gone on an extended mission to his native Norway, she relied on the help of her five-year-old son Peter, a hoe, and the dubious help of her small daughter, Sarah Ann. When the wheat did not sprout at the expected time, Sister Peterson was afraid that the seed had been planted too deep, and would not grow.

A cloud of grasshoppers descended on the crops, and despite the best efforts of the settlers, the insects destroyed the new fields of wheat before they moved on.

It was hailed as a miracle when Sister Peterson's field sprouted a week or so later. The entire community tended the field with great care, and it eventually yielded sixty bushels of wheat, which, with frugal planning, lasted the settlement through the winter. When the incident was recounted in later years, the crop was aptly referred to as "salvation wheat."

Her husband, Canute, was so moved by the story and his wife's gift of a few kernels of the miracle wheat crop in a small jar, that he requested the jar be buried with him when he died.

Dan's son tells the story of the time his father was tired of waiting for the ground to be ready to work before planting his potatoes. He rode his horse out into his field, straddled backwards, and dropped seed potatoes into the hoof prints that his horse made in the soggy soil.

ANGLEWORM OIL

I wished that Jimmy Simmons would hurry up and find me. I shifted my legs under my long party dress, trying to find a more comfortable position. I realized too late that I should have used the outhouse before I found this perfect hiding place.

I wasn't bored while I waited to be discovered in our game of hide-and-seek. The soft shadows of the unfinished loft made me almost invisible as I looked down through the rafters to the tops of the dancers whirling around on the opera house floor below. It was quite amusing to see the people from the community dancing from the top view. The women's skirts whirled out like colorful flowers, and the men looked like leggy insects as they stepped out in dark dress pants and twirled their partners. I looked until I found Mam dancing with my brother David. From where I was hidden, she looked young and pretty.

I had just decided to climb down to the main floor and make a dash for the outhouse when I heard Jimmy at the bottom of the ladder. My need for the outhouse pushed to the back of my mind and I held very still.

The footsteps got louder the closer Jimmy got to the loft. Any second now, I expected to see Jimmy's grinning freckled face appear, so I was shocked when it wasn't Jimmy's head that popped into view. It was Niel Madsen's.

As soon as he cleared the top of the floor joists, he turned and extended his hand down the ladder. A smaller hand grasped his, and my older sister Anne's face appeared.

"Watch your step," Niel said, moving aside as he balanced on the rafters to make room for her. Anne giggled and moved closer to Niel. The look on his face as he guided her to a spot to sit in relative comfort was straight out of a fairy tale.

I couldn't figure out why she hadn't married him yet, except that she wasn't selfish enough. They were both getting really old—about twenty-five. They didn't have much life left. But I figured Anne had stayed home to help Mam with our brothers and me. I thought she should have married Niel by now and had a couple of babies. Then I could baby-sit. I was old enough. I'd be their favorite aunt because I was young and so much fun.

Anne was laughing as she pointed down through the rafters to the dancers below. No one on the dance floor looked up. I guess the music was too loud. When you're dancing, you're usually talking, too. And how many people look at the ceiling when they dance? I don't. Not that I've danced much.

I would have danced with Poppy, but he died when I was a baby, before I could even walk. I didn't remember him at all.

Now Anne was talking to Niel, smiling, her eyes shining with happiness. Anyone could see she was in love.

I won't ever be like that, I told myself fiercely. *When I find the man I want to marry, I'm going to marry him and not wait for years and years.*

After a little while, I got tired of their spooning and wondered if they were ever going to leave or if I would have to give up my hiding place and be accused of spying, even though I had been here first.

At last Niel pushed himself up to his feet and reached down for Anne. As he helped her over to the ladder, I heard him say, "Well, since I climbed up first, I suppose I should climb down first." I thought I could see crinkles by his eyes as if he were laughing inside himself.

Anne had a more serious nature, though, and got a look of near panic on her face. I knew what she was thinking. If Niel went down the ladder before her, he might be able to catch a glimpse of her ankles when she climbed down. She would never stand for that.

Anne took a tentative step around Niel, reaching her hand out to grab the top of the ladder before Niel could make good his threat to climb down first. She tottered, and a look of desperation chased the modest panic from her face. Then she disappeared.

Niel grabbed at the space where Anne had been, but it was too late. The horror in his eyes as he stared down through the rafters made me want to scream.

I jumped up, my legs feeling tingly and weak from sitting in the same place for so long. "Anne!" I shrieked. Niel started and stared at me as though I was the angel of doom.

His chest was heaving when he called to me, "Bessie! We've got to get down there!"

I couldn't move. I stood and stared down through the rafters at my sister who was sprawled like a broken doll. She had hit the pile of wooden benches that had been stacked up on the side of the floor under the loft, out of the way of the dancers. Her ankles were clearly showing, but she didn't move to cover them with her crumpled skirt. She didn't move at all.

"Bessie!" Niel's sharp command pulled me out of my stupor. I moved within reach of him, and he grabbed my hand. He guided me down the ladder ahead of him and followed so quickly he almost stepped on my hands.

Mam had made her way over to her fallen daughter by the time my feet found the dance floor. She was calling to the brethren who were lifting Anne off the benches to be careful, not to twist her back or neck as they carried her to a pile of wraps that had been hastily tossed to the floor. Anne moaned and twisted in their grasp and then burst into loud sobs. "Mam! Mam!" she called.

"I'm here," Mam said, kneeling by Anne's side as the men moved back to make room for her.

"It hurts!" she cried.

"I know, darling," Mam said quietly. "You'll be all right. Everything will be all right."

Doctor Mahlmgren knelt on Anne's other side. He tested her limbs and pressed on her torso. "It looks as though she's broken her arm," he announced solemnly, "Her side is tender. It may just be bruising, but possibly some broken ribs, too."

I couldn't help but cover my ears as they loaded Anne into the buggy to take her home. Her cries of pain made me hurt, too. As I climbed in after Mam and squeezed as small as I could into the corner, I saw Jimmy Simmons' scared face peering out at me from the crowd, his cheeks so white that his freckles stood out like pox.

Mam helped Dr. Mahlmgren set Anne's arm. Mam was known as a healer, and had a lot of experience with the suffering. She had several home remedies that people swore were miracle cures. Niel waited in the hallway, pacing back and forth, running his hand through his hair when the pained cries of his sweetheart leaked under the closed door.

After I used the outhouse, I sequestered myself in the kitchen, surrounded by the comforting and familiar stove, the wood and sheet-metal pie safe that kept the flies off the bread and pastries that were stored there, and the scarred old table where the family had sat and laughed and argued for years. I longed for the good old days when May and Belle were home, and Anne didn't act like she had to carry the welfare of the whole family on her shoulders.

Trying to stop myself from worrying, I sought a normal activity. I decided to cut myself a slice of bread and spread it thick with fresh butter. I opened a new jar of blackberry preserves without even asking Mam.

Three slices of bread later, Mam came into the kitchen with the doctor. "How's Anne?" I asked, setting my half-finished, sticky bread down on the table without a plate to put it on.

"Her arm is set, and Niel is with her," Mam said.

"She'll be fine," Doctor Mahlmgren added. "I'll be back to check on her tomorrow." Mam nodded and Doctor Mahlmgren left.

Mam looked me over soberly, then sat down with a sigh. "Is there any bread left?" she asked. I got up to slice her some. "It will be several weeks before Anne's arm plaster can be removed," she said, "I'll need your help around here."

"You can count on me," I assured her fervently as I placed the bread in front of her. She smiled up at me gratefully.

In the two months it took Anne's arm to heal, I had changed my mind about her getting married and moving away. I was delegated to do most of her chores, and it ate up a lot of my free time. Maybe if Niel still wanted to marry her, they could move in to our house. Then Anne could still do her chores, and Niel could pitch in, too. It seemed like a fine plan to me.

The day Doctor Mahlmgren came to take off Anne's splint, I was in the kitchen doing my best to make a chocolate cake. It was a momentous day, calling for a momentous dessert. Anne would be back to normal. Her damaged ribs had taken almost as long to heal as her arm, but she was feeling better all over, and I would soon have my free time back.

I heard Doctor Mahlmgren leave before the cake was done. That was just as well. While the good doctor certainly deserved a piece, I wasn't disappointed that there would be more cake for me.

I heard voices in the hall. "It doesn't matter, Anne," Niel said.

Anne's tearful voice came back, "It matters to me! Doctor Mahlmgren said I won't even be able to comb my own hair! What kind of wife could I be to you?"

"A wonderful one," Niel replied firmly.

I turned as they came into the kitchen, Anne flouncing ahead, hurt and disappointment on her face clouded over by angry brows. Niel followed, his eyes pleading, his hands outstretched in a helpless gesture toward Anne's back. Her arm was free of the splint, but she still held it bent at the elbow. I was confused.

"What's wrong?" I asked.

Anne's normal good humor was nowhere apparent. "*This* is wrong," she said, flinging her arm toward me. It jutted out at the elbow in an "L" shape, as stiff and crooked as an old tree branch.

"But just straighten it," I said, demonstrating with my own arm.

"I can't straighten it!" Anne said thickly, blinking back the angry tears that crowded into her eyes.

I stared at her blankly. "Why not?" I said.

"It won't straighten! The doctor said it will be like this always!" She burst into tears and ran from the kitchen.

Niel cast a despairing glance at me, then followed Anne.

I plopped down heavily at the table, not even hungry for cake anymore. I was willing to admit that there were things more important than chocolate cake.

I propped my head up with my hand, my elbow resting on the well-worn wood. Why couldn't this have happened to someone else? Why Anne? Or why could it have not happened at all? It wasn't fair! My heart was heavy, pulling me down so that I let my head fall to my arms folded on the table.

Poor Anne. I felt the tears burning my eyes. "Father . . . ," I said. Whenever I prayed, I had a mixed picture in my head. It was partly my father's face, the one I had seen in the pictures Mam kept in the parlor, and it was partly bearded and white-robed with a patient countenance, radiating wisdom of the ages. "I know you love Anne like I do—more than I do, and because you love her, please help her." I didn't know what else to say, so I just sat there with my head down, my tears wetting my arm.

Then I thought of something else. "I'll even keep doing the extra chores if you'll help her. Please. Thank you. Amen."

I sat there, waiting for a miracle. I wanted Anne to come running back into the kitchen, smiling, showing me how her arm could now straighten and bend just like before, wrapping both arms around me in a loving hug like she used to.

I heard the kitchen door open and close. I jerked my head up. When had Anne gone outside? But it was Mam I saw. She was holding a metal can in her dirty hands. Her shoes were muddy.

She stopped when she saw me. "Bess, are you all right?" she asked.

"Yes, but Anne . . ." I couldn't say any more.

"I know about Anne," Mam said, "She's going to be just fine."

"But Doctor Mahlmgren said . . ."

"Doctor Mahlmgren doesn't know everything," Mam said quickly. "Now come take this can and put it on the stove. The stove is still hot, isn't it?

"Yes," I replied, pushing to my feet and walking over to take the can. I peered inside and made a face. "These are worms!" I said.

"Not just any worms," she replied calmly as she sat on the stool by the back door. She pulled off one of her shoes. "Those are angleworms."

"Worms are worms to me," I said.

"If you took an interest in healing, you'd learn the difference," Mam said. "Now put them on the stove."

I gingerly set the can next to the stovepipe as Mam pulled off her other shoe.

"Now stoke the stove," Mam instructed.

"But the cake is done," I said.

"It's not for the cake," Mam said, standing in her stocking feet and walking toward me.

A horrid thought struck me. "We're not having worms for supper, are we?" I asked.

"No," Mam said slowly, staring at the can of angleworms, "I hadn't ever thought of that before."

I spoke up quickly. "Don't think of it now, either."

After Niel left, Mam took Anne's supper in. She stayed while Anne ate. When she brought back the plate, Anne's chocolate cake only had one bite out of it. I didn't even feel like finishing it for her.

The next day Mam looked into the can of worms and declared that they were ready. "Ready for what?" I said suspiciously, looking over her shoulder. The worms had seemed to melt into a shiny, slick substance that floated on top of the can.

"Ready for Anne," Mam said.

"Does she have to?" I asked. I felt sorry for Anne. For all I knew, Mam was going to make her drink the angleworm oil as a cure, kind of like castor oil, which tasted very nasty.

Mam called our brother Dave into the kitchen, then went to fetch Anne. Anne came in looking red-eyed and sullen. Mam pushed Anne's sleeve up and told Dave to hold on to her waist. Although younger than Anne, Dave was taller and stronger. Anne made no resistance as Dave took a firm hold around her middle. Mam scooped up some of the warm, shiny angleworm oil with her fingers and began to rub it on Ann's elbow. At first Ann winced, but as the oil worked into her skin, she relaxed some. Mam scooped up more oil, rubbing it on Anne's elbow again, only this time she started to pull on Anne's wrist as she rubbed. Anne bit her lip, and creased her forehead. I could see Dave tighten his grip as Anne began to squirm. Mam scooped up more oil and rubbed it in, still pulling.

"It hurts, Mam!" Anne cried, as tears began to roll down her cheeks.

"It won't be for long," Mam assured her. When Mam finally declared the treatment done, David walked Anne back to her room. Her arm was still bent.

"It didn't work," I said, trying to hide my disappointment.

"It's working," Mam said firmly. "It just takes more than once."

It ended up being a year of digging angleworms, turning them into oil, massaging and pulling before Anne's arm was working as well as before. She could now comb her own hair, and do all her household tasks. Only now she was working at Niel's house because they finally got married. My prayer was answered. I got to do all of Anne's chores.

Candace Rowe's granddaughter Johannah Hafen reported to Mary Seamons that in about 1893, Anne Wilcox accompanied her curious beau Niel Madsen up a ladder to check out the unfinished loft of the opera house during a community dance. Always a gentleman, Niel went up the ladder first.

When he teased Anne by offering to be the first to climb down, Anne tried to step past him so she could preserve her modesty by not letting him see her ankles. She lost her footing, fell through the rafters, landed on a pile of benches and broke her arm.

When the splint came off, the arm was stuck in an "L" shape. Anne's mother, Candace Wilcox, would not accept the doctor's prediction that her daughter's arm would always be that way. She made up a batch of angleworm oil and massaged it into the stiff elbow as she pulled. One of her sons held onto Anne and pulled in the opposite direction. After about a year of this treatment, Anne could straighten her arm and use it as well as she could before the accident. Anne married her long-time beau Niel Madsen.

MY BROTHER'S KEEPER

I was sick and tired of Orville. "Almer, watch Orville," they would say to me. "Al, where's Orry?" "You're in charge of the baby, Al."

Orville was no baby. He was a pest on two legs, who could run and hide and would pull my hair when he got mad at me.

Ma would scold me if I ever pulled Orry's hair. "He's only two," she'd say. "He doesn't understand."

Then Orville would grin, looking at me sideways from his eyes, understanding perfectly well that he had gotten me into trouble again.

Adelia helped me with Orville at least half the time, until she found out that Mama was in a "family way." Then all she wanted to do was sit and sew baby clothes, and pester Mama about names for the new baby. Girl names. Mama didn't seem to mind Adelia sewing, but she tired of the pestering. Then she'd make Adelia help me.

Adelia was the oldest, at eight years old. I wasn't so big, being five going on six. But Orville thought I was big. I was bigger than him.

Problem was, Orville wasn't an ordinary little kid, because he could do stuff like catch butterflies. I know other two-year-olds have caught butterflies and bugs, but I've never seen any but Orry who could let them go in one piece, laughing as they fluttered away, completely unharmed—no bent wings or missing legs or anything.

Another time I noticed something different about Orry was when we visited Uncle Anthon before we left to colonize a new town. Uncle Anthon had wild cats in his barn. The only reason I even knew the cats were there was from seeing the back ends of them as they streaked away from me, their tails jerking side to side, keeping them balanced as they dodged rocks and shrubs on their flight from imaginary danger.

After we ate a wonderfully big dinner, where I stuffed myself with too many of Aunt Nolie's yummy biscuits, I was feeling sleepy. Ma asked me to find Orville, who had wandered off after dessert. I didn't want to, that's for sure, but I knew it wouldn't do any good to argue.

I walked out into the yard, scuffing my feet in the dirt. I looked around half-heartedly, but the only things I saw moving were red and gold leaves drifting down from the branches of the trees. No sign of Orville. I didn't call out, because I really didn't care if I found Orry.

My eyes focused on the barn, and my mind turned to the dry green hay stacked inside that was so fresh it still had a spring to it. I imagined myself snuggling into the fragrant softness for a rest. I didn't think Ma would come looking for me for a while, not when she had Aunt Nolie to talk to.

Inside the barn was twilight. The lazy flies were humming lullabies to the farm dog spread out in slumber by the milking stand. I climbed the ladder to the loft and paused at the top, looking for the most likely spot to lie down and rest.

My sleepy eyes popped open wide-awake when I saw Orville sitting in a little nest of hay with two wild barn cats. One was a big gray with a torn ear, his fur rough and scarred from years of fighting. The other was a thin calico with a tail bent at a comical angle.

The calico was sprawled on Orville's lap, it's eyes closed to blissful slits as its thin chest rumbled in ecstasy. The big gray was sitting up, looking into Orry's eyes as he patted its battle-scarred head and made sympathetic noises.

"Orville!" I shouted.

Both cats sprang up as though they'd backed into a porcupine. The calico scrabbled its feet in the air a couple of times before it hit ground and sped off in a flurry of hay. The big gray shot like an arrow into a crack in the wall and was gone.

"My tikis!" Orry wailed.

"They're kitties!" I corrected him, "and they're wild! They might scratch you!"

"No! Want tikis!" Orry cried, pushing up to his feet and stepping unsteadily onto a small mound of hay.

"No! Want Mama!" I mimicked him unsympathetically. I took hold of his hand and pulled him toward the ladder.

"No! Tikis!" Orville yelled, stretching his hand back toward the hay.

I finally got my brother back to the house. Ma was upset that Orry was crying. She thought "tikis" sounded like "kick me" and began to scold me. I told her I did not kick Orville. She stopped scolding, but looked at me doubtfully, and she didn't even believe it when I told her Orry had been holding two wild barn cats on his lap.

Nevertheless, this time she didn't punish me. We were getting ready to go settle in a new place called Sanpitch, and her mind was full of packing and moving.

We didn't get to Sanpitch until November when it was cold and snowy. There were no houses there.

I looked over the cold, frozen valley. "Pa," I said, "Can we go back to Uncle Anthon's house?"

He said no. He said that Heavenly Father wanted us here, and that we were having an adventure. Pa said he'd dig out some dirt and make us a house in the hillside.

I was very interested as he began digging. I wondered how Ma would cook on a dirt stove, and would a dirt bed be softer than the ground?

It turned out that we just put a few of our normal old regular things in the dugout after Pa was done. Even though he made some lattices out of bendy willow branches for a sort of wall, it was still kind of dirty. And when Orville cried, there was no place to go to get away from the noise. I told Pa I didn't like adventures. I would rather live in Uncle Anthon's barn with the wild cats.

It seemed like winter would last for the rest of my life. It was still snowy and cold when Pa took Orry, Adelia, and me over to the Shoemaker's dugout to spend the night. While we stayed there, Sister Shoemaker had a sleepover at our dugout.

When she came back the next morning, she said that a stork had come in the night. I was pretty mad, I can tell you. I wanted to see that stork, so I hurried back to our dugout, slipping and sliding along the way, leaving Adelia to bring Orville. I was too late. The stork was gone. All that was there was a new baby in Ma's arms.

"Where'd he come from?" I asked.

"Heavenly Father sent him," Ma said, smiling at me.

I was suspicious. Ma looked so pale and sickly that her smile couldn't be real.

Orville said, "Baby!" and tried to touch the baby's eye with a grimy finger.

I pulled his hand away. "No, Orry," I said.

"Just touch his hair, Orry," Ma said softly, like she was real tired, then smiled again.

I looked doubtfully at Ma. She was acting strange. "But Ma," I said, "He doesn't have any hair."

Adelia burst into tears when she found out the baby was another boy. After awhile she got over the disappointment and had a good time cuddling and dressing our new brother Delaun. It was a good thing, because Ma didn't seem like herself for a long time. She mostly laid in the bed with the baby when Adelia wasn't fussing over him.

Adelia warmed up the broths and thin soups that the other ladies in the dugouts made from melted snow and scant provisions and shared with us. And I watched Orville.

When it was finally warm enough to follow Orville out of the dugout and onto the flat ground, I was glad to get muddy. I didn't even worry about Ma or Pa scolding us about the dirt because practically our whole house was made of dirt.

When we got back from building our mud pies, Pa wiped our faces and hands with a dampened cloth.

"Well, boys," he said, "It looks to me like it's time to build a house out of something besides dirt and willow sticks."

I looked at Pa's eyes to see if he was teasing. He was smiling, but his eyes looked serious.

"Tomorrow, Pa?" I said.

"I can start it tomorrow," he said.

"Will it be done tomorrow?"

Pa laughed, a deep rumble in his chest. I couldn't help but smile. I liked it when Pa laughed.

"I'll build it as fast as I can," Pa said, "But it will take more than one day."

"I'll help you," I said hopefully.

"You can help me best by watching Orville," Pa said, rubbing his hand over my dusty hair, then wiping his hand on his trouser leg.

Orry again. Sometimes I wished there wasn't any Orville.

It was only two days later that I woke up scared, the sounds of screaming in my ears. First I thought it was Orville having a bad dream. "Ma!" I called, desperate for someone to stop the screaming that was so frightening it felt like it was stabbing into my chest like a knife.

But it was Ma that was screaming, clutching Delaun to her chest while Pa was beating on the floor with a stick. Adelia was crying. I started crying, too.

Then something grabbed me from behind by the neck. I couldn't even breathe. I grabbed at the choking thing with my hands and found Orville's arms. I pried them apart.

"Awmer," Orry cried piteously, "Awmer!" His arms were open wide, beseeching me for comfort. His little face was wet with tears, and he was shaking.

I pulled him awkwardly onto my lap. In spite of not having a lot to eat over the winter, Orville had grown some.

Just as I got Orry settled in my arms, Pa lifted up a thick, limp rope with the stick he held. Only it wasn't a rope. It was a dead rattlesnake.

All day we found snakes crawling out of crevices and slits in the rocks. At first I was scared, but when some of the older boys cut some of the rattley buttons off the dead snake's tails, I got interested. They made a shushy, rattly sound, like whispering ghosts wandering through tall dead grass.

I tore a strip of loose fabric off the bottom of my raggedy shirt and wound it around a couple of snake tails as I held them onto the end of a stick. After I tied the fabric tight, I handed it to Orry.

"Here," I said.

Orry pulled back, not wanting to touch the stick.

"It's okay," I said, "Look. Shake it." I showed him how.

Orville tilted his head, then hesitantly reached out and took the stick from me. He shook it, heard the soft dry rattle, and smiled.

For the rest of the day while anyone who was big enough swung shovels, hoes, and heavy sticks at the rattlesnakes as they kept coming, Orville drove us all to distraction by shaking his new rattle over and over and over.

That night after he fell asleep, I took his rattle and buried it so we wouldn't be bothered with his incessant rattling the next day.

Over the next few days, more snakes were killed. Ma was up more now than she had been since Delaun appeared. She seemed kind of twitchy and nervous, but it was good to have her up and around almost like normal.

Pa had begun our new house, which was a short distance away across the flat from the base of the hill. I went to see it every day. Orry came with me, as usual. But what was unusual is that he just stood and watched Pa, his big eyes fixed on every movement Pa made. He didn't run around or get into things like he usually did. He wasn't even noisy. Sometimes Orry would curl up on the ground, his head on Pa's coat, his little face white against the dark fabric, alternately staring and sleeping. Yet Orry hated naps. After a couple of days, Orville quit tagging along. As Ma got better, Orry seemed to feel worse.

At first I was glad. I was free of Orry at last! But then it turned out I wasn't free of him after all. As I watched Pa and helped him when I could, I caught myself looking around to see where my brother was. Then I'd remember he was back at the dugout with Ma, and my heart would drop a notch. I decided it was easier to be looking for him and find him than to look for him and remember that he wasn't there.

The next day I tried to talk him into going with us, but he wouldn't.

He just lay back on his blankets and closed his eyes, as listless as Adelia's baby doll, as pale as porcelain and looking just as fragile.

I put my hand to his forehead like I'd seen Ma do, but I didn't know what I was supposed to feel. I smiled down at Orry in a hopeful way and left with Pa.

That night I had bad dreams. I couldn't find Orville anywhere. I was even looking inside of trunks and under the beds. Frantic in my sleep, I searched under bushes and behind trees. I started crying helplessly because I couldn't find my brother.

I was relieved to finally wake up, even though my eyes were wet and puffy. Pa had already left for his day of house-building, and I was too tired to follow him.

Ma served me and Orry some breakfast. There was crumbled bread in our bowls with a portion of milk from a milk cow that had survived through the winter and had even managed to freshen three weeks before. The families in the settlement took courage from the sight of the skinny-legged calf tottering around after her mother as the cow found tender new growth to graze on in the warming days of late spring.

I sat on the bed with my breakfast. Orville took his toward the dugout entrance.

"Where's he going?" I asked Ma.

She looked up from changing Delaun. "He always eats out there," she said, "He says he needs his tiki, whatever that is." She shrugged delicately, and bent back over the baby.

His tiki? There were no cats in the settlement that I knew of. What was my brother up to? I had to find out.

Without knowing why I felt such urgency for silence, I crept carefully and as noiselessly as possible to the dugout entrance. Orville was sitting on the ground in the morning sun, talking to himself. His little knees were bent out like grasshopper legs as he sat.

When he lifted his spoonful of bread to his mouth, I could see his bowl balanced on his lap. With a shock of horror, I saw more than bread and milk in his bowl. Fear slid down my neck in cold little prickles when I spied the scaly head of a big diamondback rattlesnake draped over the side of Orry's dish. The snake was eating from my brother's bowl.

I could only imagine how scared Orville must be. He probably didn't dare move or run away because that snake was so close. I didn't dare yell because the snake might bite my brother.

On shaking legs I turned back into the dugout. "Ma," I said in a voice that wobbled out of my throat, "You've got to help Orry."

Ma snapped her head up. "What's wrong?" she asked sharply.

"The shovel," I said, "Snake . . ."

Without any further explanation, Ma snatched up a hoe. "Addy, watch the baby," Ma said as she headed for the dugout entrance.

I followed at a safe distance and saw Ma cautiously approach Orville. Then she gasped.

"Hi, Mama," Orville smiled up at her in a tired sort of way. "My tiki," he said.

The snake seemed to sense danger. It pulled itself away from the bowl in strong, loopy coils of muscles and mottled scales. It headed away from my mother and Orry, twisting itself across the ground toward a hole between some rocks.

Ma brought her hoe down with a crack. I don't know how she did it on the first swing, but she cut that snake in two. She kept swinging the hoe, chopping again and again with the blade, even after the snake quit moving. By the time Ma stopped, that snake was surely dead.

It was only after it was over that I realized Orville was crying. He spilled what was left of his breakfast on the ground as he scrambled awkwardly up to his feet and tottered toward the snake. Ma scooped him up before he could reach it.

"My tiki!" Orville sobbed, "Want my tiki!"

"Hush now, darling," Ma said, smoothing Orry's hair, "The tiki made you sick. Almer will get you the buttons so you can play with your tiki's tail any time you want to."

Orry put his head down on Ma's shoulder and wept as she carried him back inside.

My heart was thumping hard enough to hurt my ribs. I didn't like rattlesnakes. They made me think of screaming and pounding and fear so thick in the air you could almost feel it. I could barely breathe when I got close to one. But I couldn't stand to hear my brother's broken hearted sobs, either.

I reluctantly stepped toward the dead snake and saw with some relief that there was a detached tail segment with the rattles on it laying a little way from the rest of the body.

I picked it up before I could think about it, and hurried into the dugout. Ma smiled delightedly as though I'd just carried in a bucket full of ripe, red apples. "Look, Orville, here's your tiki," she said. She took the buttons away from me and deftly trimmed the remaining meat and bone off. Then she carefully threaded the whispery dry rattles onto a string. When she handed it to Orry, he stopped crying. Somberly, he studied the small token of his deadly friend. He shook the string, and then sighed. Pulling the crude necklace over his head, he patted the buttons with his hand and said, "My tiki."

This story is reported by Norma Wanlass as happening to Orville Cox in 1850. The baffled family could not understand why their two-year-old was getting sicker and weaker as the days were warming and plants were sprouting. Then one day they found him sharing his bread and milk with a rattlesnake. The snake was immediately killed. Although it seems unlikely, the family suspected that when the poison was no longer transferred from the snake's fangs to the child's food, the toddler recovered. He was said to have kept his pet snake's rattles on a string even when he grew into a teenager, swinging them along beside him as he walked the dirt trails.

MESSAGE RECEIVED

"Take this, Katrina," Mama thrust a warm, cloth-covered plate into my hand. I knew what it was even before I lifted the corner of the napkin to take a peek. Danish pancakes. My tongue tingled in anticipation even though I'd just finished eating a few minutes ago.

"Where are we going?" I asked as I copied Mama and pulled my shawl off the peg. I had to set the plate down to adjust the fabric over my shoulders.

"Bertha's," Mama said as she pulled the door open.

"Maybe I should stand on the sidewalk and hold the plate out to see if we can get her to come out of her house!" I said as I followed Mama out the door.

Mama closed the door behind me with a thump. "Now, Katrina, be kind," she said firmly. "Bertha has had a hard life. Besides, what is wrong with a person staying home if they want to?"

"But why would anyone want to?" I asked.

"You have a lot to learn," Mama scolded me gently. I knew she was wrong. At fourteen years old, I knew just about everything.

When we got to Bertha's house, Mama knocked firmly on the door. After a minute or two, the door opened a couple of inches. A pair of large blue eyes looked solemnly out from the crack, then crinkled up at the corners as Bertha smiled in recognition. She opened the door wider and motioned us to come in. Her eagerness at having visitors tugged at my heart. She was like a prisoner in her own house, but it was her own fault. If only she would go out, meet people, and at least try to speak English, she wouldn't be cowering here like a mouse in its hole.

"How are you, Bertha?" my mother said in Danish. Although she'd been in America for over a year, Bertha only spoke and understood Danish.

"I could be better," Bertha replied, a little quaver creeping into her voice. It sounded as though she might start to cry again. I thought Bertha cried too much, usually when she was reminiscing about her homeland and the hardships and blessings that came with accepting the Gospel. Before she had a chance to let the tears loose, I pushed the plate into her hands. She smiled at me as though I had thrown her a lifeline as she was sinking in the ocean. I smiled smugly as Bertha led us into her parlor. I had cleverly averted a disaster.

"Bertha, I have good news," Mama said after we sat down. "Elder Smith is coming here."

Bertha's eyes got moist again. "A prophet," she whispered. I knew they were talking about the Apostle Joseph F. Smith.

"He'll be speaking in the Tabernacle," Mama said.

Bertha's smile suddenly collapsed into a frown. "But I won't understand him," she said woefully. "He will speak in English."

Mama was silent for a moment. I couldn't think of anything to say that wouldn't get me into trouble. I wanted to tell Bertha to learn English, for goodness' sakes!

Mama finally answered, "But you could at least see him, maybe even shake his hand."

Bertha sighed and looked down at the hands she had clasped in her lap. "It has been my dream since I joined the true church in Denmark to hear an apostle speak." She looked up at Mama. "Would you go with me?" Bertha asked, her wide eyes harboring worry in their depths.

"Yes, of course," Mama assured her, "And I will tell you what he said when the meeting is over." Bertha smiled gratefully.

Finally it was time to leave. As we made our way home, I said, "Mama, how could someone as fearful and timid as Bertha ever leave her homeland? How did she ever dare to even step onto a boat?"

"She had great faith," Mama said in a gently chiding voice. "You don't realize what great courage it took for her and Lars to join the church."

I was still trying to picture it. Even though Brother Anderson obviously got his wife on board somehow, perhaps pulling her along with her eyes closed, I could almost see her sitting in a corner of the ship with her hands clasped so tightly that you couldn't tell which fingers went with which hand as underneath her she felt the vast, rolling waters waiting to swallow the ship and everyone on board into its great blue belly with the first opportunity.

My mother's voice broke into my thoughts. "Bertha's family turned her away," she said, "In Denmark it is almost a crime to become a Mormon. Some people are very hateful."

"But she won't even talk to anyone unless they're Danish," I said.

"She doesn't understand anything but Danish," Mama said. "Just imagine if you went to someplace like . . . well, China. You wouldn't understand anything they said. You wouldn't know their customs or be used to their food. Then how brave would you be?" Mama looked at me sideways out of her eyes.

My heart began to flutter. I examined my feelings, and then said truthfully, "I think it would be exciting! I would go out every day and talk to people until I learned what they were saying. I couldn't stand to not know what they were talking about! And I wouldn't just sit at home and peek out at the Chinese through my curtains!"

Mama smiled and nodded. "Yes, I believe that you would do that. But Bertha is a different kind of person than you."

I heard a door close and turned toward the sound. Carrie Jensen was stepping down off the porch of her house. She waved at me.

"Mama, could I walk with Carrie and meet you at home later?"

Mama smiled. "Yes. Just don't be too long. There are chores to do."

I groaned. I would much rather work at the telegraph office with Carrie than to be stuck at home stuffing mattress ticks and scrubbing wallpaper. Carrie got messages from all over the world, and sent messages everywhere, too, even to New York City. I had begun to study Morse code so that I would be ready as soon as there was a job opening in Carrie's office. Of course, Carrie was sixteen, but I was a very mature fourteen, so I was confident that I wouldn't have to wait two more years to get a job as important as Carrie's.

"Hi, Kat," Carrie said as I fell into step beside her. Warmth bloomed in my chest when I heard the nickname she had given me. It made me feel as though we were the best of friends, although I know a lot of people knew Carrie. She was popular.

"Hi, Carrie. What's new?" I asked. Carrie always knew what was going on.

"Well, I received a proposal of marriage yesterday," she said, lowering her lashes demurely.

"Oh, who was it?" I said, clasping my hands together, "Was it Willard Hanks?"

Carrie's eyes slid sideways to me. "No. You'll never guess."

"Ferdy Oleson!" I declared, naming the old, toothless man who tottered around town on a cane.

Carrie burst out laughing. "No! It was a Chinaman!"

"A Chinaman?" I said doubtfully, "You don't know any Chinamen!"

Carrie smiled smugly. "One came in the telegraph office yesterday. He had a black silk suit on, with wide-legged trousers and a long coat with a little collar that stood up around his neck," Carrie showed me by running her fingers around her slender throat. "It was all embroidered in yellow and red dragons."

"Was he handsome?" I asked, trying to picture this exotic man in my mind and hoping desperately that he was still in town so I could get a look at him personally.

Carrie shrugged. "I suppose so, for a Chinaman. He had a single long braid down his back, longer than the Indians wear."

"And he came into the office to ask you to marry him?" I said.

"Not at first. He came into the office to send a telegram. I could see him watching me as I worked. It made me feel uneasy. I didn't know if it was just the Chinese way, or if he had something on his mind, but I figured if I needed to, I could scream and someone on the street would hear me."

I shuddered deliciously. "Could he speak English, then?" I asked.

"After a fashion," Carrie said. "When I finished the telegram and asked him if he needed anything else, he said, 'You mally me. Me no mind if you Amelican'."

"Did he really say it like that?" I asked. "That is so funny! Couldn't he say his r's?"

"There aren't any r's in the Chinese language," Carrie said as she turned off the street and headed toward the telegraph office. "Here we are."

I looked up, surprised that we had reached our destination already. "But what did you say?" I asked as Carrie unlocked the door, "What did he do?"

"I told him I'd have to think about it," Carrie said, then burst out laughing just before she pulled the office door shut behind her. I knew she was just teasing me. She wouldn't marry a Chinaman that she had just met yesterday. As I turned toward home, I envied Carrie and her adventurous life.

On the day that Elder Smith came to town, the air itself felt alive. We put on our Sunday-best clothes and walked to the Andersons' to pick up Lars and Bertha. Bertha held my mother's arm while Lars and Pa walked side by side, discussing farming, temple building, and weather. They switched from Danish to English, depending on which language suited their conversation best.

We found some seats on the hard wooden Tabernacle benches. The room was abuzz with people trying to whisper, yet trying to be heard above everyone else's whispering. I caught bits of English, Danish, Swedish, and Norwegian. I only really understood Danish and English, but I could at least identify the other languages.

When we were all settled, I found myself seated behind Bertha. She kept glancing down at her lap and back up again, occasionally darting looks to the sides. If she saw someone she recognized, she would waggle her fingers at them from her safe place in between her husband and my mother. I felt kind of sorry for her, but I also felt that it was her own fault for being so timid.

I caught sight of Carrie Jensen in the balcony. Her modest pearl gray dress looked anything but matronly on her young figure. I wasn't surprised that the Chinaman had proposed to her.

It didn't take me long to notice that she was behaving rather strangely. She was blinking her eyes a lot. I wondered if she had something in them, especially when she pulled at the outside corners of both of them until they turned up into slants. Then she let go and smiled, her gaze fixed on the balcony across the room from her. After a time, she started blinking rapidly again.

I looked across to the opposite balcony and tried to see what Carrie was looking at. Before long, I found Christine Willardson, another telegraph operator, and she seemed to be having the same problem with her eyes. Suddenly I smiled to myself. I had figured it out. The telegraph operators were sending messages to each other in Morse code, blinking out the dots and dashes as they silently exchanged the latest news. I renewed my determined to learn the code as quickly as possible.

I saw Carrie turn her face toward the front of the room when a sudden hush fell throughout the Tabernacle. I followed her gaze, then joined the congregation in rising to my feet. Elder Smith was walking onto the podium, his face pleasant and smiling, although it was only obvious around his eyes since his beard obscured most of his mouth.

After we sat down to sing the opening hymn, I kept sneaking peeks at Elder Smith. I noticed Bertha dabbing at her eyes with a handkerchief as we sang, "Come, Come Ye Saints."

The first speaker at the conference was Brother Henry Beal. In his usual big booming voice, he thanked everyone for coming and being where the Lord wanted them to be. Then he said, "Last conference, Bishop Dorius told me that when he and his family were headed across the yard on their way to meeting, his wife noticed a pair of shoes sticking out over the side of the hammock in their yard," he smiled genially. "She went over to see who was shirking their church attendance and found their hired hand with his hat over his eyes.

Being the good church-going woman that she is, she snatched off his hat. 'What are you doing lying there when you should be going to church?' she asked him.

'Well,' he replied, 'I heard that Henry Beal is preaching today, and

I can hear him just as good from this hammock here as if I was to go to the meeting house.'"

Brother Beal exploded into booming laughter as the congregation joined his merriment, all except Bertha, who looked around with a puzzled expression on her face.

At last Elder Smith's turn came and he moved to the pulpit. As he began to speak, I could feel warmth enveloping me. Bertha stopped moving her head and hands. She pointed her face straight at the prophet. I imagined that she was wishing she could understand what he was saying. Perhaps she was trying to make sense of any word that came out of his mouth, or maybe she just enjoyed the sound of his voice.

When he was done, and after the heartfelt thunder of "Amen," we joined in the hymn "Abide With Me." I noticed that Bertha was wiping her eyes again.

After the closing prayer, Mama turned to Bertha. Before she could offer to translate the Apostle's message for her, Bertha said, "Oh, that was beautiful, more beautiful than anything I have ever heard before. The message, and the language . . . in Denmark even they do not speak such beautiful Danish!"

Mama's face must have looked like mine as we both stared at Bertha in confusion. "No," Mama said, "It was not Danish he spoke. It was English. There were some things he said that I did not know the words myself."

Bertha did not argue. She simply smiled and said, "It was changed for me, then. God changed it into Danish for me."

LuGene Nielson wrote that in the mid 1880s, Bertha Katherine Anderson, a recent immigrant from Denmark, was feeling displaced because she couldn't speak or understand English in her adopted home. She had long held a great desire to hear an apostle speak, and she got her chance when Elder Joseph F. Smith visited the Ephraim Tabernacle. Although President Smith spoke in English, Bertha heard his talk in Danish.

Carrie Jensen ran a telegraph office. A visiting Chinese gentleman proposed to her. Carrie and her telegraph operator friends would sometimes blink Morse code messages to each other during meetings.

Sister Dorius found her hired man in a hammock on a warm Sunday morning. He defended his position by declaring that he could hear Brother Beal's talk just as well from the comfort of the hammock as if he were sitting on a hard bench in the meetinghouse.

THE EMPRESS'S NEW CLOTHES

"Well, Sarah, fancy meeting you here."

I turned and peered around the edge of my bonnet. I would have rather seen a rattlesnake than Elizabeth Wilcox. "Hello, Elizabeth," I said, because my mother had taught me manners and I couldn't help myself.

Elizabeth smirked at me from underneath her parasol. In spite of the dust on the faded pink fabric and the slightly tattered edges, I envied that parasol.

"You're doing a good job on those sugar beets," Elizabeth said. The way she said it, I could tell that she was rubbing it in that I was down in the dirt on my knees while she was the one walking past in the shade of the parasol.

"Love the sugar, hate the beets," I said.

Elizabeth laughed. "Oh, Sarah, you're so funny!"

"Then stay awhile and enjoy my company," I said. "Ma says I can't go back to the house until I finish thinning this row. You can help me."

Elizabeth's mouth opened in alarm. Oh, but I can't," she said, "Mother's expecting me." She twirled her parasol. "'Til we meet again, Sarah." As she walked away, her threadbare dress hem swished in the dirt behind her hurrying feet.

I attacked the sugar beet row with renewed vigor. I imagined that each tiny beet top I had to pull out of the ground was one of Elizabeth's hairs. Wouldn't she look funny to be as sparse on top as this row of beets? I smiled grimly. She wasn't in any better shape than the rest of us, she just acted like it.

She must have been used to having everything she wanted because her father once owned a general store, but that was before they moved in next door to my family. I could just imagine Elizabeth roaming the store, lifting the lid on a jar of licorice whips or horehound candy and helping herself whenever she wanted. She could pick out fabric for a new dress before her old one even wore out. And her bonnets would be the newest styles, straw maybe, with little flowers circling the crown. If I had ever had a hat like that, I would carry my head high, too.

I pulled the shade of my old calico-brimmed bonnet hard enough to scoot the crown down over my forehead, using the seam to scratch the itch from the sweat that had beaded there. Then I impatiently pushed the bonnet back into place with my dirty fingers.

I continued my lonely task, not made any better by remembering that Elizabeth had moved here in newer clothes than I had. But she wasn't wearing new clothes now. Except for her manners, or lack of them, she was pretty much like all the other girls in town. Poor.

Yet there were ways to overcome deprivation. My cousin had told me of a young man named Tommy in Orderville who had gathered up all the lambs' tails that were cut off and thrown aside at shearing time. After the other workers were done for the day, Tommy sheared the tails of their precious little wool.

Over time, and with perseverance, he accumulated enough wool to trade for a new pair of store trousers in the latest style.

When he showed up in his proud new finery, he was called before a town council where he told his tale. The town leaders decided that he really hadn't done anything wrong as the sheep tails were destined to be thrown out. Yet how could he be allowed to put himself above the other boys by wearing his new pants? That was not the way of the United Order.

After some discussion and prayer, the town elders decided to enlist the help of the Orderville seamstresses. They carefully unpicked the new pants and laid them out for a pattern. Tommy received the first pair of pants made out of homespun fabric in the new pattern. Over the course of the next few weeks, every young man in the town received a pair of homespun pants cut in the latest style.

I grinned to myself as I imagined what a hero Tommy must have been, then slapped at the tiny flies that were trying to land on my eyelashes. Thinning beets was bad enough without the added torment of the flies. How much hardship could one girl take?

When I peeked sideways to see how much row was left before I could be free, my heart skipped. I was at the end. Time had passed so quickly for me as I fumed about Elizabeth that I gave her a silent thanks for stopping by.

The next Sunday, I pulled on my best dress. The scent of sun and air and sage from the washing Ma and I had done the day before filled my head as I pulled it down and settled it on my shoulders. It was too worn-out to feel stiff and new, but the clean softness felt comforting on my skin.

I walked with my family to the meetinghouse, feeling light and cheerful. There would be no worries of beet-thinning on this, the Sabbath Day.

"May!" I said as I caught sight of my friend in the churchyard. "You look happy today."

"As well she should be," said a voice coming up behind me.

"Minerva!" I said, greeting May's sister. I creased my forehead. "Why should she be happy?" I asked.

Instead of answering my question, Minerva lowered her voice. "Look out," she said, "The empress is coming."

"The empress?" I said, turning my head.

"Shh!" Minerva warned, "Don't let her hear you!"

Elizabeth was approaching, her nose tilted up almost as high as her eyebrows. She didn't look at us as she walked past, that ever-present parasol perched on her shoulder like a huge bristly cocklebur.

I giggled and turned back to my friends. "The empress is a perfect name for her!" I said.

The three of us linked our arms and walked into the meetinghouse.

Ma insisted that we sit as a family, but with May and Minerva's family sitting right next to us, I was still beside my friends.

It wasn't until after the opening hymn and Brother Munk's interminably long prayer that I had a chance to whisper to May, "Why should you be happy?"

May whispered back, "We're getting new dresses!" Her eyes were bright with the news, and her voice had a tremor of excitement in it.

I felt my heart jump. "Where? When?" I said.

May leaned in a little closer and whispered earnestly, "We're earning money to buy some fabric."

"How?"

"We're picking ground cherries and drying them on our shed roof. We're going to sell them when we have enough."

"But that could take forever!" I said.

"Shhh!"

I turned guiltily and bent forward to look down the row. Ma was leaning toward me, a finger to her lips, her forehead creased into a disapproving frown.

I obediently sat back with my face forward. Ground cherries! They were hard to pick, since you had to bend over to get them off the shrubs. After you got them, you had to pop the pod open to get even one small cherry. That was as much work as thinning beets, except that you could sit in the shade to pop the pods.

I imagined that May and Minerva would be picking cherries until their far-off future wedding days! Then maybe they could buy some white fabric for a wedding dress, but they'd probably have to share it! Well, I guessed that some people were desperate for new clothes, like everyone I knew of in our settlement.

As I walked out into the warm spring air, the back of my neck prickled. Someone was watching me. I could feel eyes on the back of my head.

I looked back and saw Empress Elizabeth following us. May and Minerva stopped and turned to see what I was looking at. Elizabeth hesitated.

"Hello, " I said, just to break the awkward moment.

"Hi," the empress responded with a smirk. "I couldn't help but hear you talking about dresses." She twirled her parasol, her frayed cuffs rubbing against her wrists. "My father is bringing some fabric for my mother and me from Salt Lake City. He should be back any day. I can hardly wait!" The empress turned and walked on. "See you girls later," she said.

We were silent for a few moments. "I hope I see her much, much later," Minerva grumbled, "like never."

Three days later, as I reached for a plate from the sideboard, I felt something suddenly give at my shoulder.

"Sarah! Your dress!" Ma said.

I stretched my left arm around behind me and felt a gap where the sleeve had pulled away from the bodice at the shoulder seam.

"I'm sorry, Ma," I said.

Ma pressed her lips together and shook her head sadly. "It's not your fault," she said, "The dress is too small for you besides being worn-out." Ma pulled the edges of the fabric together. "If I hadn't already cut the homespun into trousers, I would have used it to make a new bodice for you, at least," Ma sighed. "I suppose I can mend this with the leftover scraps, but we've got to find a way to get you a new dress. I don't think we can wait until the next shearing."

Then an idea blazed bright in my mind. "Ground cherries," I said.

Ma opened her eyes wide. "What?"

"Ground cherries!" I repeated. "May and Minerva Rowe are picking ground cherries to sell for new fabric. I think they'll let me help them."

Ma looked pleased. "That's a good idea," she said.

As I had thought, the sisters were glad to have me along on their ground-cherry excursions. Although the work was tedious, it was more fun to pick ground cherries with my friends than to thin beets by myself.

Elizabeth's father returned from Salt Lake as she had predicted. When I saw her that Sunday, I felt hot with envy. Her new dress was a rich, dark blue, scattered with little white flowers that looked cheerful and bright as they swished along on the skirt behind their new owner. There was also a matching bonnet. I wondered if Elizabeth had even had to take the time to carefully unravel a section of the fabric and gather the thread onto a spool to use in sewing her dress—or had her father brought her a spool of store thread?

Almost as astonishing as the new dress was the absence of Elizabeth's parasol. Perhaps she realized that a scruffy pink parasol would not complement her beautiful new dress.

"Her mother must have stayed up nights sewing for her," Minerva muttered behind me. I turned to see Minerva and May with their eyes fastened on the empress. She was acting every bit the part of snooty royalty, too.

"She would have had to help," I said. "All that sewing by hand would have had to take at least two people."

"Maybe her father helped," May said. The three of us burst into laughter at the thought of Brother Wilcox wielding a needle and thread in his thick, work roughened hands as he stabbed it in and out of layers of fabric.

The laughter made me feel better, until I saw Elizabeth seated in a pew as though it were her throne, arranging her skirt around her as though she really were royalty. She fussily picked an imaginary piece of lint off her sleeve.

That week I threw myself into ground-cherry picking as never before. My fingers flew as fast as bird wings in flight as I popped the pods and dropped the small green cherries into my bucket. May and Minerva caught the spirit and stepped up their efforts, too. The sooner we had enough dried cherries, the sooner we'd have our dresses.

Saturday was washing and bath day. Standing out by the washtub in my nightdress, I carefully stirred my two limp, worn dresses in with the other laundry. My new dress would become my good Sunday dress. Then my tired Sunday dress would be my everyday dress. My ripped one might be cut down into a smaller dress for a little girl, or made into rags if there wasn't enough usable fabric to be found.

In Elizabeth's yard, the laundry was almost done. I watched Elizabeth as I stirred. In a long white apron over her oldest dress, she lifted her handsome new dress out of the rinse water. She wrung it out, then shook it and laid it over the sagebrush. I thought she was going to leave it to dry, but she hurried to the house and came back with her hands clasped together in front of her.

What was she doing? It looked like she was praying over her laundry.

She walked over to the rinse water and slowly opened her fingers, moving them constantly in a circular motion as a white powder sprinkled out from her grasp. She stirred the powdered water with her hands. As she picked up her new dress and carefully lowered it back in the water, I guessed what she was doing. She was flour-starching her dress.

I perked up with an idea. Maybe if I flour-starched my old dresses they would hold their shape better. It certainly couldn't hurt them. But then my shoulders sagged. Ma would never let me use any of our precious flour just to starch a dress.

I watched enviously as Elizabeth spread her finery out on the sagebrush bushes, brushing the sleeves and skirt with her hands to make them as smooth as possible.

"Sarah," Ma called from the doorway, "We're washing clothes, not making them into soup!"

I stopped stirring and lifted the steaming clothes with my paddle, purposely stepping around the wash kettle so I had my back to the empress. I couldn't stand to watch her fussing with her new dress any longer.

When the washing was all spread out to dry, there was little else I could do in my nightdress but stay around the house, helping Ma bake bread for Sunday dinner and do some mending on clothes she had found in need of repair as we sorted through the laundry.

The sun was going down when Ma pushed up from checking the bread in the oven and rubbed her back as she stretched backwards. "Sarah, would you please bring in the wash?" she asked. Her face was shiny with sweat, and there were big patches of wet staining the dress under her arms.

"Yes, Ma," I said as I carefully poked my needle partway through the fabric on the trousers I was mending.

I stepped outside, glad to feel the cooler air of the evening on my skin after the thick, hot air from the baking in the house. I paused to look for an early star to wish on, but there were several stars flung against the sky like chicken scratch. Wishing was best with only one star, so tonight there would be no wishing for a new dress.

I dragged myself down the steps toward the flat clothes spread out like scarecrows that had fallen down and died on the sagebrush. They would all need a good, hard shaking before I folded them up to carry them in. We didn't want any insects that had snuggled inside our unmentionables to overstay their welcome and be rudely awakened when we got dressed the next day.

I had just picked up Pa's shirt from the nearest bush when a soul-piercing wail reached my ears. I stopped still, shocked by the anguish that reverberated in my bones. I whipped my head toward the sound and saw Elizabeth standing in her yard, her hands clasping both sides of her head. She fell to her knees as I watched.

I dropped Pa's clean shirt on the ground and ran to Elizabeth. "What's wrong?" I cried, "What is it?"

Elizabeth moaned. I wondered with dread if maybe she had been struck by an Indian arrow. I ran my hand quickly across her back. There was no sign of any wound.

"Are you hurt?" I asked.

Elizabeth covered her face with her hands. "My dress," she moaned. I didn't understand at first. I thought she meant the dress she was wearing. Was it too tight?

"My beautiful new dress," she said thickly. Then the great, heaving sobs came.

I turned to look at the sagebrush that had held Elizabeth's prized new dress. It was gone. All that remained were shreds of ragged fabric attached to a collar, the front placket sagging crookedly down through the spindly branches, and a sad straggle of fabric lying in the dirt where the hem used to be.

I bent and picked up the puddle of fabric from the ground, but dropped it as though it had scorched me when several grasshoppers pinged off of it and bounced out of sight into the underbrush.

"The grasshoppers ate your dress," I said, sliding to the ground beside Elizabeth. She continued to sob, her shoulders shaking so piteously that I couldn't help but encircle them with my arms and lean my head against hers.

"They never ate our clothes before," I said, trying to help. "I think it must have been the flour starch they were after."

Although I didn't think it was possible, Elizabeth cried harder. I patted her back awkwardly, not knowing what else to do.

Before long, her sobs settled into small hiccups, but she still didn't take her hands away from her face. I started to stand up. Elizabeth mumbled something I couldn't understand.

"What?" I said.

"It's all my fault!" she yelled.

"No, it's not," I assured her, "The grasshoppers did it, not you."

Elizabeth pulled her hands away from her blotchy face. "I starched my dress so I could look better than you," she said angrily.

I pulled back a little. "It's not hard to do," I said, "With the rags I wear, you'd look better than me in burlap cloth!"

"I want to be your friend, but I don't know how," Elizabeth blurted, "You're always running around with the Rowe girls, and they don't like me either." She wiped her sleeve across her face. "Since none of you like me, I thought at least I could look better than you. But I was vain, and now I am being punished. God sent the grasshoppers to take down my pride." Elizabeth started crying loudly. She buried her face in her arms.

I sat and thought for a minute. "Elizabeth," I said. She didn't answer. "Listen," I said, "We don't know why things happen. Remember the scripture? *'My ways are not your ways, nor are your ways my ways, saith the Lord.'* What if he sent the grasshoppers so that we could be friends?"

Elizabeth stopped crying. She lifted her head. "You want to be my friend?"

I hesitated, thinking about the way Elizabeth gloated and showed off. Yet she had said she did it from the hurt of being rejected, trying to get back at me. But I hadn't meant to reject her. She'd been so unpleasant that I hadn't known she wanted to be friendly. If we were friends, then maybe her annoying behavior would stop. It was worth a try.

"Yes!" I answered.

"How about May and Minerva?" Elizabeth asked.

"The more friends, the better," I said.

Elizabeth nodded slowly. "All right. You can be my friend," she said decisively. She stood slowly and with shaking fingers gathered up the scraps of her dress. Her chin began to quiver.

"Elizabeth," I said, before she could start sobbing again. "Will you come with me and the Rowe girls to pick ground cherries? We're saving them up to sell so we can buy fabric for new dresses. If you'll come picking with us, you could get a new dress, too."

"Ground cherries?" Elizabeth asked doubtfully.

I shrugged. "It's the only way I know how to get another dress, unless you want to go find some sheep tails to shear." Elizabeth looked at me with her head tipped into a question. "I'll tell you tomorrow," I laughed. "Right now I need to take the laundry in."

Later that fall, May, Minerva, Elizabeth and I walked to church arm-in-arm, our four cranberry-colored dresses turning heads as we made our way to a pew.

And the empress never flour-starched her new clothes again.

Luella Rogers reports that in 1865, her fourteen-year-old grandmother Elizabeth Wilcox worked hard to earn the money for her first dress of store-bought fabric. Anxious to keep it looking new, she flour-starched it the first time she washed it. When she went to get her dress at the end of the day, she found to her horror that the grasshoppers had eaten all of it except for the double-fabric thickness such as the collar, cuffs, and hem.

In an article titled "Destroying Angels," Davis Bitton stated that grasshoppers in the nineteenth Century would sometimes eat green clothing. The insects mobbed a little girl with green stripes in her dress, and by the time her older brother came to her rescue and carried her into the house, the green parts of her clothing were chewed to tatters.

In reality, Elizabeth was a sweet-natured, industrious girl, but the author took the liberty of making her snobbish for the interest of the story.

Ruth Scow tells the family story of the time May and her sisters spent a summer gathering and drying ground cherries. They sent the fruits of their labor, which filled a flour sack, to Salt Lake City where the money they brought was used to buy fabric for new dresses.

In a Utah town called Orderville, which was founded for the purpose of living the United Order (sharing all things in common), lived an enterprising young man. He noticed that at lambing time, the tails of the community's sheep were docked and thrown out. He gathered up the unwanted tails and sheared them. When he had enough wool, he traded it for store-bought trousers. A pattern was made from the pants so that all the young men could have a pair of the latest-styled trousers in homespun.

LIMBS IN LIMBO

I cringed as the words were hurled down from above, even though they weren't directed at me.

"Hey, Henry," Adam Salter yelled from his perch on the scaffolding. "When are you going to match me in a footrace?"

Henry, also known as Peg Leg, stopped pounding his mallet. He relaxed his grip on the splayed end of his chisel. "Well, Brother Salter," he said, squinting up at the younger man's laughing face, "On Resurrection Morning, I will hop on the first boat to Wales, get my leg, and beat you soundly!"

"I want a crack at outrunning you, Peg Leg!" another voice sounded. Laughter followed along with several other challenges to race. Henry John raised his calloused hands, one with fingers outstretched, one clutching his pocked mallet.

"I'll take you all on!" he declared, sweeping his open hand to include all the men on the scaffolding, "And I'll beat you all!"

When the laughter died down, I sidled over to Brother John. I wasn't quite sure what to say, so I said nothing. I stood there because I felt he should have at least one friend. Cursed with big feet and a bad complexion, I knew what it was like to be teased and taunted.

Brother John returned to pounding his chisel, chipping the creamy white oolite stone for the Manti Temple to the proper shape and size with expert strokes. I studied the scarred wooden peg that stuck out below his trouser leg, ending in a metal cap where his foot should have been. I wondered how he had lost his leg. How badly would it hurt? Had it been blown off in an explosion? Maybe it was shot off, or maybe he got a big cut that got the infection in it so bad that his leg had to be cut off. Was it hard to walk on a peg leg? If I bent one knee and used a stick, maybe I could see how it felt.

"Do you want to know how it happened?" The unexpected voice so close to me made me jump. I looked into Brother John's somber eyes. I'd been so busy with my wondering that I hadn't even noticed him stop his work. I nodded in answer to his question.

"I'll tell you only if you promise not to ask any more questions about it," Brother John said. His solemn eyes let me know how deeply the subject of his handicap affected him.

I was honored that Henry John was willing to trust me with the innermost feelings of his heart, and I would respect his trust in me. Besides, once I knew how he'd lost his leg, there would be nothing else I needed to know.

"I promise," I said, squaring my thirteen-year-old shoulders and looking straight into Brother John's blue eyes.

Brother John regarded me thoughtfully. "Well, Karl," he said slowly, "It was bitten off!" Then he burst into laughter, rocking back on his seat so far that his wooden leg lifted up from the ground.

He finally stopped laughing long enough to look at my face. "Now Karl, don't look so somber," he said. "The Lord giveth, and the Lord taketh away." He wasn't laughing now, but his eyes were bright with hope. "I'll get my leg back. It's promised in the scriptures, and I believe the scriptures." Henry John looked me over thoughtfully. "It's all right to smile, boy."

"Karl! We need mortar!" So I left Henry John and took up my task of hod-carrying without even asking him what it was that had bitten off his leg.

When it was time to put my carrier away, the shadows were getting long, staining the mountains a bruised purple. I hurried to the bottom of the hill before most of the men, decidedly before Peg Leg John, who needed to use the towrope to hang onto as he maneuvered down the steep incline.

As I had hoped, the Parry mules were being unhitched from the stone boat that they used to drag the heavy oolite blocks up the hill. Jack lowered his head when he saw me. I reached up and rubbed his soft muzzle. Bodeen stuck his face over to Jack's and mouthed my fingers with his velvety lips.

"Sorry, Bodie, no sugar today," I said.

"You just keep on spoiling those mules so they'll keep wanting to come to work." I turned at the sound of the voice and saw the building foreman, Edward Parry, smiling at me.

"Yes, sir," I said, returning the smile. Brother Parry was one I counted as a friend. He had known my mother and father before they were murdered by the Indians.

I could remember Ma and Pa some, but the images were shift-changing, like pieces of dreams. After we were orphaned, my older sister Maitlyn and I had been taken in by the Helean family.

"You're a good man, Karl," Brother Parry said, clapping a warm hand on my shoulder and letting me walk with him as we each led a mule toward their pen in Brother Parry's yard a few blocks away. My step was light in spite of the size of my feet, and my chest felt a size and a half bigger than it had that morning.

After throwing some hay to Jack and Bodeen, I headed for home. My sister had recently married Matt Helean, a son of our foster family, and she had insisted that I move in with them.

"Ma and Pa have more room," I'd overheard Mark say, "and he's used to it there."

"But he's my brother," Maitlyn had replied.

"He's old enough to look out for himself," Mark had reasoned. That was easy for him to say. He didn't have to deal with his brothers like I did, and endure pitying glances from his sister. I could understand how the Heleans had been willing to take me when they had Maitlyn in the bargain, but just plain old me was no prize.

"He's still a boy," Maitlyn had insisted.

Mark's voice was pleading now. "You're my wife. We'll have our own children. And besides, Ma likes having Karl around."

"So do I," Maitlyn shot back.

Eventually Mark had given in, but he made no secret that it wasn't the way he would have it. Truth be told, it wasn't the way I would have it, either. There were many days when the thought of living like a mountain man tugged at my mind like a rope on a runaway horse. My head would conjure up visions of me and my pack animals up in the mountain valleys, away from everyone. In my mind I was doing what I pleased, when I pleased, and there was no one to answer to.

As I got closer to home, I noticed the doctor's horse tied to the hitching rack. My mind flew to Maitlyn and the baby that she had shyly admitted she was expecting. But it was too soon. I ran to the house and opened the door. An awful stench hit me in the face and twisted in my stomach. Ma Helean was holding my sister in her arms as Maitlyn cried on the older woman's shoulder. It sounded as though my sister's heart was breaking clean in two.

Inside the add-on room where I had feared to see my sister lying was Mark. The doctor was working with bandages, but I couldn't see exactly what he was doing, since Pa Helean was standing in my way.

"What happened?" I asked the room in general.

"Karl," Ma Helean sounded surprised to see me there. Her blotched and anguished face seemed almost unable to register who I was. "Matt's had an accident," she blurted, then burst into a crying fit that left her unable to continue.

Indians? Had Indians attacked Mark even after the Black Hawk

War treaty had been signed? There were always renegades to worry about, no matter what the chiefs said they would do. I was surprised to realize that I was shaking.

Maitlyn turned away from Ma Helean and put her arms around me. "He lost his hand, Karl," she explained thickly.

"His hand?" I replied stupidly. I could feel Maitlyn's head nod as her shoulders shook.

A wave of dread ran through me like a bucket of cold well water as I identified the bad smell in the house at last. Dr. Oldroyd must have had to sear Mark's wound with a hot iron to stop the bleeding. The odor of scorched flesh was repulsive, and I found myself pulling away toward the door.

"Karl?" Maitlyn said as she felt me moving away from her.

"You can go visit with John and Archie," Ma Helean said as she wiped her eyes. She turned toward her oldest son's bed and squared her shoulders. "God's will be done," she said, and she marched into the sickroom.

As Pa Helean moved aside to meet his wife, I could see the figure on the bed. I wished I hadn't. Mark was as pale as temple stone, and lay as still as a slab of rock carved into the shape of a man. Dr. Oldroyd was packing his bag, and when he turned away from Mark, I could see a red-spotted bandage covering the end of his arm exactly where you would normally expect to see a hand.

"Chores," I choked out the word as my stomach flopped with fear and revulsion. I made it out the door before I let loose all that was left of my mid day meal.

I took a long time to do chores, not wanting to return to the house. But I didn't want to go to the Helean's, either, where John and Archie would surely have something to say about my spotted face or wearing boats for shoes. I didn't belong anywhere.

Eventually I had to go back in. Maitlyn welcomed me as warmly as if I had just returned from an extended mission overseas. She busily sat me down to a bowl of stew. Doctor Oldroyd was gone.

The simmering medicinal herbs were pungent enough to mask the remaining traces of the smell of burned flesh. I shifted in my chair so that I couldn't see Mark. For all I knew, he was actually lying there dead while his mother held his hand and spoke futile words to her son's maimed corpse.

I stared at Maitlyn so long that she finally turned to me and said, "What do you want?"

"Was it Indians?" I whispered.

She caught her breath, and then shook her head. "No. He was cutting lumber with his brothers, and had an accident." She pressed her lips together and covered her mouth with her hand.

"I'm sorry," I said, ducking my head and taking a spoonful of the soup I didn't really want. She needed to know that I appreciated her efforts. Giving her a chance to fuss over me a bit seemed to calm her down, and she didn't give in to her tears. As soon as I could get away from her mothering, I crawled into bed.

I was up before first light and hurried outside to do chores. I took care of Mark's as well as Maitlyn's after I did my own. By the time I got back to the house, Maitlyn was up and fixed me something to eat. I gulped a hasty breakfast of boiled milled wheat, bread, and cured side pork, doing my best to tune out the moans of pain that were coming from the bedroom. "My hand, oh, my hand!" I heard Mark mumble. He was definitely not a corpse.

I gladly hurried away from the house and toward my day of work at the temple site. As usual, I went first to the Parry mule pen. I was disappointed to see that it was empty. Had Brother Parry left without me?

Confused, I looked around and saw a familiar figure walking away. I hurried toward it as fast as my awkward feet would let me until I caught up to Brother Parry.

"Where's Jack?" I asked without even saying hello. "Where's Bodeen?"

Brother Parry twisted toward me, his eyebrows lifted high over anxious eyes. "They're missing," he said, his shoulders rising in a helpless gesture as he spoke. "They weren't in their pen this morning."

"Indians!" I said, my blood running hot and fast through my body.

Brother Parry shook his head. "I don't think Indians took them," he said.

"Why not? They take whatever they want, kill whoever they want, and don't think there's a thing wrong with it," I spat out angrily.

"There are no horse tracks, there were no pioneer warning drums last night, and no evidence that I can see of Indians being here." When Indians were spotted, especially ones mounted on horses, the warning drums within the fort were sounded so that people were alerted to possible danger and had a chance to take cover. I hadn't heard any drums either, but I wasn't so willing to shift the blame.

"Indians are sneaky," I insisted stubbornly. All my enthusiasm for getting to work had gone flat with the disappearance of those mules. I couldn't feel at peace while worrying about Jack and Bodeen.

"Brother Olaf," I heard Edward Parry call.

I noticed a stocky, round-faced man walking toward us on his way to temple hill. "Ja, it's me," he answered cheerfully.

"Have you seen my mules?" Edward Parry asked.

"No, but I vill help you look," Brother Olaf answered.

In short order, we had men searching all around the corral and nearby outbuildings for those two mules. There was no sign of them anywhere. I was sure in my heart that they had been stolen, but I knew it would do no good to insist on it.

At last Edward Parry admitted defeat. "Let's assemble for morning prayer and do what we can today," he said. "We have done all we are able. Now it's up to the Lord." I trudged behind the group of men as they moved toward the partly-finished temple.

When we came within sight of the base of the hill, I heard a great shout go up from the men at the front of our column. I dodged around the group and looked ahead to see what the fuss was about. My feet started to run and my heart lifted like a meadowlark as I ran toward Jack and Bodeen. Those two mules were standing patiently beside the stone sled, looking back at us latecomers with an expression close to reproach in their eyes.

"Couldn't wait to get at it, could you, boys?" I said, hugging each of their necks in turn. Jack blew noisily at me in reply.

I got to work carrying mortar for the stonelayers, feeling a surge of happiness every time the mule team appeared over the brow of the hill with another stone for the wall. At mid day, Peg Leg called me over to him. He offered me a piece of jerked venison from his lunch bucket, and in return I gave him a slice of Maitlyn's starch cake. He sighed blissfully at the offering before he spoke to me. "Heard Mark had some trouble yesterday," he said.

I nodded, my mouth full. After I swallowed I said, "Got his hand cut off."

Peg Leg nodded solemnly, but didn't pursue the subject.

Over the next couple of weeks, Mark complained of pain in his hand.

"I know it hurts," Maitlyn would sympathize, "But it's healing. At least you're alive."

"It's not the wound that hurts," Mark would insist, "It's the hand."

"But there isn't a hand there anymore," Maitlyn would say, her hands clasped helplessly at her thickening waist, her voice rising, "I'm so sorry, but your hand is gone."

"But it hurts just the same," Mark insisted, holding up his stump and staring at it with tear-filled eyes. "It hurts awfully."

I thought Maitlyn should check her husband for a fever, yet he didn't act delirious. In time, Mark began sitting at the table for meals, but his frustration at only having one hand was so apparent that I didn't stay around him any longer than I had to. I couldn't stand to hear him crying about the pain in the hand that wasn't there.

One night while out doing chores, I saw Henry John stumping down the road toward our house. "Hey, Karl!" he called out cheerfully. "I'm paying a social call! What do you think of that?"

"Coming to see me?" I joked. "You missed my company after working with me all day?"

Brother John shook his head woefully. "You didn't bring me any cake," he chided me.

"Mark ate it all," I said.

Brother John stopped joking. "Is he having visitors?"

"The doctor comes," I said, "And his parents and some elders to give him blessings sometimes. Oh yes, and the Relief Society ladies."

Brother John smiled. "And now you can tell him a peg leg man has come to call."

I took Henry John into the house. Mark was sitting in a chair at the table. He looked up when we entered. His eyes were red-rimmed, his forehead creased in pain.

"Hello, Henry," he said.

"Have a chair, Brother John," Maitlyn said. "Would you like some biscuits and honey?"

"Yes, ma'am," Brother John replied. Then he turned to Mark. "How you getting along?" he asked.

Mark waved his stump despondently. "It's healed. But it still hurts."

Henry John nodded his head in agreement. "Mine does too."

"Your hand?" I said.

"My leg," Henry John said firmly. I felt my face grow warm from embarrassment. "Even though it's missing, it still hurts me sometimes."

Mark sat up straighter. "You don't mean the place where your peg leg fits? Where you feel the pressure of your body on the wooden peg?"

Henry John was shaking his head. "No. I mean the part of my leg that is no longer there."

Maitlyn set a plate of biscuits and honey in front of Brother John.

At the sight of the food, I felt as though I hadn't eaten in a week, even though we'd finished supper only an hour earlier.

As Brother John took his first bite, I spoke up. "His leg got bit off," I said to Mark in an effort to help him understand.

Mark stared at me in disbelief. "He lost it in a mine crusher," he corrected me.

I whipped my head toward Henry John, looking for him to back me up. The sheepish expression in his eyes as he chewed the biscuit made the heat rise in my face again. "You said it was bit off!" I accused him.

Brother John shrugged. "It makes for a more interesting story, don't you think? Besides, that crusher felt like it had teeth." He shuddered. "I would never want to go through that again."

"But the pain," Mark said, "Doesn't it ever go away?"

Henry John shrugged. "I haven't lived forever yet, so I don't know about the 'ever' part. But mine hasn't. And I have an idea why." Brother John leaned forward with an arm on either side of his plate. "You see, when you're born, your body and spirit are stuck together, supposed to stay together until it's time for you to die."

Mark was nodding without knowing he was. Brother John continued. "When a part of you gets lost, I mean from your physical body, then your spirit body leg or hand is still there, and I believe it misses its companion. The spirit of the missing part grieves for what is gone as though it was dead. And you feel the pain of that sorrow."

Mark nodded again, his eyes with a faraway look.

"My leg was crushed into so many little tiny pieces, it just stayed right there in the coal crusher in Wales," Henry John said. "I didn't even get a bone to bury. Maybe if I could have put my missing leg into a proper little grave, my spirit leg would give me some relief until the resurrection. I know it's looking forward to winning many a footrace!" With one more huge bite and an equally huge sigh of contentment, his biscuit was gone.

That night in bed I thought over what Henry John had said before I fell into a troubled sleep with dreams of body parts chasing after me. There were legs and arms and feet and fingers and even a head. As I ran from the nightmarish limbs, my own legs and arms became loose. I held onto my thigh joints the best I could, but my arms were separating from my body at the shoulders. I awoke with a jolt. And an idea.

After morning chores, I walked over to the Helean's house. John and Archie were outside, throwing knives at a board. I couldn't see for the life of me what good that would ever do, unless someday they ever needed to kill a house.

They turned from the board at the same time when they saw me. They looked comically like a couple of wind up men on a cuckoo clock. "Hey, Karl-pox," John said, "It's been a long time." He pulled his knife out of the board. "But not long enough."

"Hey," was all Archie said.

I didn't want to be here any longer than necessary, so I came right to the point. "I heard that you two were out with Mark when he had his accident."

"So what?" John said, stepping up to me with his chest out and his chin down.

"So, I'd like to know where you were when the accident happened."

"Why?" Karl's stance did not relax.

"I want to find Mark's hand."

Karl stared at me as though I'd told him I was a full-blooded Ute Indian and was ready to take his scalp. "What's wrong with you?" he said, "Are you touched in the head?"

Before I could reply, Pa Helean came around the side of the house calling, "John! Archie!"

John turned away from me and hurried toward his Pa, his voice trailing behind him. "Did you hear what Karl said?"

Archie hung back. He said to me in a low voice, "We were up Willow Creek. Meet me at the fork mid day, and I'll show you." Then he followed his brother.

"Karl," Pa Helean called to me with false cheer, "How are you?"

"I'm doing well," I assured him, although his face remained doubtful. "I need to go now. I'm late for work."

At the temple site, I told Edward Parry that I had to leave at mid day. He said he'd somehow manage to drag the mules home by himself.

I made my way to the fork without seeing any sign of Archie. I wasn't surprised. This could be a trick of his, or even of John's. They could be in on it together, hiding somewhere to watch me, or maybe not showing up at all.

I probably was a little early. Archie might show up. And he might not. I sat down to wait. The warm sun and the restless night I'd had combined to make me sleepy. Even though I closed my eyes, the flies kept me from getting a really sound nap. As I irritably swished another one away, I heard a voice say, "Careful. Don't hit yourself." I sat up to see Archie grinning down at me. "Good thing you waited," he said. "I would have hated to hike up here for nothing."

"What took you so long?" I said as I unkinked my back and stood up.

"Had to lose John," Archie said. "He gets the creeps about stuff like this."

Archie began moving along the trail and I followed.

"John?" I asked, hardly believing that John ever got the creeps about anything.

"Yeah, well, don't say I said it, but he thinks he saw a ghost once, so now anything that's close to death makes him scared. But he'll never admit it. So don't say I told you."

Archie's voice sounded anxious. He tripped over a low bush and slowed, as though he was considering stopping and turning back. "I won't say anything," I assured him. He hesitated, then picked up his pace, and we were soon off the trail and into a stand of dead timber.

Archie stopped and looked around him. Then he pointed. "That one," he said, aiming his finger at a tree sprawled across the broken branches of a spindly young evergreen. The top of the downed tree rested on a row of rocks that looked as though they'd been swept along in the mighty current of some ancient river, and then abandoned in these dry mountains when the river died.

A breeze blew through the dead branches, sifting itself into smaller gusts that tugged at my hair. The leaves whispered secrets to each other that we couldn't hear.

"Where exactly was Mark when the accident happened?" I said.

Archie pointed again. "He landed on those rocks under the tree." He seemed as reluctant as I felt to go any closer. If I'd had any curiosity about this place, it was satisfied now. Besides, I reasoned with myself, what good would it do to look for Mark's hand? This whole situation had been prompted by a nightmare. Anyway, some wild animal had probably dragged it off by now. And how could it really help Mark if I did manage to find it?

Now the tree limbs were tapping impatiently. I thought I could feel eyes on the back of my neck. My heart began to beat faster, in a sense of urgency that I had to act fast or forever miss my chance.

I stepped toward the rocks. "Help me, Archie," I said without looking back. I peered in between the saddle-sized rocks that were tumbled together under the fallen tree. Archie stepped past me and bent over a crack that was further along the tree trunk. I could see a dark brown stain splashed over the rocks where he stood. The sight of it made me shudder as cold fingers of dread slid along my backbone.

Archie moved his eyes back and forth as he worked his way along the rocks where the blood stain was the biggest. Suddenly he stopped as though he'd hit a wall. "I think I see it," he said.

I felt a wash of relief. "Well, get it," I said.

Archie's head came up fast. "Me?" he squeaked.

"Yeah. You're closer," I reasoned with him.

Archie quickly backed away. "Now you are," he said.

"He's your brother!" I said.

"You wanted to do this!" Archie retorted.

I sighed. I would have to do it myself. I took Archie's place where he had seen the hand. Below me, and half-obscured in the semi-darkness between the rocks, was what looked like an old leather glove that had been left out in the rain and sun until it was ruined. It was shriveled and hard, a throwaway thing.

I poked it with a stick. It rolled like a broken old half of a seed pod from some gigantic flower. After a minute or two of futile prodding, I realized I'd have to use a different method, so I took my handkerchief out of my pocket and wrapped it around my hand. Then I reached down and groped for Mark's dead hand. After I got a hold on it, I tried not to think about what it was as I raised it to the surface of the rocks. It looked much worse in the sunshine than it had in shadow.

I folded my kerchief around the stiff, mummy-like fingers, then headed home. Archie walked beside me, casting furtive glances toward the hand I carried in my kerchief. At the closest point to his house, Archie turned off the trail.

"Thanks, Arch," I said to his back.

"Yeah, Karl," he said without stopping or turning around. That was the first time he'd used my given name without some kind of tag on it.

It was getting onto evening by the time I got home. Time to do chores. But first I had to take care of something else.

I stepped up to the cabin door. "Mark?" I called. Maitlyn looked at me with a question in her eyes. "It's all right," I assured her.

Mark met me at the door. "Come outside," I said. He followed somewhat reluctantly.

As I began to dig a hole in the corner of the yard, Mark said, "What are you doing?"

I stopped and pulled out my handkerchief. I set it on the ground. "I found your hand," I said, "and now we're going to give it a proper burial."

I continued digging. Out of the corner of my eye, I saw Mark squat down by the little bundle on the ground, and then carefully unwrap it with his right hand. He was silent as he studied the sorry-looking appendage for a while. Then he folded the handkerchief back over it.

The little grave was done. I stopped shoveling and Mark dropped his dead left hand into the hole. When I started to throw dirt on it, he put his hand on my arm. "Let me," he said.

I watched him as he awkwardly pushed dirt into the hole, grasping the shovel handle with his right hand and pushing against it with his stump in order to move the dirt. I turned away from him and searched the ground until I found a medium-sized rock that was roughly in the shape of a tombstone. I carried it over and set it at the head of the small grave. Mark looked up at me. "A headstone," I explained.

He thought a moment, and then smiled sadly. "No, a hand stone," he replied.

I turned away from the little grave and headed toward the barn. "Chores," I explained to Mark as I walked away from the burial site.

I felt Mark's right hand come down on my shoulder as he fell into step beside me. "I don't know what we would have done without you, Karl," he said. The unexpected praise struck my chest with warmth. "Now I'm going to help with the chores. I can now, because do you know what?"

I looked at him, simply waiting for him to tell me. He broke into a genuine grin. "My hand doesn't hurt any more."

In "The Story of the Life of Henry John," Rozella D. Anderson writes that the musician lost his leg in a coal crusher accident in his native Wales. It wasn't until the 1880's that he found a job chipping and shaping stone for the Manti Temple. When other men teased him good-naturedly about racing with him, he was overheard to say that on Resurrection Morning, he would retrieve his leg and beat them all.

Glen Stubbs' thesis titled "A History of the Manti Temple" contains the account of the morning the Parry mules were nowhere to be found. The searchers finally gave up and went to the building site without them. They found the runaways standing patiently at the base of the temple hill, waiting for their harnesses so they could get to work.

According to June B. Jensen, Mark Helean lost his hand in an accident. Phantom pain was a constant companion until he retrieved his hand and buried it in a small grave.

WEBS

I knocked on Grannie Annie Jensen's big wooden door as hard as I could, but it didn't sound very loud to me. I shivered as a swirl of clattery brown leaves blew across my shoes, twisting the hem of my skirt around my legs. I raised my fist to knock again, but my knuckles swung through the air as Grannie opened the door.

"Missy!" she said, as I stepped through the doorway to catch myself from falling. I think people shouldn't move their doors when other people are knocking on them.

"Come in," Grannie said, but I was already inside. "Warm up by the fire," she said, steering me to a chair beside the stove in her kitchen. Even though I'd just come from next door, the heat from the stove tucked itself around me like a comforter as it soaked into my face and hands.

"Where's Julius?" I asked. Grannie didn't scold me for calling her husband Julius. That's because he told me to call him that. He said he had enough kids calling him Grandpa that he'd really get mixed up if I did, too.

"He's gone to the mountains to get more firewood," Grannie said as she picked up her bonnet. I watched her tie it on. Mama didn't wear a bonnet. She had a smaller hat with feathers. She said bonnets were old-fashioned, but since Grannie wasn't my real Grandma, I didn't tell her that.

"Are you ready?" Grannie asked. My face was beginning to feel like a piece of toast, so I nodded and took Grannie's hand. We stepped out into the October afternoon, a cool All Hallow's Eve.

Mama had loaned me to Grannie Annie for her shopping trip. I was convenient, because I was her next-door neighbor. I was good to hold onto for walking, and I was also good company. I could also give good opinions about shopping, only Grannie wasn't too interested in good opinions. She seemed to like her same old things, like high black shoes and long, dark dresses and bonnets.

Today we headed for Taylor's Emporium. The wind hurried us along, Grannie clutching her long black coat around her with one hand and holding onto me firmly with the other hand so I wouldn't blow away.

As we swept in through the Emporium doors, Jeffrey Switch looked up and smiled at us. Grannie always called him "that nice young man," but he didn't look young to me. After all, he had a bald head. Julius was more wrinkled up than Mr. Switch, but he still had hair.

Mister Switch was nice. He wasn't one of those cranky old men who yell at you for laughing too loud or running when they think you should be walking or standing still.

"What can I do for you ladies today?" Mr. Switch asked us. I stood a little taller. I liked being called "lady."

It wasn't like being called "young lady" by Mama at home. She said, "What do you have to say for yourself, young lady?" and then I couldn't think of anything to say.

Grannie smiled at Mr. Switch. "I'd like to see some shoes," she answered.

We followed Mr. Switch to the chairs by the shoe display. When I saw the new red shoes, I couldn't stop myself. "Ooooo!" I said, picking one up. "These are so beautiful. Look, Grannie. I'll bet Julius would love these on you."

Grannie frowned at me. "Julius doesn't have to wear them." She said, "they're too bright," and she lowered herself into a chair.

I sighed as I set the pretty red shoe back by its mate. When I was old enough to buy my own clothes, I promised myself I would buy red shoes.

Grannie placed her foot up on the little stand that Mr. Switch had brought over for her to use. He unlaced her shoe and pulled it off as Grannie modestly smoothed her skirt down as far as she could on her lower limbs.

Grannie seemed pleased when Mr. Switch pulled out a new black shoe very much like her old one, only free of the permanent creases and worn-down heels that her old shoes had. He knelt in front of her with the shoe in his hand. I giggled. Wouldn't Julius be mad if Mr. Switch asked Grannie to marry him while he was down there on his knees?

"What's so funny, Missy?" Grannie asked.

I didn't want to tell her it looked like Mr. Switch was proposing, so I said, "Maybe you should get some brown shoes instead."

Grannie looked surprised. "Why?"

I thought about it. "So that people know you have new shoes," I said.

"I don't care if other people know I have new shoes or not," she said, giving me her "lecture" look.

"Then you could get brown shoes just to be different," I said.

"Why? What's wrong with me the way I am?"

"Nothing," I said, walking over to her and standing by her shoulder.

Mr. Switch had his head bent low and close to Grannie's knee as he fastened her shoe. Grannie glanced down at him, gave a loud gasp, and threw the skirt of her coat over his head.

"Grannie!" I said, as surprised as if she had danced the can-can on the Emporium roof. Had Mr. Switch pinched her? This was certainly something different. More different than brown shoes. Maybe there was hope for her after all.

Mr. Switch pulled the coat off his head and looked up at Grannie with puzzled eyes.

"I'm so sorry," Grannie said, her hand over her heart. A red color had spread over her face. Now if she'd only get the red shoes, she would be color-coordinated.

"Are you all right?" Mr. Switch asked without his usual smile. He smoothed his hand down over the short fringe of dark hair sprinkled with gray that grew on the back of his head.

"Yes, I'm so sorry," Grannie repeated quickly. "I'll take them."

Mr. Switch tipped his head to the side, like he was asking a question without saying any words.

"The shoes," Grannie said, "I'll take these shoes."

I was surprised. Usually Grannie tried on several pairs of shoes, walking up and down the store aisle to test the fit before she decided on the perfect ones.

Mr. Switch sat back on his heels and extended his arms as far as he could, presumably to stay out of reach of Grannie's coat as he took the new shoe off her foot. He quickly replaced the old shoe as Grannie sat stiff and unsmiling.

It was only after we left the store that Grannie's face turned back to its normal color.

"Grannie," I ventured to say.

"What?" she replied.

"Why did you do that?"

"What?"

I knew she knew, but I said it anyway. "Throw your coat on Mr. Switch."

She looked down sideways at me. "Because when I looked down and saw the top of his head, I thought for one second that it was my knee," she said.

"Your knee?" I repeated.

"Yes," Grannie replied, shrugging her shoulders, "I was so embarrassed to have my knee showing, I had to hurry and cover it up."

I couldn't help myself. I started to giggle. I heard Grannie make a noise and thought she might be angry with me, but when I looked over at her, I saw that she was laughing quietly.

"He looked so surprised," she said, "But I couldn't explain! I couldn't tell him that I thought his head was my knee!" That made me laugh even harder.

It was getting dusky as the swirling leaves chased us home.

When we came in sight of Grannie's house, she said with a frown, "I thought Julius would be home by now!"

"Should I wait with you?" I asked, wondering if there were any cookies in her kitchen.

"No, Missy, you'd better run home. Thank you for going with me."

"You're welcome," I said, and started for my house next door.

"Missy," Grannie called to me. I turned to look at her. "Don't tell Julius!" I knew what she meant.

The next morning I looked outside to check for snow. There wasn't any, but there was a whole evergreen tree on top of Julius' wagon load of wood. "A Christmas tree!" I yelled. Papa came over to see.

"I'd better go help Julius get it inside," Papa said.

"May I come too?" I asked eagerly. Papa nodded. We put on our coats and made our way across the yard. Papa's knock on the Jensen' door was good and loud.

Grannie opened it. "Hello, Sister Jensen," Papa said.

"Come in, come in," Grannie said, shutting the door behind us.

"Would Julius like a hand with that tree?" Papa said.

"I'm sure he would," Grannie said sourly. "Why he got one as early as October, I'll never understand. I told him not to bother with cutting a tree at all this year."

"No Christmas tree?" I said, hardly believing what my own ears had heard.

"All our children are married and moved away," Grannie explained. "There's no one to have a tree for."

It was obvious to me. "You and Julius," I said.

"That's what he thinks, too," Grannie replied, smiling at last.

"Hello, Paul. Hello there, Miss Missy," Julius boomed at us in his cheerful voice as he walked into the room while fastening his suspender to his pants.

"Julius!" Grannie scolded.

"What?" he looked at her with wide eyes. "I'm dressed. There's nothing showing that's not supposed to, is there?"

Grannie threw up her hands in surrender. "I'll fix some breakfast," was all she said.

Julius rubbed his hands together. "Paul, would you help me set up that Christmas tree? I know I got it kind of early, but when I saw it, I knew it was perfect." Papa followed Julius to the back of the wagon, and jumped up to take hold of the thick evergreen. "Now I don't have to worry about getting one after the weather turns." Pa heaved the tree off the end of the wagon, and Julius helped pull it down onto the ground. "Can you believe that Annie didn't even want a tree at all?" Julius said.

It was rather amusing to watch the two men struggle with a tree that was taller than Papa and wider than Julius. They eventually got it through the door, hauled it across the house and set it up in the parlor right in front of the bay window. As they attached a tree stand, I clasped my hands around my arms.

"Why is it so cold in here?" I asked.

"The heat from the stove doesn't reach this far," Julius said. "We keep the door closed when there's no company, because that way the stove heat stays in the kitchen and bedroom that we use. You run along, Missy; we're almost done anyway. Go get warm by the fire."

Julius didn't have to tell me twice. When I sat down by the stove in the kitchen, Grannie handed me a mug of hot apple cider. Papa and Julius were not far behind me.

"Thanks, Paul, now it feels like the holidays around here," Julius said as he and Papa accepted cups of hot cider from Annie.

"Glad to help, Julius." Papa took a sideways look at me, but he still spoke to Brother Jensen. "Now you've got to be good so that Santa Claus will come and put a present under that tree!"

"I always am," Julius said with wide, innocent eyes. "In fact, I'm so good that I'm going to let you help us decorate it, Missy!"

"May I really?" I asked. Decorating two Christmas trees in one year would be fun.

"No one else but you," Julius smiled.

"That's right," Grannie said. "I'm too old to help. Besides, no one is going to come home for Christmas anyway."

"I'm someone," Julius said in a huffy voice.

"Time to go home, Missy," Papa said, taking my arm to steer me toward the door.

"Good-bye!" I said, "Thank you for the cider."

I didn't get a chance to go over to Jensen's until the next Saturday. When I knocked on the door, it didn't open. Remembering the last time, I wasn't going to knock again. So I got my foot ready to kick on the door when I heard Grannie's voice sounding soft and mushy through the wood.

"Who's there?" she said.

"Missy!" I yelled, "I've come to decorate the tree!"

"You can't! Not today! Julius is sick with a fever and can't get out of bed. You need to go on home. I don't want you to get sick."

When I told Mama, she put some soup in a bowl and walked over to Grannie's house. I watched from the window and saw Grannie let Mama in! I was upset. When Mama got back, I was waiting for her.

"If Julius is too sick for me to visit, why did Grannie let you in?" I said.

"Because I'm an adult," Mama said.

When Papa came home, Mama told him about Julius in whispers. I couldn't hear the words, but I knew she was talking about him, because Papa put on his coat, got his little bottle of consecrated oil, and went over to Jensen's. If Papa was going to give him a blessing, he must be really sick.

It was after Thanksgiving before Grannie came over to our house. She was wearing a tired smile as she stamped the snow off her new shoes. "Julius is going to be fine," she told Mama. Mama gave Grannie a big hug, then I hugged Grannie, too.

Mama let me bake some gingerbread men for Julius. I made one with white icing hair because we didn't have any gray icing and Mama said Julius would know it was him. I followed Mama across the yard along the trail that Grannie had made in the snow. Julius was sitting in a chair by the stove with a blanket over his lap.

"I've missed my Missy!" Julius said when he saw me. When I gave him the gingerbread men, he said, "Sweets from the sweet!" Then he picked up a cookie and bit its head off.

"Hey, that was you!" I said, kind of indignant that he didn't recognize himself.

Julius stopped chewing and looked at Mama, then back at me. He swallowed, and then said, "Of course it was me! I didn't want Annie to eat me, so I had to do it first. And am I ever delicious!" I laughed.

Mama only let us stay long enough for Julius to eat the rest of himself. "After all," he said, "My head would be awfully lonely down there in my dark stomach without the rest of me to keep him company!"

My cousins came to visit a few days later. We had lots of fun sledding and building snowmen. On the day before they had to leave, we were moping around, sorry that they had to go so soon, and bored of the winter games we'd been playing.

"Why don't you go caroling?" Mama said.

"That's a good idea!" I said. We bundled into coats and hats and scarves and gloves. Mama promised to have a pot of hot chocolate for us when we got back.

We started down the street, stopping at the neighbors' houses as we went, singing Christmas songs at the top of our young voices. Brother and Sister Caroll gave us sugar cookies, and old Sister Bennett cried as she sang along with us. Everyone smiled and thanked us, and we kept going until our toes got cold.

On the way back home, I said we had to sing at one more house. My cousins started to complain until I told them it was right next door. I was heading around to the back, but Emmalinda said we had to sing at the front of the house. She said it was tradition. I thought it was a dumb tradition if the people in the house couldn't hear you, but I didn't want to argue. I wanted hot chocolate.

We positioned ourselves in front of the bay window and started singing "O Tannenbaum." I could see the Jensen's Christmas tree dimly through the glass. It stood lonely and silent, like a ghost left over from All Hallow's Eve. Julius and I had never had a chance to decorate it, yet there was something different about it. It wasn't green any more.

I stepped closer, forgetting the words to the old Christmas song as I studied the tree. I wondered if it had turned into a ghost tree, since it had been cut down dead on All Hallow's Eve and dragged down the mountain into strange surroundings, only to be forgotten.

Yet the branches didn't look haunted and lifeless. They were soft and silvery, like a magic tree from a fairy tale. Without pinecones or popcorn strings or cranberries, Julius had found the most charming decoration I had ever seen. Whatever it was looked far too delicate to be wool, but was spread evenly all over the tree with a most sensitive and precise hand. Or maybe it had been done without hands. Maybe the tree was enchanted.

Just as I knew would happen, no one came to the front door. My cousins trooped back to my house without me. "Tell Mama I'll be there in a minute," I called to the retreating figures.

I hurried around to the back of the house and knocked on the kitchen door. Grannie opened it. "When did Julius decorate the tree?" I demanded.

"He didn't," Grannie said, pulling me inside and shutting the door behind me against the cold. "We haven't been in the parlor since the tree was set up."

"But someone decorated it," I insisted.

Julius came walking slowly into the kitchen, his face twisted into a question. "Who decorated our tree?" he asked.

"I don't know," I said, "But it's the prettiest I've ever seen. It's all silvery. Go and see."

Grannie followed Julius to the parlor door with a lantern in her hand. He twisted the door open. I was right behind them.

As soon as the light hit the Christmas tree, Grannie gasped. Julius said, "Well, I'll be!" But he didn't say what he'd be. I just stared. Every single branch was covered with fine little silver threads crossed and criss-crossed over and under each other into a soft covering as delicate as silk. It was so dense that you couldn't even see the spiders that had busily spun the thread while the tree was abandoned all those long weeks as it waited for Christmas all alone with only the spiders for company.

Dorothy Buchanan's father ran a dry goods store. At about the turn of the twentieth century, he saw an elderly woman come into his shop to buy some shoes. Unfortunately, the clerk who helped her try them on was bald-headed, and when she caught sight of his bald head hovering close to her lap, she was horrified because she thought her bare knee was showing. She threw her coat over his head to cover her embarrassment, and only succeeded in embarrassing herself further.

A forgotten Christmas tree in the closed-off parlor of Julius and Annie Jensen's house was found to be totally covered with delicate silvery spider webs by the time they remembered to take it down.

FINDERS KEEPERS

I put my hand out to steady myself as I climbed down the steep cellar steps. The rough stone wall felt cold and a little bit damp, even though the air outside was the hot, dry air of late summer. It was no wonder that Mama kept the cheese, milk, eggs, and produce down here.

Mama had sent me down to get an apron-full of apples. I knew right where they were, but I paused at the bottom of the narrow steps to let my eyes adjust to the grayish dark of the cellar. I pulled my apron up into a pocket and held it with one hand. My other hand would fill the pocket with the fragrant apples recently harvested from our orchard. I hoped Mama was going to bake them, so we could eat them with cream. I smiled at the tantalizing thought.

When I looked up from gathering my apron, I saw a movement on the milk table. At first I thought it was a mouse. But what I saw next to the flat pan that held our fresh milk as we waited for the cream to rise to the top was no mouse. It was a snake.

It didn't seem to see me, and kept right on with its task. I couldn't believe what it was doing. Coiled loosely, the end of its long, pointed tail was moving across the top of the milk pan. Now loaded with thick, rich cream, the snake pulled its tail sideways through its mouth before it swung the tail out and around to make another pass across the top of the pan.

I couldn't move. I stood there with my apron in my hand, fascinated and repulsed as the snake helped itself to a few more mouthfuls of our family's cream.

Suddenly, the snake stopped. It turned its scaly head toward me and fixed its shiny cold eyes on mine. It's thin tongue whipped out at me in a gesture that was so like my sister Marjorie that I stopped feeling scared and started to get mad. That snake was taking my apple cream!

I raised my fist and stepped toward that sneaky snake. The snake turned and slithered quickly up along the cracks in the rock wall and out a small hole at the top. I was glad to see it go. I don't know what I would have done if it had stayed and challenged me. I wouldn't have really hit it, because even though I could tell it was just a water snake that wasn't poisonous, it still had needly-sharp teeth.

I turned and ran up the stairs. "Mama! Mama!" I hollered.

"What is it, Ethel?" Mama asked as she turned toward me. Philip was balanced on her hip, struggling to get down.

"A snake in the cellar!" I yelled.

Mama set Philip down on his sturdy little legs, creased her forehead into annoyed lines and said, "You don't need to yell. I can hear you just fine." She didn't seem at all concerned that I had seen a snake in our cellar.

"It was eating the cream!" I said. Mama's annoyed lines sprang up in surprise. "Come and see!" I insisted.

I let Mama go first as we climbed down the cellar steps. When she saw the drips of cream on the table as evidence of the snake's thievery, the only thing she could do was believe me. I even pointed out the hole where the snake had escaped.

To my surprise, Mama shrugged. "We left the milk laying out, and the snake found it," she said. "It didn't know it was taking our cream."

I could hardly believe what she was saying. "You mean snakes can claim finders, keepers?" I asked.

Mama laughed. "Yes, I think so. I'll ask Papa to fix that hole in the wall so we can have some cream tomorrow." She gently pulled at the side of my apron that I was still holding in a pocket shape, and saw that it was empty. "As long as we're down here, how about if I fill that up with apples?"

Marjorie scoffed at me when I told her about the snake. "You must have been dreaming," she said.

"No!" I yelled, "The snake was eating our cream with its tail, just ask Mama!"

"She didn't see it," Marjorie teased, "She just believed you. I don't."

"But it was real! I saw it!" I insisted.

"Girls, go outside to argue," Mama said from the rocking chair where she was cuddling Philip. I knew that Mama especially liked Philip's naptime because she could get more done when he was asleep than when he was awake.

We didn't talk back to Mama. I stomped outside and Marjorie followed me. I automatically curved around the house to the right, away from the side by the foothills where Papa had killed the coyote last spring.

I still got the shudders when I remembered the day that the sinister gray shape came slinking out of the shadows beneath the trees, moving out into the open and toward our house, its head down, ears back, belly low to the ground. It looked more like a demon than a coyote. My oldest brother, David, saw it first. He grabbed up Penelope, our younger sister who was calling, "Doggy! Doggy!"

"Pa!" David yelled, the desperation in his voice making the hair rise up on the back of my neck.

Papa came running from the corral. He took one look, yelled, "Get back!" and ran into the house. He was out again in an instant, his Winchester rifle clutched in his hands. He dashed through the knot of us children as David herded us onto the porch. Papa stopped, took aim, and shot at the advancing coyote, his shoulder jerking back as the bullet spit out of the barrel.

The coyote kept coming. Its narrow eyes were fixed on Papa and his rifle. Papa shot again. The coyote didn't even flinch as the bullet kicked up the dust on the ground beside him. He kept his steady, ominous pace straight for Papa. The coyote was close enough that I could see white foamy stuff dripping from his mouth, sort of like the smelly sour milk that Philip used to spit up when he was a little baby.

"Rabies," David said. Even though he said it low and whispered, I knew it was something bad. I started to cry, because it seemed as though the coyote would never stop. For some reason, Papa's bullets kept missing it.

Pa bent down, his hand on the ground. Had he given up? A few more paces and the coyote would be on him. I knew it wouldn't stop. Once it had killed Pa, it would come after all of us as we huddled together on the porch, and kill us one by one, and none of us could stop it. It seemed to possess an evil power, something unearthly that would even let it walk through the door and into the cabin where it would kill Ma and Philip. We would all be dead from this devilish thing that came creeping down from the mountains.

I was shaking with fear when Pa stood up and drew back his hand. I could see the rough rock that fit inside his fist. He hurled the rock at the coyote, his foot coming up off the ground behind him with the force of the throw.

Like David against Goliath, that rock smacked into the coyote's head with the sound of a bundle of wet laundry plopping into a basket. The coyote dropped instantly to the ground. Papa stood for a few minutes between his children and the threat that was now still, watching to see if the animal moved at all. It didn't. It was dead.

Mama pulled all of us younger children inside the cabin while Pa and David took care of the dead coyote. Mama made us some hot chocolate with whipped cream and read us a story from the scriptures.

It was a good one, about Daniel in the lion's den and he didn't get eaten up. It reminded me of how we hadn't been eaten up, and I felt better.

When Papa and David got back, we all hugged each other. Later, David told us that they had buried the coyote, but he wouldn't say where. That night at family prayers, Papa said an especially long one, thanking Father in Heaven for His protection of our family.

Now when I went outside, if I avoided the side of the house where we had first spotted the coyote, I could play without glancing constantly at the foothills.

Marjorie started out down the path toward the orchard. I followed her to see what we were going to do for fun while Philip had his nap. Even though Marjorie was bossy, she usually had good ideas. I was almost ready to say, "What are we going to do?" when Marjorie stopped dead still in front of me, her head turned toward the foothills. I was scared to look. It couldn't be another coyote, it just couldn't. We were too far away from the house to make it back in time. And Papa was out in the fields with David. I'd never seen Mama shoot a gun before, and I knew she couldn't throw a rock very far.

"Look!" Marjorie said. Her voice wasn't a scared voice. It was excited, as though she'd made a great discovery. I looked the direction she was looking, but didn't see anything.

"What?" I said.

Marjorie walked along the edge of the orchard a little ways, then stooped down beside a bush. She lifted up a dark-skinned little baby with shiny black eyes and no teeth. It looked to be about the size Philip had been last year when he was really good at spitting up sour milk.

"It's a baby!" I said, staring at the round little face. At the sound of my voice, the dark eyes turned toward me, and the chubby cheeks lifted up into a smile. The baby raised its fist and made little gooing sounds.

"It likes us!" Marjorie said. "Let's take it home!"

I had a suddenly brilliant idea. "This can be our baby!" I said.

"Yes!" Marjorie agreed delightedly, as she cuddled the brown baby against her neck. The baby thumped her back with its tiny fist and bit down on her shoulder with its gums.

"We can feed it and dress it and put it to bed and it will call us 'Mommy'!" I said, as my heart raced with the lovely picture in my mind.

"This is much better than playing dolls," Marjorie declared as she started for the house.

"I want to hold him," I said.

"What if it's a *her*?" Marjorie answered in that superior tone that I hated.

"I want to hold whatever it is!" I insisted.

"After we get home," Marjorie said, "I don't want to make it cry."

"I won't make it cry!" I promised as I trotted behind Marjorie. But she wouldn't let me hold the baby.

We made our way up the porch steps. I was so eager to show Mama what we found that I held the door open for Marjorie without being asked.

Mama looked up from her sewing, a little frown of annoyance on her face that disappeared as soon as she saw what Marjorie had in her arms.

"What on earth . . ." she said, putting her hand over her heart.

"We found it, Mama," I said, before Marjorie could have a chance to say anything.

"Where did you find it?" Mama demanded, standing up and walking over to Marjorie.

"Under a bush by the orchard," Marjorie declared. "It was all alone."

"Someone must have thrown it away," I said eagerly, "So Marjorie and I are going to be its mamas."

"You can't," Mama said. "This baby belongs to someone."

"But it was alone," Marjorie insisted, hugging the baby tighter to her chest.

"Its mother knew where it was," Mama said. "Maybe she left it there asleep while she went to take care of something. I know she'll be back for it. I know she wants her baby."

"Then she shouldn't leave it lying around," I said, my face stiff with indignation. "Finders, keepers."

Mama shook her head slowly. "Not with babies," she said, "Babies aren't like puppies and kittens. You can't just bring one home and keep it. You must take it back." Marjorie's bottom lip was beginning to quiver, and I could feel the hot sting of tears in my eyes.

"But, Mama!" was all I could say before I heard a strange wail outside our house. It stopped me cold, a sound like an injured wildcat, and I shrank against the wall. I noticed Marjorie move a step closer to Mama as she turned to face the doorway and boost the baby up in her arms. The baby was smaller than Philip, but it was still a big baby for Marjorie to carry for so long.

The wail sounded again, closer this time. The coyote Papa killed had stalked us silently, yet steadily and relentlessly. Maybe rabid wildcats made that kind of noise. The wail seemed to penetrate my ears and slide down my arms, pushing up goose bumps along the way. Mama went to the window and looked out.

"It's too late, girls," she said solemnly. I shuddered at the tone of her voice. I didn't know what it was too late for, but I was scared of whatever it was.

Mama opened the door, and an Indian woman, still wailing, walked into the house. When she saw Marjorie, she pointed an accusing brown finger and began to speak rapidly, but I couldn't understand her language. Her face was wet with tears, and when she was done speaking, she let out another wail.

Mama pulled the baby from Marjorie's arms, then held him out to the Indian woman. She took hold of him and held him close, wailing the whole time. He looked worried as he stared up at his mother's face. Then his little mouth opened and he started wailing, too. That was too loud already, but then Philip woke up and began to scream.

Mama looked grim as she picked our little brother up from his bed and began to rock him against her shoulder. "I'm sorry," she said to the Indian woman, "My girls didn't know you would be back for your baby. They were just trying to take care of him."

The woman seemed not to understand, and kept on wailing, right along with her baby and my brother.

Suddenly Mama turned toward me. "Ethel, get some squash from the cellar." She turned toward my sister. "Marjorie, get a loaf of bread. Give it to her."

I hurried down the cellar steps, not even thinking about snakes as I scooped up a couple of squashes. I wanted to stay in the cellar where the thick walls offered some protection to my ears, but I trotted obediently back up to the noisy room and handed the squashes to the Indian. She dropped them into a sling of fabric that also held her baby. She took Marjorie's loaf of bread under her arm, immediately stopped her loud wails, and shot us a dark look before she turned and carried her baby and her edible peace offerings out of our house and down the stairs. As she hurried down the road, I saw what looked like an apple tumble from the folds of her clothing and roll across the road into the weeds.

When Mama closed the door, Philip's cries were blessedly quiet compared to what we had just heard.

"Mama," Marjorie said, "I think I'm going to wait and have my own babies."

"Me, too," I said, "And no more finders, keepers!"

At around the turn of the century to the 1900's, Ethel Hermansen Madsen went down into the cellar and saw a water snake skimming cream off the surface of the milk pan with its tail, then draw the tail through its mouth to eat the cream off.

Marjorie Madsen Riley's father shot at a rabid coyote that had come down out of the foothills and was advancing relentlessly toward his family. His rifle shots did not deter it, nor did the bullets find their mark, so at last in desperation, he threw a baseball-sized rock at the animal. The rock hit the coyote in the head and killed it.

Jenny Lind Brown's grandmother told two of her daughters to return an Indian baby they had found under a bush. They resisted their mother's advice, not believing that the baby belonged to anyone who wanted it. When the baby's mother came to claim her child, she could not be comforted until a gift of bread and vegetables was given to her in repayment for unknowingly stealing her child.

STRANGE CURE

The baby scared me. The sight of her little face put such a twist of pity and revulsion in my stomach that it was hard for me to even look at her.

When I had first heard the midwife, Sister Tilley, solemnly announce that it was a girl, I had grinned triumphantly at my older brother Soren. "The girls still outnumber the boys!" I said gleefully.

He scowled back at me. "C'mon, Charles," he said to our younger brother, "Us guys have to stick together." He put his hand on Charles' shoulder and they marched outside.

I paid them no mind. After twelve years of being the oldest girl, I knew exactly how to help care for a baby sister. I was an expert.

Sister Tilley wasn't smiling as she led Papa outside, but I didn't suspect a thing. Anxious to welcome the new little girl to the family, I tiptoed into the bedroom where my mother lay.

Tears were sliding down Mama's pale cheeks, dripping off her chin. Her nose was running, the thick wetness sitting on her upper lip. She made no effort to wipe her face dry.

"Mama?" I asked, my happy heart suddenly thudding heavy in my chest. "Are you okay?"

"Oh, Caroline. Caroline." Mama held her arms out to me. I approached her warily. When she pulled me against her full, soft breast, I wanted to snuggle in, to be comforted. I wanted to hear Mama tell me everything was all right. But I held back a little because I didn't want the wet on her face to get in my hair. Bath day was still five days away.

"Caroline," Mama said again.

Suddenly fearful, I pulled back from her grip. "Mama, is the baby dead?"

Mama looked shocked, as though I had placed a horny toad in her hand. "No! Why, no, of course not!" she said. "She's right here beside me." She pointed to a small bundle on the bed. "Your Papa and I even named her already. She's Annie."

"Can I see her?" I asked.

Momma lifted the sheet that was draped over her small hill of a tummy and wiped her face with it. "She's not the same as the other babies," she said slowly.

I snorted a laugh. "Of course not! She's our own special girl, cuter than any baby in the territory!" I smiled at the cherished thought of another baby sister. I'd dress her up in a bonnet and booties with her little white dresses made out of factory cloth. I would smock the dresses myself, and she would look just like a little angel. I'd show her off to all my friends. I'd teach her how to walk, and I'd knit her little socks. We were going to be the best of friends. The best sisters in the whole territory.

I leaned over Mama and gently pulled the blanket down from the baby's face. A tiny little mouth made a small "o" of surprise as the squinty new eyes blinked slowly out of a face that was blotched an angry red. The entire right eye was surrounded with the deep stain, from above her eyebrow down past her cheekbone.

Shocked, I let the blanket fall and stepped back. "Sister Tilley didn't clean her off!" I protested.

"She's clean," Mama said quietly.

"No. She missed a spot," I insisted.

"It won't come off," Mama said.

"Yes it will!" I shouted, "Give me a cloth. I'll get it off."

"You can't."

Refusing to listen, I found a clean rag left over from the birthing and dipped it in a basin of still slightly warm water. I gently wiped it across the redness on Annie's little face. She squirmed and let out a mew of protest. The ugly patch of red stubbornly stayed where it was. The damp cloth came away perfectly clean.

"No!" I said.

"It's God's will," Mama said, the tears dripping off her chin again. "Remember when that stray dog spooked the horses and they bolted?"

My mind spun back to the day of the nightmarish incident four months ago when we had all been tipped out of a runaway wagon. Most of us had escaped with a couple of bruises and scrapes as we tumbled out onto the hard desert floor. But Mama's long skirt had been caught on the wagon box. She had been dragged away from us, screaming. Papa desperately limped after the grimly stampeding horses until exhaustion from dragging their burden overtook them and they stopped themselves, blowing and snorting in fear.

Mama was still alive, but scraped and badly bruised. I remember that she had worried whether the baby she was carrying was dead. Her battered face had suddenly lit into a smile through her bleeding lips, her swollen eye shining with joy when she felt the baby move at last.

There was no joy on her face now. Annie was alive, but she was marked.

Mama began to sob. I didn't know what to do. I just stood there, each sob from my mother wrenching my soul, twisting my heart into a big, painful knot.

Papa came in and said, "Go on, Caroline." He gently pushed me toward the door and turned to my mother's bed.

I was glad to go, to get out of that room of pain and shattered dreams.

For the next couple of days, Mama pretty much kept to herself. I knew she was wondering why I didn't stick to my promise to be her helper. She and I had discussed my role of holding the baby and changing its diapers and burping it, just like I had done with the other girls.

My sisters were too young to be of any real help, but when Mama asked if I wanted to hold Annie, I said, "No, I'm busy." I could see the hurt in her eyes, but I couldn't bring myself to hold my sister. The red mark over her eye looked like blood, as though she'd been half-scalped. Even though Mama assured me that the birthmark didn't hurt, I just knew Annie was in terrible pain when she cried. I could tell by the way her dark red cheek bellowed in and out with each breath and wail.

The next morning, Mama came out of her room, her little blemished baby held close in her arms.

"We need to help her," Mama announced, her face set as firmly as the mountains we had come to live among. "We all must pray for her, for a miracle to heal our little Annie's face."

I joined the rest of my family in prayer for Annie that night, but I didn't feel it would do any good.

The next day, Sister Tilley came to check on Mama and Annie. Annie was crying, wrenching my heart with each wail of pain that seemed to herald her disappointing future. I was washing dishes in the corner, trying to distract my thoughts from my disfigured sister.

Mama put Annie to her breast. In the blessed quiet that followed as Annie suckled, I heard Sister Tilley say, "Have you heard of Thessla Rhodes?"

"No. Is she a new settler?" Mama asked.

"She's new to Pleasant Creek," Sister Tilley said, "They say she's a healing woman."

I stopped what I was doing, but I kept my back to the room.

"Is she a doctor?" Mama asked.

"No, not exactly," Sister Tilley seemed to be searching for the right words. "She knows cures."

"And do they work?" Mama asked.

I glanced over my shoulder and saw Sister Tilley shrug. "She cured John Albany's warts."

"I want to see her," Mama announced.

"She's coming to town tomorrow to visit her sister," Sister Tilley said."

"Can you tell her I need to see her?" Mama's eyes were fastened hopefully on her visitor.

"Of course," Sister Tilley assured her. Then she reached over and patted Mama's shoulder. "It will be all right," she said.

Mama nodded and wiped her eyes. "I know," she answered softly.

Thessla Rhodes appeared the next evening, when the shadows were long and Annie was getting fussy, her cry becoming more insistent as Mama walked the room and patted her tiny little back, trying to comfort her after her feeding.

Sister Rhodes was smaller than Mama, white-haired and pink-cheeked, pleasantly round and wrinkled with a perpetual smile on her face.

She gently took Annie from Mama's arms. With pleasant little shushing sounds and words of comfort, she teased Annie out of her bad mood. The baby stared up adoringly at Sister Rhode's face from the safe crook of the little woman's arm.

"Such a sweet little thing," Sister Rhodes cooed. I sagged a little at her words. Couldn't she see that glaring red birthmark that ruined my sister's face? She wasn't sweet! She was frightening!

After a minute or two, Thessla Rhodes said quietly, "There is a cure. But it must be done soon. And it won't be easy."

"I'll do it," Mama assured her fervently, "Just tell me."

Sister Rhodes tilted her face as she looked up at Mama. "Do you know any women who are close to their time?"

I wondered what time she meant. But Mama knew. "Yes. My friend Johanna Hansen is due to deliver any day."

Sister Rhodes nodded. "That's good." She reached out a small finger and gently caressed the discoloration on Annie's face. "You must take Annie with you to the birth."

"Why?" Mama asked.

Sister Rhodes' hand wandered to my baby sister's head. She touched her hair as lightly as she would a stem full of dandelion fuzz that she didn't want to scatter. "There are miracles in the process of creating new life," Sister Rhodes said. "You must be there at the moment of delivery. When the afterbirth is delivered, you must take a portion and completely cover Annie's mark with it. Hold it on until it dries. You must cover every bit, and don't let it slip off. When it's dry, you can remove it. Repeat this process as often as you possibly can, with as many new mothers as will let you."

"The afterbirth?" Mama looked doubtful.

Sister Rhodes looked at her keenly. She spoke with authority that belied her small size. "Are you willing to do everything you can to help your baby?"

"Yes!" Mama answered without hesitating.

"There are healing powers in new life that we cannot comprehend," Sister Rhodes said, "It's as if these babies are so newly come from our Father in Heaven, they're still surrounded by his great love and power." Sister Rhodes stared down at Annie, and then spoke without looking up. "I did not teach myself healing. It is a gift from God." She sighed. "All I can tell you is that you can't wait. If Annie gets much older it will be too late."

Annie twisted uncomfortably in Sister Rhodes' arms. She let out a small sound, a forlorn little "aaaaa" that made me think of an orphaned lamb.

I was ashamed. It wasn't Annie's fault that her little face was disfigured. She was an innocent little baby who would grow up having to bear people's stares and whispers and the cruel taunts of children. She might take to wearing veils, or maybe not going outside at all, shut up in her house, a prisoner of her birthmark.

"I'll help," I said. Stepping over to Annie, I slipped my finger into her tiny fist. She hung onto me with an endearing little squeeze of her fingers. I knew that she needed me. I was going to help her in any way I could. And no ugly old birthmark could keep me from my sister's side.

Sister Rhodes lifted Annie and placed her on my shoulder. Annie quit fussing. She snuggled in and curled up like a contented kitten. My heart welled so full of love that it actually pained me.

Sister Rhodes smiled. "Good luck," she said softly, "May God be with you," and she let herself out the door.

Mama was crying. She put her arms around me and Annie and held both of us at the same time.

A message from Sister Hansen's came three days later. She was having her baby. Mama and I hurried to her house with Annie wrapped up snug and secure in my arms.

As we stepped through the door, I could hear Sister Hansen moaning. Sister Tilley had hung a blanket up in front of the bed for a little bit of privacy. Brother Hansen was pacing. He stopped when we came in.

"Do you think I ought to chop some wood for the fire?" he asked Mama hopefully.

"I'm sure that would be a good idea," Mama said. Brother Hansen was out the door before I could close it behind us.

Mama went behind the curtain to help Sister Tilley. I snuggled and bounced and cuddled Annie as much to comfort myself as her, because the moaning and occasional cries of distress were troubling to hear. Soon I heard a prolonged squeak of the footboard and a sustained wail as Sister Hansen pulled against the knotted rope of fabric that was tied to the bed in order to help her bear the pushing pains.

As I tried to ignore the noises of distress, I wondered if it was worth it, to go through such pains to have a baby.

I looked down at Annie, now sleeping on my lap. I gently covered the damaged side of her face with my hand. Now all I could see was pink and white skin, smooth as cream and as beautiful as a cherub.

Love flooded my heart. I knew that having a baby straight from heaven was worth anything I eventually had to go through to get it.

Now a different sound came from behind the blanket. A thin, tentative wail that was distinctly different from Sister Hansen's earlier one. I stood up even before I heard Mama call my name. I stepped around the blanket, and then stopped. Sister Hansen lay on her pillow, her eyes closed, and as pale as bread dough. Her deathly-still face was surrounded by loose, damp hair that looked like tangled yarn. A naked, wrinkled and red little baby lay on her tummy, it's hair plastered down flat and wet to its head. Sister Tilley was cutting the cord that twisted thick and purple from the baby's belly. The spurt of blood made me gasp.

Sister Hansen opened her eyes and smiled at me. "It's a girl," she said through dry lips parched almost white. Sister Tilley was expertly swaddling the newborn in a clean white cloth.

"Bring Annie," Mama said urgently.

I took careful steps over to the foot of the bed. Mama lifted a piece of warm, pinky-purple afterbirth to Annie's face. She pressed it onto the red stain, spreading the edges with her fingers until the red stain was blotted out. Annie squirmed and stretched at Mama's touch, but didn't wake up.

"Hold it, Caroline," Mama said to me, "Hold it tight and don't let it slip. Mind her nose, keep it clear."

I hesitated. I didn't really want to touch the afterbirth. But when I thought of Annie going through life with a red-stained face just because of my reluctance, I knew I couldn't live with myself if I didn't at least try the cure. I placed my hand carefully over the warm poultice, then walked gingerly back to a chair on the other side of the blanket.

Mama spent a few more minutes helping Sister Tilley. I heard her whisper congratulations to Sister Hansen, and promise that she'd send her husband in with an armload of the wood he'd gone out to chop.

"I don't know why," Sister Hansen replied weakly. "The wood box is clear full!"

"A lot of chores get done by husbands when their wives are having babies!" Sister Tilley said cheerfully.

Mama appeared around the edge of the curtain with a canning jar full of the same pinky-purple that I was holding on Annie's face. She noticed the question in my eyes. "For tomorrow," she said.

The next morning, I awoke to see Mama sleeping in the rocking chair, Annie on her lap. I walked over and looked down at my sister. The poultice was dry and cracking. Annie stirred, and Mama woke up.

"Let's see," I whispered. Mama lifted the dry afterbirth off of Annie's face. She rubbed at the stain. Like the peeling skin of a sunburn, a layer of red came off under the gentle insistence of Mama's finger. The birthmark was noticeably lighter.

Mama's shining eyes met mine. "It works!" we both said at the same time. I fell to my knees and put my arms around my little Annie.

"Thank you, Father," Mama said. Her face was tilted up to heaven as she stroked my hair.

"Yes, thank you," I said, my tears soaking Mama's knees.

We reapplied the poultice from the jar. When it was gone, whenever we could, we would take Annie with us when a woman was having a baby and gather more of the precious afterbirth. As Annie got older, she would often squirm to get away from the treatment, but I would sing to her and tell her silly stories about her fingers and toes, keeping her occupied as long as I could so the poultice could dry and work it's healing wonders.

By the time Annie was learning to take her first steps, the red stain had faded to a single faint line as thin as spider web silk that ran over her eyebrow and onto her cheekbone like a fairy trail. Although it stayed with her the rest of her life, every time I noticed it, it made me think of the finger of God caressing a precious little baby's face as He bestowed His gift of healing.

In 1873, Annie Jacobson was born with a bright red birthmark over her right eye. It was common in that time period to believe the superstition that trauma to the mother during pregnancy could cause birth defects. Annie's mother Christinia was sure the mark was caused by an incident a few months earlier when she was dragged by a runaway horse after the buggy she was riding in tipped over. A newcomer to the settlement with a reputation for healing told Christinia to cover the stain as often as possible with new afterbirth. When the instructions were carried out repeatedly, the birthmark was reduced to a faint pink line.

A SHOT IN THE DARK

"Chris!" The harsh whisper cut through the slow waltz music that was playing in my ear as I swirled Sophie Sergeant around the dance floor. It was not in Sophie's nature to speak so harshly.

"Chris!" Sophie roughly shook my shoulder with her hand as we continued to whirl. I was beginning to feel annoyed. If she didn't want to dance with me, there were plenty of other young ladies who would love to dance with a suave young man of fifteen.

Yet something was wrong. Sophie never called me Chris. She always called me Christian.

I opened my eyes from my dream in order to check the face of the girl I thought was Sophie. Instead of round blue eyes and rosy cheeks, I found myself looking into small brown eyes narrowed against the lamp light and cheeks bristling with stubble. I was face to face with Hector Keyes, and he didn't smell like Sophie, either. The dance floor, the music, and all the pretty girls waiting in line to dance with me were gone in the blink of an eye. My heart sank clear down to the soles of my feet when I recognized the sheep camp. I was somewhere in the middle of a soggy summer night, and I was looking at Hector instead of Sophie. It might as well have been a nightmare.

"I heard something," Hector said.

"Was it waltz music?" I asked sourly.

Hector looked at me quizzically. Although he was older than me by a few years, I had decided he was certainly no wiser. "No," he said, shaking his head slowly as though seriously considering the possibility of dance music. "It was an animal noise."

I groaned. My first man-sized job was not turning out as I expected. The thought of herding sheep for the summer had seemed idyllic. I could picture myself following the flock, shouldering my new gun as I stood on a craggy outcropping of rock, stoically guarding and protecting my charges as I earned my princely wage.

Reality was grimmer than my daydream. The sheep were stupid. If one walked into a mud bog, they all walked into the mud. They bunched, then ran, if a flurry of leaves blew across their path. They tried to crowd each other off cliffs in their hurry to see what was up ahead, even if it killed them.

There didn't seem to be such a thing as sleeping through the night anymore. Bears and coyotes would invite themselves to the sheep supper-table whenever they felt like it. Eagles would dive out of the sky and snatch a newborn lamb in the daylight. Big cats would skulk up in the darkness. You never knew just what you would find when you stumbled outside in your skivvies. If the moon was bright, you had to keep to the shadows and strain your eyes for a disturbance in the flock. Getting a clear shot at a bobcat or coyote was nearly impossible, as they were small enough to blend in with the sheep.

It made me wonder whose side the sheep were on, the way they milled about between the predator and the rifle, getting in the way of the bullet that could kill the enemy and save their woolly hides.

If it was a cougar or a bear, you could spot them right off. One day only last week, I'd gotten a good shot off at a cougar—even drew blood, but I never found the cat. Might've been that it wasn't wounded badly enough to drop it. At least with the sting of a bullet in it's hide, it would think twice before making an easy meal of my sheep again.

After being initiated into the very real hazards and dangers of herding those woolly idiots that some people thought were soft and fluffy enough to count themselves to sleep by, I was dubious when we met up with Dave, a young man whom Hector introduced to me as an exceptionally good sheepherder. I didn't believe Hector. Dave was deaf. I could grant him the possibility that he was a sharp lookout in the daytime, but how could he protect the sheep in the dark of night if he wasn't able to hear a predator as it slunk it's way toward the flock?

It was late in the evening when our flocks joined up. We decided to eat together that night and trade news. For the most part, Dave followed the conversation so well that I almost forgot he was deaf. When I turned my head to talk to Hector, Dave put his hand on my arm and said, "Face me when you speak, even if you're talking to Hector." He smirked, "I'm better-looking than him anyway." Dave was quite skilled at reading our lips.

Dave's camp wagon was parked next to ours. That night, I heard the dogs barking, and then the chilling sound of a coyote howl. I leapt out of bed and grabbed my rifle, hurrying outside to save our flock. I was ready to defend Dave's, too. I knew he would need some help.

To my surprise, Dave was already outside of his camp wagon, rifle at the ready. He saw me and gave me a little salute before he faded into the night to circle around his flock and deal with the danger.

I didn't figure the moonlight was bright enough to carry on a lip-reading conversation with Dave, so I confronted him the next morning at breakfast. "How did you know there was a coyote out there?" I demanded as soon as I saw him face-to-face.

Dave smiled smugly. "I felt the vibration when the dogs barked," he said, "And I could feel the answering vibration of the coyote howl." It didn't seem possible, but it had to be, because I couldn't think of any other explanation.

We had parted our flocks, and now Dave was off somewhere with his sheep, probably sleeping soundly through a still night, while I was stuck with Hector and his keen hearing.

"Time to go, Chris," Hector said, "You check around west and I'll circle around to the east. Meet you back here," and he was gone.

I pulled on my shoes and shrugged into my jacket. I grabbed my rifle and stepped outside. The ground sucked at my shoes like a giant leech. The air was damp from the earlier rain, and the cool wind blew, sending shivers down my uncovered neck. I had discovered that summer nights in the mountains could be downright cold, and tonight was no exception.

I turned up my collar and decided I would make a quick circle, then get back to my bed before it could cool off completely. After all, I hadn't heard any noise. It was Hector who'd heard it. Let him get the varmint, if there was one.

I started out with my customary long strides. I could keep my bearings for a few yards beyond the camp, but once I was well out into the open, I realized what my haste had prevented me from noticing before. With the tired-out rain clouds resting in the sky, covering the moon and stars like a thick comforter, there was no heavenly light.

I slowed, and then stopped. I briefly thought about turning back, but I wasn't going to let Hector needle me about getting lost in the dark. He sometimes thought he was superior because he was a seasoned herder and this was my first year. I didn't plan to give him reason to harass me tonight.

I grasped the rifle in both hands and extended it before me, feeling my way with my feet, using the rifle as a sort of barrier between me and whatever was out there. I slipped my finger into the trigger guard and gripped the stock firmly with my other hand. The world was strangely silent, as though the clouds muffled out sound as well as light. The cold breeze stirred my hair, making me shiver and regret not pulling on my hat. Even the sheep were silent, and I found myself wishing to hear a small bleat or the hollow clopping of a sheep's bell. But there was nothing—nothing except the disembodied whisper of leaves as the invisible breeze stirred them to momentary life. The sound seemed unnatural in this total darkness. It should have been quiet, like a cave. Or a tomb.

The thought flashed through my mind that maybe I was dead. But dead men didn't carry rifles, did they? A shiver tickled my spine as I took another careful step.

Suddenly, my feet slipped in the traitorous mud, forcing me down to one knee as my hands flew out to catch my balance. Somehow I managed to keep my grip on my gun. In a desperate effort to save myself from falling forward, my arm brought the weapon back toward my body. The wooden stock slammed into my knee, making what I knew would be a large, colorful bruise. The impact on my leg caused my finger to squeeze off a shot.

The blast tipped my precarious balance and I ended up on my seat in the mud. I didn't care. I'd had enough. Hector could say whatever he wanted to, I was returning to camp.

I turned and blundered back the way I had come. I worried that in the darkness I would miss the wagon, but like a homing pigeon, I found it with only a few stumbles over low brush and one bruised shin.

I stood my rifle it its corner and crawled into bed, jacket and all. I trembled and shivered like a pup kicked out in the snow.

"Hector?" I whispered hoarsely through my chattering teeth, although I didn't think he was there. I got no reply. That was odd, since he had left before me and he was a young man with long legs. He could easily have finished his circle and returned by now, unless he had trouble finding his way in the dark, too. But he'd never admit that.

I began to warm up and to relax, letting my body sink into the straw tick and my muscles turn to mush. My mind was drifting pleasantly back toward my dreams when suddenly the awful thought struck me that maybe Hector wasn't back because he couldn't get back. Maybe I had gotten disoriented out there in the impossible darkness of this eerie night and had crossed over into the path of Hector's circuit. It could be that when I slipped and fell he could have been standing right in front of me and I wouldn't have seen him. He could have been standing right in the path of the bullet.

I sat up and started shivering again, but not from cold. Had I killed a man? I had to find out. But how would I ever find him in the dark? I desperately groped toward the table, searching for the lantern or a candle or any source of light so that I could find Hector. Maybe he was just wounded. Maybe I could help him, save him from bleeding to death.

My hands stopped their scrabbling search when I heard a scraping sound outside. Was it a branch? Or an animal claw? I strained my ears. Nothing but a low moan from the wind sounded outside.

The wagon shifted, and I yelped in surprise. Something was coming in.

"Chris! What did you get?" Hector said as he clumped inside.

"Are you all right?" I blurted.

"Kind of cold, but nothing ate me while I was out there. Where were you? Not doing your job? Out shooting just for fun?"

"I had an accident."

The banter left Hector's voice. "You hurt?" he asked.

"No."

"What did you shoot at?"

"I just fell and my gun went off," I said, with more edge to my voice than I meant it to have.

I thought Hector would say more, get in a few more digs, but he just rolled himself into his blankets and said, "Sweet dreams."

In the morning, Hector was shaking my shoulder again. "Chris!" he said.

I swatted at him. "Go away!" I said. I was still tired and anxious from the night before, and had no desire to get out of my bunk yet.

"Chris, you've got to come see!" Hector persisted. He was almost squeaking, he was so excited.

"What?" I said, flinging back the covers and staring him hard in the face.

"Outside," Hector said, leading the way.

I stuck my feet in my boots and made my way outside. The sky was clearing of clouds, a few ragged tatters moving reluctantly toward the horizon. The sheep were trading their morning news with muffled "Baa's." It seemed that the events of the night before had been more of a dream than waltzing with Sophie.

Hector was following the dents my feet had made in the wet soil the night before. Becoming curious now that I was up, I looked around to get my bearings on the path I had taken. I was off by a few yards from where I thought I was, but all in all, I was pretty close, and proud of it.

"This is where you were standing," Hector said.

I turned my attention back to my fellow herder and stopped dead in my tracks. Lying about four paces beyond Hector was a mountain of black fur.

"A couple more paces and you would have been bear bait," Hector laughed shrilly. "Instead, you got him right between the eyes!"

When my legs would move again, I examined the bullet wound, then circled the huge black bear, measuring the scant distance that had been between him and me and counting my blessings with every step I took.

In 1874, fifteen-year-old Christian Munk got his first real job herding sheep in the mountains, and for this job he was equipped with his very first rifle. One dark night, he went outside with a fellow herder to investigate a noise. In his own account, he states that he "shot from the knee" into the darkness before going back to bed.

In the morning, he was amazed to discover the body of a huge black bear, with a fatal bullet wound between the eyes, a mere ten feet away from where he had been when he shot his rifle. He had no idea the bear had been there when he pulled off the shot in the dark.

POOR PETER

I wished the stranger would go away. I checked the window again. He was still there, sitting on the porch, facing the road. Pa was nowhere in sight.

When the stranger had come to the door asking for Pa, he hadn't smiled or said, "Howdy." The dusty metal star pinned on his coat had seemed to put a fright into Aunt Julianne. She had gone to her room and firmly shut the door. Aunt Toddy had politely told the man that if he wanted Pa, he'd have to wait outside. Then she busied herself in the kitchen, rattling pans and clicking dishes together.

Ma and Aunt Irene had gone to town, and I sorely wished they would return.

Staring at the back of the stranger's head as he waited for my Pa sent trickles of fear through my veins like warm molasses.

"Charlie," I jumped and whirled from the window to face my Aunt Toddy. Her eyes were soft and kind. She was holding a plate with a thick slice of buttered homemade bread crowded by a generous piece of smoked ham. In her other hand was a glass of buttermilk so cold that the sides were beginning to sweat.

"Would you please take this out to our visitor?" she said.

My mouth dropped open. I would have liked to put some of that bread and ham into it, but apparently it wasn't for me.

"Why?" I said indignantly.

"Now, Charlie," Aunt Toddy scolded me gently, "he looks like he's traveled a far piece, and I'd be surprised if he's not hungry."

"But he's not friendly," I protested, "I think he might be dangerous." The star on his coat represented a government that wasn't always kind to Mormons.

Aunt Toddy's eyes flicked to the window, then back to me. Her smile looked more forced. "We don't know that, Charlie. Regardless of why he's here, we're supposed to love our enemies as well as our friends. Now, friend or foe, I need you to take this out to him."

She pushed the plate and glass into my hands, then stepped to the door and opened it.

There was nothing else for me to do but walk through it onto the porch.

The stranger was perched on his chair like a vulture, his shoulders hunched up and his pointy nose jutting forward as his small eyes took in every movement around him.

He turned his head toward me. When he saw what I was holding, he sat up straight and searched my face for an explanation.

"Here," I said, holding the plate and glass out to him. His eyebrows went up and he hesitated. "Aunt Toddy thought you were hungry."

He slowly took the offerings from me, then glanced at the doorway. I looked behind me, but there was no one there.

I turned back to the stranger who was staring at the plate as though he didn't know what to do with it. "Thank you," he said softly, as though he wasn't used to the words. "Tell her thank you."

I sat on the other side of the porch, stealing glances at the stranger as he ate every bit of the bread and ham and swallowed every drop of the buttermilk.

Just as he finished, I noticed a horse and rider moving toward the house. "Pa!" I yelled with relief when I recognized my father. Pa dismounted and hesitated, looking questioningly from me to the stranger.

I hopped off the porch and took the horse's reins. "This man wants to see you, Pa," I said.

The stranger stood and carefully placed his plate and glass on the porch chair. He came down the steps and Pa extended his hand for the stranger to shake. The man was slow to take it and quick to let go.

"Peter Ammons?" he said.

"Yes, I'm Peter Ammons," Pa said.

The stranger pulled a piece of paper from his pocket and put it in Pa's hand. "This is a subpoena to appear before Judge Moore and answer to the charge of polygamy," he said. Then he turned away from Pa, mounted his own horse, and rode away.

Pa unfolded the paper and read it, his face set in a frown of concentration, his eyes moving over the written lines in quick jerks, like an animal seeking a hole in the fence to escape through.

"What is it, Pa?" I asked as he folded the paper and put it in his pocket.

"Charlie, my boy," Pa said, putting his hand on my shoulder, "Some officials think that I shouldn't be married to your mother, and Aunt Irene, and Aunt Julianne, and Aunt Toddy.

I felt a shock of surprise. "Why not?" I asked. I couldn't imagine life without my mother, or any of my aunts, either.

"That's a good question," Pa said, "and I don't have a good answer." He lowered his eyes to the ground and stroked his beard. "But I have to come up with some answers when I go before the judge."

"Does that paper mean you have to go?" I said.

"Yes, I do," Pa said.

My heart squeezed tight, and I almost couldn't ask the question that was burning on my tongue. "If you don't, will they put you in jail?"

Pa looked me in the eyes. "Charlie," he said softly, "They could, but whether they do or don't is of no great consequence. The prophet Joseph Smith was jailed."

Tears burned in my eyes. "But he was killed!" I said.

Pa put his hands on my shoulders. "Son, it's all in the Lord's hands. Whatever happens will be all right. There are worse things than dying."

I grabbed my Pa around his waist and cried into his coat. He gently stroked my head. "It's all right, son," he said to me, "Just remember good will always triumph over evil. God is over all. He will provide." I finally pulled away and wiped my eyes.

"Charlie!" Frederick Stahli was hurrying into the yard, a fishing pole balanced on one shoulder. "D'you want to come down to the river with me?" Fred stopped suddenly and looked confused, glancing from my Pa back to me. When he noticed my tear-streaked face, his ears turned red.

"Go ahead, Charlie," Pa said, "but come back in time for supper."

Fred fell into step beside me, and then glanced back over his shoulder before he spoke. "Did you just get a whuppin'?" he asked in a sympathetic whisper.

"No," I said, "Some man came and gave my Pa a paper that says he has to go talk to a judge about having four wives." I shook my head miserably, "He might get put in jail." I ground my teeth together to keep from crying again.

"I'd hate it if my Pa had four wives," Fred said.

I snapped my head toward him. "What do you mean by that?" I said, jutting my chin out at the boy I thought was my friend.

"It's nothing against your family," Fred said, putting up his hand as though to defend himself in case I was going to hit him. "It's just that when my Pa brought Aunt Jean home, everything got worse."

I scuffed down the road for three paces before asking, "What happened?"

"Well, we've only got that one bedroom downstairs," Fred said, "It's not like your house where each of your aunts has her own room with an outside door."

I nodded. I had been to Fred's house and knew what he was talking about.

"So Pa brought Aunt Jean home, and told Ma she'd have to sleep with us kids up in the loft because Aunt Jean was going to be in the bedroom with him."

We skirted around a clump of young willows and saw the lazy, winding river before us. At this spot, I could have waded across it in ten steps, but fishing was as good on one side as the other.

As we made our way down the bank to the water's edge, I asked, "What happened?"

Fred smiled sourly. "Well, Ma was put out, to be sure. When she wasn't mad and muttering, she was crying. But when we showed her the knotholes in the floor of the loft, she cheered up some." Fred settled himself on the bank and began baiting his hook.

I remembered the loft, and knew it was built right over the top of the main bedroom in Fred's house, the room where his father slept.

I settled myself beside Fred in the thick riverbank grass and watched him cast his line out. "Why was she so happy about a bunch of knotholes?" I said.

Fred looked sideways at me with a grin. "Because she could drop things down on Pa and Aunt Jean while they were trying to sleep."

I laughed. "Did she really?" I asked, trying to imagine it in my mind.

Fred nodded emphatically. "She did. Once the sun goes down and the lights are out, you can't see anything down there. It's as black as an outhouse hole. But Ma must have known right where the bed was. She started dropping dead flies, but that didn't seem to be enough for her. She sent us boys outside for twigs, pebbles, and worms if we could find any. She must have sent my sisters for the wash basin, because when we snuck back upstairs as quiet as we could, she was dripping water down through the holes."

Fred jerked his line and stood up to pull in his first catch. I waited as he unhooked the fish, then he handed the pole to me. As I baited the hook, I said, "What'd your Pa do?"

Fred chuckled dryly. "He yelled for us kids to stop it, and Martha, would you get those children to behave? It sounded like he even tried to move the bed, but Ma just adjusted herself over new knotholes and kept dropping things through them."

I cast my line and settled back into the fragrant grass. I batted at a fly. "Didn't he ever go up to the loft to put a stop to it?"

"No," Fred said, picking a wide blade of grass and fitting it in between his thumbs. "I guess he figured we'd go to sleep sometime and the pestering would stop." He put his thumbs to his lips and blew a loud, piercing whistle.

"You did fall asleep, didn't you?" I said as I watched my line drift carelessly downstream.

"Well, we kids did, but Ma didn't," Fred said, shredding his grass blade between his fingers. "I woke up in the middle of the night and saw her sitting over the knotholes, Grandma's shawl draped over her shoulders. Her arms were folded on her knees and her head rested on her arms. I don't know if she was sleeping or not." Fred threw his shredded grass blade into the water. "It's been more of the same since. To say truthfully, I'd rather be most anywhere than home."

I pulled my empty line in, thinking of my Ma and my aunts. They didn't always get along. Sometimes they disagreed, but I couldn't imagine them purposely hurting one another, or throwing dead bugs and sticks at each other.

I handed Fred the fishing pole. "Sorry to hear it, Fred," I said, meaning it. I was glad that Fred caught a fish on his next cast. He needed something good to happen to him

It was about two weeks later when Pa gathered his family together in prayer. We knelt in a circle, holding hands, while Pa asked Father in Heaven for his protection and guidance, finally stating that His will be done.

Then we all headed for the wagon. Aunt Toddy, being the first wife, was respectfully helped up onto the driver's seat by Pa. I knew that she wouldn't ride there the whole time. She would insist on taking turns with the other wives.

Ma and Aunt Julianne and Aunt Irene settled themselves on the bench that Pa had installed for their comfort. It was back-to-back with the driver's seat, so it faced the wagon load of quilts and picnic lunch boxes and children. The quilts were meant to cushion our ride, but it still seemed like a long and hard journey. We stopped once for a bathroom break, and Aunt Toddy insisted on giving up her seat on the driver's bench. Aunt Julianne settled beside Pa and we took off for another long, rattling stretch of road.

When we caught sight of the trees that signaled the town with the courthouse ahead, we all cheered, ready to get out so we could walk the kinks out of our legs.

Pa pulled the wagon into the shade of the trees in the quiet cemetery. The gravestones stood straight and tall, waiting patiently for the resurrection day.

Pa stopped the wagon beside an unused section of the cemetery grounds. The quiet stillness was broken as the large Ammons brood began to scramble out of their forced confinement. Pa climbed down, then held his hand up to Aunt Julianne.

I jumped out of the back of the wagon and took a picnic box from one of my sisters as she handed it down. Aunt Julianne pulled a quilt from the wagon box and shook it out, expertly smoothing it in one motion into a colorful ground cloth as Pa helped his other wives climb down from the wagon.

Soon everyone was scurrying around like ants before the picnic. The food was laid out and the children eagerly surrounded the quilt, tucking their legs in under them as they impatiently waited for the prayer.

Pa remained standing, bowed his head, and asked a blessing on the food, as well as for protection and safety for all of us.

When he said "Amen," he solemnly put his hat on and turned toward town.

Seeing him walking away from the circle of the family, a lone figure, his hands in his pockets and his head bent, pulled at something in my heart. Impulsively, I left the food behind and ran after him.

"Pa," I said.

He turned, his eyebrows raised. "What is it?" he said, "are you all right?"

"Yes, Pa," I tried to catch my breath. "I just want to go with you."

Pa's eyebrows went up another notch. "If you don't eat now, there might not be any food left for later," he said.

My stomach tweaked with discomfort, but I squared my shoulders. "God will provide," I said.

Pa's eyebrows relaxed and he smiled at me. "I'd be proud to have your company," he said, putting his hand on my shoulder as we continued on our way.

We easily found the tall, angular courthouse. As we approached the front steps, I felt my feet dragging. The stark building looked as unforgiving as a jail cell. I knew that there were men sitting in jails just because they were married to more than one woman, yet it was beyond my understanding why. I could see why murderers were in jail, and people who stole things. But why put polygamists in jail—except for maybe Fred's Pa for making his Ma sleep in the loft?

Pa and I walked up the stone steps together. I followed his lead as he went through the front door and found the judge's chambers.

Judge Moore was more than a little frightening. He looked like a bull dressed in a long, black robe. His chin rested on his chest, his nose was wide, his eyes were small, and his ears stuck out.

"Mr. Ammons," he bellowed.

"Yes, Your Honor," Pa said.

"And who is this young fellow with you?" The judge fixed his stern eyes on me. If I hadn't had bones in my body, I would have melted to the floor like a lit tallow candle under the heat of that gaze.

"This is my son, Charles," Pa answered respectfully.

I bobbed my head and mumbled, "Sir," unsure if I was supposed to approach the bench and offer my hand or not. Since Pa stood still, I stayed where I was, fiddling nervously with the hat I had removed from my head when we entered the courthouse. I knew if this bullish man decided to charge, Pa and I would both be flattened and crushed, yet standing by Pa gave me a small measure of courage.

"Do you understand the nature of the accusation levied against you?" Judge Moore boomed.

"Yes, Your Honor," Pa answered calmly. He wasn't even twisting his hat in his hands.

Judge Moore looked down at a paper on his high desk. "So, Mr. Ammons, how many women have you married in your lifetime?"

"Four," Pa replied.

The judge drilled Pa with his eyes. "And where are your four wives now, Mr. Ammons?"

Pa returned the judge's gaze without flinching. "They are in the cemetery," he said.

Judge Moore blinked, his eyebrows shooting up as he leaned back in his chair. He twisted his pen in his fingers as he looked from Pa to me. His voice was softer when he spoke. "All of them?" he asked.

Pa's voice was soft, too. "Every last one," he replied.

Judge Moore appeared to be at a loss for words. He opened his mouth, and then shut it. Finally he leaned forward and gave me a look of such pity that it took me completely off guard. He reached in the folds of his robe and pulled out a handkerchief.

"Mr. Ammons," he said, shifting his eyes from me to Pa, "Your case is dismissed. My regards to you and your son, sir."

Pa bent his head. "Thank you, Your Honor," he said. As we turned and walked out of the courtroom, I heard Judge Moore give a great big bellowing blow into his handkerchief.

With each tread down the courthouse steps, my heart felt lighter. I was fairly skipping when we reached the road and headed toward the cemetery.

As we approached Ma and the aunts sitting on the quilt, watching over their children as they played hide-and-seek among the headstones, Ma was the first to ask, "What happened?"

"The case was dismissed," Pa said, as he gave my shoulder a squeeze.

"Oh, thank Heaven!" Ma said, and all the aunts broke into smiles.

"Come and sit down, you two," Ma said. "I saved you each a plate of food."

With a smile, I reached up and squeezed Pa's shoulder. It was awkward, but it seemed like the right thing to do.

In the family stories of Deneice Blackham, an unnamed polygamist was summoned to court in Provo, Utah, to answer the charges of polygamy. As his six wives rested in the cooling shade of the cemetery trees, the man faced the judge and truthfully told him that all of his wives were in the cemetery. The judge dismissed the charges and the man took his wives home.

Helen Reeder told the author of a different unnamed polygamist who brought his second wife home and sent his first wife up to the loft to sleep with the children. In retaliation, the first wife dropped unsavory things down through the knotholes in the loft floor onto her husband and his new bride as they tried to sleep.

PART III
ODD PEOPLE

REMEMBER ME?

"I have a bad feeling about this," Abe said.

I turned to him, my surprise showing plainly on my face. "Why? We said our prayers this morning."

Abe shook his head. "If you pray for safety and then jump off the ship into the ocean to take a swim, do you deserve to be saved from drowning?"

I smiled. Maybe I didn't share my companion's gloomy outlook because I'd had enough experiences in the past fifty years to make me feel confident throwing my lot in with the Lord's.

"We've been asked to perform a survey by the leaders of our church, and that's just what we're going to do."

"Yeah, but can't we wait until this Indian war is over?" Abe asked, looking back over his shoulder.

"We don't know how long the war is going to last," I answered. "And we need the survey now."

"Who is going to want to move to a place with angry Indians everywhere?" Abe asked. "I know I wouldn't."

"This war won't last forever," I said. "I know Black Hawk. He's just got a misguided sense of what's right—at least to our way of thinking. As far as he knows, he's doing the right and noble thing by declaring war on us."

"How come you know him so well?" Abe asked, his eyes abandoning their search of the shadowed places in the brush by the roadside and settling on my face.

"When I first came to Utah, Brigham Young asked me to start a school."

"You were a schoolteacher?" Abe asked, his eyes wide. Then his brow furrowed. "I just can't picture it."

I chuckled. "Well, it's true. I was Mr. Jesse Fox, teacher of a school of white children and one Indian boy by the name of Black Hawk."

"You had Chief Black Hawk in a room full of white students and they all came out alive?"

"Of course. He's not like you think," I said, wanting Abe to understand the Black Hawk that I knew. "The kids included him in all their games until the massacre."

Abe leaned in closer. "Who did he massacre?"

"Not Black Hawk. He was just a boy. Some of the other Indians killed an entire family and stole their cattle. If the family hadn't tried to stop them they probably wouldn't have been killed."

"Yeah, what were they supposed to do, just let their livelihood walk off?"

I shook my head. I really didn't have an answer. "It was a tough situation. You've got to understand how Indians think. They figure that anything on their land that they can take is theirs. They were only trying to survive in the best way they knew how."

"So what happened?"

"About what?"

"With Black Hawk."

I opened my mouth to answer but snapped it shut when I saw the face of an Indian moving toward us.

Abe turned his head to follow my gaze. Just then, more Indians appeared from behind the trees. As soon as he saw what was coming, Abe squealed, "Lord have mercy!" and ducked his face down, wrapping his arms over his head.

"Don't show fear," I hissed.

Abe didn't answer. I could feel him trembling beside me.

"Sit up, or it will be worse for you," I said.

Abe lowered his arms and raised his head but kept his eyes down. I glanced over at him. His face was shiny with sweat and his skin had a sickly, green pallor. His chin made a prune shape as he bit down on his bottom lip so hard that I was sure he'd draw blood.

"Calm down," I said.

Abe answered in a voice so shaken that it was hard to make out the words. "So much for prayer."

Several Indians surrounded our buggy. Two of them grabbed the bridle of our horse, and the animal danced backward. Their bows were nocked with arrows; I caught sight of a spear held at the ready, its black, flint tip as dark as death. What would it feel like to have that spear buried in my heart?

The Indians probably didn't know that I could understand them as they argued back and forth. Some wanted to kill us on the spot and steal our horse and buggy. Others disagreed, and said that they should take the prize of two finely dressed white men in a horse and buggy to the chief. Some of them poked fun at Abe, calling him a woman. I was glad that he didn't know what they were saying.

Eventually, the ones who wanted to present us to their chief won the consent of the others. Our horse was taken by the reins and led away. There was no chance for us to leap to the ground and run for safety. We had mounted warriors moving along both sides of our buggy, glancing our way as they hefted their spears, clubs, and bows.

Once in camp, we were ordered to get down. Abe trembled so badly that I wasn't sure that his legs would hold him up. Several of the Indian men pointed at him and jeered. I could feel their hostility as though it were a blanket wrapped around us.

Some of the men at the edges of the group quieted and turned away. I wondered why until I saw a tall Indian approaching with dignified steps. When he got close enough, I looked into the haunting, dark eyes of Chief Black Hawk and felt myself transported back in time.

I remembered when the other kids shunned young Black Hawk after the massacre, and he chose to spend the recess break in the schoolroom with me. I opened my lunch pail and took out the starch cake that my wife, Eliza, had made for me. It was an extra-large piece. She knew how fond I was of good starch cake, and her cakes were always delicious.

I set the cake down on the desk before the lad. His eyes flew open wide in surprise, and he looked up at me.

"Look at this," I said, grinning at the boy. "The fox feeding the hawk!"

Young Black Hawk smiled for the first time since news of the massacre had reached our settlement. Sacrificing my dessert was worth seeing that smile. Besides, I could always get more cake at home. "Thank you, Mr. Fox," he said, and then he ducked his head.

In time, I rang the bell to bring the students inside. We finished our afternoon lessons, and I dismissed them. All the boys and girls scuttled out the door except for Black Hawk. He moved to the front of the room, hiding his slate behind his back and stopped in front of my desk. I looked up. He pulled the slate into view with some hesitation and turned it so I could see. There was a crude drawing of an animal with a long tail and pointed ears running along the bottom of the slate and a bird flying across the top.

"I drew this for you," Black Hawk said.

"Ah, yes, the hawk and the fox," I said, stroking my chin. "Quite an unlikely pair, wouldn't you say?"

"Both hunters," Black Hawk said. "Both friends."

"Yes," I said, standing and clapping Black Hawk on the shoulder. "Friends."

I like to think that our exchange increased Black Hawk's confidence, because he was soon playing games with the other children again.

Now I looked upon Black Hawk the man, who was taller than when I'd last seen him, with craggy features that didn't betray a shred of recognition. It had been almost twenty years since he'd been in my classroom. I had to admit that he had changed quite a bit.

Black Hawk barked an order to his men. "Put them inside."

Rough hands grabbed my arms and pushed me into a tepee. If Black Hawk had recognized me, he would have acknowledged it by now. It wasn't surprising that his anger at the white man was stronger than the memory of a single piece of cake.

Abe collapsed onto the ground inside the tepee. "They're gonna kill us," he moaned. "It's gonna be torture."

My heart quailed at the very thought of his dire prediction. I wasn't afraid of dying, but I was familiar with Indian torture methods and I didn't relish the thought of enduring any of them. A mark of manhood for Braves in warring tribes was to test how well they could tolerate their opponents tortures.

I had never aspired to die that way. Yet, whatever the Lord was willing to have happen to me, I would go through. Eventually it would be over and I would meet my maker.

Please protect us if it be thy will, I prayed. *Let them know we bear them no ill. May we, thy children, all learn to get along.* "Amen."

"You praying again?" Abe asked. "It's kind of late for that." In the dim light of the tepee, I could see him biting his lip again.

The scuffing sound of moccasins made us both turn toward the entrance to the tepee. Abe's eyes filled with abject fear as he beheld the notorious Chief Black Hawk enter our leather prison. I faced my former student and greeted him with a nod.

Black Hawk looked at me for a moment, and then bent down and drew something in the dirt. I leaned closer and adjusted my spectacles to better see what he was doing. He had drawn a dog-like creature with a bushy tail and pointed ears. Without looking up at me, he moved his finger to a place above what I recognized as a fox and drew a bird with outstretched wings.

"Fox and hawk," I said.

Black Hawk rose to his feet and faced me, a smile tugging at the corners of his mouth. "Did you think I had forgotten?" he asked.

"Perhaps," I said.

"I had to get you out of the way until I could send some of my more angry and bloodthirsty warriors away," Black Hawk said. "I have told the others that you are my friend. They will escort you to the fort. You will have no further trouble."

My heart filled with gratitude. From the corner of my eye, I saw Abe looking at Black Hawk with his eyes opened wide in a mixture of hope and disbelief.

"Thank you," I said.

Black Hawk nodded and left the tepee.

I pulled Abe up off the ground and walked him out into the sunshine, but he pulled back when he caught sight of a passel of Indians surrounding our buggy, staring at us with glittering dark eyes.

"They're an escort," I reminded him.

The Indian guard parted their horses, and we climbed into the buggy and started down the mountain. The Indians moved when we moved, keeping us surrounded until we came within sight of the fort. Before we got within firing range, the Indians peeled off and disappeared into the brush.

"Thank you, dear God, for saving us," Abe whispered, his hands folded in front of him, but his wide eyes fixed on the fort ahead.

I nodded in agreement. "Amen."

Black Hawk was a student in Jesse Williams Fox's school in Manti. After an Indian massacre, the white students shunned Black Hawk, but Fox befriended him.

During the Black Hawk War of 1865–1867, Jesse Fox was riding in a wagon with Abe Doremus to survey a site. Indians surrounded the wagon until Black Hawk saw who was in it and waved them on. He appointed an Indian guard to see them to their next destination.

In another account, the captives were taken into a tepee where Black Hawk joined them later. He drew a picture of a hawk and fox in the dirt, letting his former teacher know he hadn't forgotten him, and then set the men free.

Sources: *The Manti Temple*, Manti Temple Centennial Committee (Provo, Utah: Community Press, 1988), 22; *Saga of the Sanpitch*, vol. 15 (1983), 29.

FIRST IMPRESSIONS

I had never seen a paleface, but I wanted to. My friend Lame Horse said they had strange, light eyes that were as blue as the sky or as green as deep, swirling pools of cold river water. He said that a very few of the palefaces had true eyes—eyes that were as dark as ours. I longed to see for myself the eyes of sky and water. I couldn't help but wonder how they could see. A shiver of apprehension shook my spine. One who had pale eyes could not be trusted.

Another strange feature of the whites was their hair. I knew about this firsthand because I had seen paleface scalps. Even the dark hairs were different from my people. Strands of lighter brown intermingled with dark ones, and some of their hair twisted into curves like a river. There were yellow hairs too, and once I'd seen a scalp the deep red of a fox pelt. What kind of demons were these, with colors that didn't belong on a human head? Perhaps the palefaces were more like animals than men.

When I was chosen to join a raid on the palefaces, I was both excited and nervous. I would not let anyone read those feelings on my face; if they saw what I was feeling, they would call me a mouse, and refuse to let me go.

The word had come that some of the palefaces would be moving through a narrow pass on the other side of the river. They would be strung out along the trail and more helpless in the pass than they would be on the plain, where they would circle and face out like bison guarding their young. Lame Horse said that every night the palefaces gathered in a group and counted everybody, to make sure the old and sick were keeping up. How barbaric it was that they would never leave the old or weak ones behind to either become strong or die. They kept dragging them along, prolonging their suffering and forcing them to delay their passage into the happy afterlife that awaited them. The whites were stupid.

We rode out to the pass on our swiftest horses. When we reached the hill that crested the pass, an older warrior named Tamuk told us to leave our horses so that we could scout the strangers without arousing their suspicion. I crept up the hillside behind Lame Horse, my bow over my shoulder and my arrows resting in the quiver on my back.

On the hilltop, we laid ourselves down on the ground and directed our gaze between the rocks so that the palefaces below would not see our heads. What I saw then was a sight stranger than I could have ever dreamed. The women were dressed in long skins, but the colors were unlike any animal I'd ever seen—they were the colors of sky and flowers and grass. The men wore strange little round animals crouched on their heads with wings that spread out all around them. Later, Lame Horse told me that they weren't animals at all, but hats that the whites wore to keep the sun from burning their pale skin. When Lame Horse told me that burned palefaces peeled like a snake shedding its too-small skin, I couldn't suppress a shiver.

The palefaces pushed and pulled big wooden bundles that moved along on two full moons with lines drawn through them. Although I could only see one moon shape, Lame Horse assured me that there was one on the other side as well. He called them "wheels." The white men moved their belongings on these strange carts, much like we used our travois, which were two long poles fastened to either side of a horse. The dragging ends were fastened together before loading up folded tepee skins, stone grinding bowls, extra clothing, and other items we used to survive. But we used horses to pull our travois, and if we were short of horses, our women pulled them.

Now I stared at the palefaces below us, not believing the strangest thing that they were doing. The men pulled and pushed the paleface travois right alongside the women. I'd never seen such a gathering of rabbit-hearted men in my life.

I snorted. "How can we attack men who do women's work?"

Lame Horse looked over at me, his face split in a grin of derision. "We can't fight such men. It would make us weak and without honor in our own village."

I nodded in agreement.

Tamuk shook his head, and I could hear the sounds of a chuckle rising from his throat. His amusement was contagious, and I started to laugh. Lame Horse joined me, and then the other warriors, and soon we were laughing so hard that we forgot we were supposed to be silent.

A shout from the palefaces brought us to our senses. We looked down on the travelers and saw a few of them pointing at us. Some of the women wrung their hands or covered their faces. A few ducked behind their strange travois.

A handful of men dug through the bundles in the back of their travois, but one man threw back his head and began to bray, his eyes squeezed shut with the effort. I was startled by the eerie sound, and felt a shiver run down my back.

"Hee-haw, hee-haw, hee-haw."

Others soon joined him in the most unnatural sound that I'd ever heard, which was like a pained laughter.

"They make the sound of a donkey," Lame Horse said.

"They are crazy," Tamuk said. "We must not molest them, or else their crazy spirits will follow us and torment us the rest of our lives."

I wanted nothing to do with crazy palefaces. They were frightening enough when they were sane.

I lost no time in scooting backward down the hill. As soon as I was sure that I could safely straighten up and be out of sight of their pale eyes, I stood and hurried to my horse. I swung myself up on his back and didn't even look to see if my tribesmen were following me. There was no honor in running from a fight, but there was no shame in escaping a tribe of crazy people.

Norma Pyper Mitchell, author of Prophecy Checklist, *told me these stories that were related to her by her daughter-in-law, a descendent of Shoshones, who verbally passed on the story of the time their ancestors crept up on a handcart company intent on ambush but backed off when they saw the men doing the women's work of pulling the handcarts.*

On another occasion, the Shoshones were intent on raiding a group of pioneers when one of the white men spotted the Indians and began braying like a donkey. Other pioneers joined him, and the Indians left them alone so that the crazy white men's medicine wouldn't contaminate them.

DO UNTO OTHERS

At first glance I thought it was just another log, but then I saw the toes. What I stared at was no stick, but a human leg poking out from under a bush. My heart nearly crawled out of my throat. The leg was brown, but I couldn't tell if that was its natural color or if it was dirty. The only thing I knew for sure is that the leg wasn't moving.

"Eleazer, what have you gotten yourself into this time?" I whispered. I had no way of knowing if the person attached to that foot was friendly or not. I could have kicked myself for being such a fool as to come out gathering wood alone.

I moved closer, with my rifle at the ready; my stomach turned over in somersaults just as my three-year-old, Samuel, did when he was looking for attention.

Soon I was close enough to see the dirty fringe of an Indian dress.

"Hello?"

There was no answer to my call. Now what was I supposed to do? Perhaps this woman was dead and I was on sacred burial grounds, and now I would be cursed forever. Even though part of my brain was telling me I ought to hightail it out of there, another part was compelled to see the face of this woman who'd met some unfortunate end in the wilderness.

I walked closer, angling my approach. When I could finally see her face set with high cheekbones and a slack jaw, her eyes were closed. Dead, sure enough.

Strands of her long hair were already buried in the dirt, so I couldn't be sure if the gray streaks were from old age or from the fine, gray dust that sifted through her hair.

What should I do? Should I bury her? It just didn't seem right to leave a human being lying out on the ground for the wild animals to scavenge, even if she was an Indian.

I wished I hadn't been the one to find her. Perhaps I should return to the fort and ask someone who'd been here longer what I should do. They'd been around Indians a lot more than I had.

As if I didn't have enough trouble already, the dead Indian rolled her head toward me and moaned. I was shocked into rigidity when one black eye opened and stared right at me. Then her eye closed and I was left wondering if I had actually seen the woman move. Had I looked into the blackness of her eye and seen pain and fear there?

"Hello?" I called in a voice almost too soft to be heard. It's not that I wanted to bring that single, eerie eye back to life, but I needed to know if she really was alive.

Both of her eyes opened, narrowed against the daylight, and stared a hole right through me. "Ayusta." The word was a tortured whisper, spoken through a mouth with a tongue so thick from thirst that I could barely understand her. I didn't know what it meant, of course, but maybe someone back at the fort would.

The Indian woman coughed, and I hurried back to my wagon as though the very devil himself was grabbing at my heels. I scooped up my canteen and ran back to the Indian. Her eyes were closed again, and it looked as though she had shrunken into herself—totally devoid of any hope, just waiting to die.

I knelt at her side and put the canteen to her lips. She twisted her head away, her eyes wide with alarm. But when she saw what I held and tasted the water on her tongue, she raised a hand and grabbed for the canteen. I lifted her shoulders and let her drink.

"Come with me," I said. "Let me help you."

The woman didn't seem to understand, but she didn't resist when I lifted her up onto her feet and put my arm around her to keep her from falling. I had to use both arms to support her.

We made our way to my wagon, which was mostly filled with firewood. I had no blanket with me to lay her on, so I pushed her up onto the wagon seat. She slumped over onto her side, nearly falling off in the process.

"Here, here," I said, trying to project some authority with my voice. Now that I was used to the idea that she was alive, the last thing I wanted was for her to fall to the ground and crack her skull.

It was a trick to climb onto the wagon while trying to keep her steady. I boosted myself up and stepped over her. Then I sat down and leaned her against me so that she wouldn't tumble off in the other direction.

I couldn't help but glance around before I took up the reins and started the horses toward home. What if she was being watched over by someone for some reason? I didn't see another soul, however—white or brown.

The return trip to the fort was slow. I had to keep boosting the Indian up to keep her from sliding down. She eventually slumped to the floorboards at my feet, where she jostled as we rumbled over rocks and through the wagon ruts. I couldn't stand the sight of her head bouncing up and down on the footrest. Lacking any other padding, I pulled off my shirt and wadded it up underneath her head. I couldn't tell if she was grateful or not because her eyes remained closed. Maybe the trip was killing her. What if she'd died already? I shuddered at the thought that I might now be carrying a corpse back to the fort. I slapped the reins over the backs of my team, as though, if I hurried, I might outrun the ghosts of worry that chased me.

As soon as I reached my destination, I called out, "I need help!"

Fred Scow came running. "What did you drag in?" he asked, staring down at the Indian crumpled at my feet.

"I found her just lying out there," I said, flinging my arm back in the direction I'd come from.

"You should have left her," Fred said, backing up a step.

"How could I?" I asked. "She was alive when I found her, and thirsty."

"Well, she don't look thirsty now," Fred said. "She looks beyond thirsty. I think she's dead."

I climbed down from the wagon just as my wife, Mary Caroline, came hurrying over, her skirt lifted in her hands just enough for her to run without tripping. "Eleazer, what is going on?" she asked. Her eyes found the Indian woman lying in the wagon. "Who is that?"

I shrugged.

"How did she get in your wagon?"

"I put her there."

"Oh, for heaven's sake, don't just stand there, bring the poor woman into the house."

"What if she's dead?" I asked.

Mary Caroline did a quick survey of the body with her eyes and touched the woman's throat. "She's not dead—not yet anyway. Bring her in, Eleazer. There's no time to waste."

I turned to the Indian and tugged at her. "Somebody help me," I said. A couple of men who had gathered to see what was going on helped me pull the Indian off the wagon and carry her into my house.

"Nothing good can come of this," Fred said.

"Why not?" I asked, tired of his pessimism.

"Last year, Sarah Ellen Cox saved Chief Walkara's mother after he stabbed her seven times."

I recoiled in horror. "What?"

Fred shrugged. "It's the Indian way. When someone is either old or too sick to contribute to the tribe any longer, they are put out to die. They figure it's the natural order of things. They don't usually hurry them on their way like Chief Walkara—that's just something he came up with on his own. They usually just lay them out on the ground, like this one you found here, and let the elements take care of them."

"Put her on the bed," Mary Caroline instructed. We laid the Indian on my bed. "Now, out."

"Out?"

"Yes, go. Shoo! Shoo!" Mary Caroline flapped her hands at us, and I turned to go. Before I stepped outside, though, I swept our small cabin with my eyes. "Where's Samuel?"

"He's playing at the Miller's," Mary Caroline answered. "You can keep busy by unloading the wood." She shut the door behind me.

I went to do my wife's bidding.

By the time Mary Caroline let me back in, the Indian looked like a different person, laid out in one of Mary's old nightgowns—faded and soft from wear. Mary Caroline had even washed the Indian and braided her hair. The Indian's face looked even browner next to the white pillow slip.

"Now, tell me how you found her," Mary Caroline said.

After I told her everything, Mary Caroline said, "She must have gotten sick and been left to die."

I shuddered inside. I couldn't imagine leaving Mary Caroline lying on the ground no matter how sick she was.

"What's ailing her?" I asked.

"I'm not sure, but she feels hot. Whether that's from lying in the sun or from fever, I just don't know."

In the afternoon of the next day, the Indian woke up. She soon tired of the broth that Mary Caroline tried to spoon-feed her and graduated to bread. She ate everything we gave her and some things that she helped herself to. She drank a lot of water, and guzzled milk. When I complained, Mary Caroline said, " It's good for her."

"It's good for Samuel too."

"It's all right, Eleazer," Mary Caroline said. "There's enough."

The Indian watched our exchange. Then she said the same word she'd said up in the foothills: "Ayusta."

"I think that's her name," I said.

"It's kind of pretty," Mary Caroline agreed. So we called her Ayusta.

Later on, Fred told me that "ayusta" meant "abandoned." The name seemed to fit.

At first, Samuel was afraid of the dark-skinned woman lying in our bed. Ayusta watched Samuel from her nest of pillows, her black eyes brimming with merriment. When he decided to ignore her and go about his usual play, she pointed at him. "Ha!" she said, laughing at his antics.

Samuel soon learned that there was nothing to fear from Ayusta, and he grew fond of her. He climbed onto the bed and let her pat his blonde hair. Somehow, Ayusta communicated to Mary Caroline that she wanted some straw, which she used to braid a little straw horse for Samuel. He watched her closely, but not until it was nearly finished did he recognize what it was.

"Horsey!" he exclaimed in delight. When Ayusta gave him the toy, Samuel gave her a hug in return.

"Samuel, what do you say?" Mary Caroline prompted.

"T'ank you!" Samuel said.

"T'ank you!" Ayusta repeated, grinning from ear to ear.

The straw horse became Samuel's favorite plaything. He was so fond of it that he even slept with it.

After a couple of weeks, Ayusta was up and about—poking into this and that, tasting everything, and following Mary Caroline everywhere she went. She picked up some English words, and taught Samuel a few words of the Indian language.

A little while later, some Indians came to the fort, looking to trade skins for cloth and flour. When Ayusta saw the women who carried the bundles they had to trade, she squealed and spoke to them in her native tongue.

"These are her friends," Fred told me. "She wants to go back with them."

"What if she gets sick again?" I asked.

"They'll probably abandon her again. It's just their way." He shot me a look. I must have had a pained expression on my face, because he said, "They probably don't understand the things we do either."

Ayusta left with her friends, talking and laughing as they made their way back across the foothills to their camp. I wondered if she was talking about her rescue, Samuel's antics, or the kindness of my wife.

With Ayusta gone, I thought our adventure was over, but I was wrong. The worst was yet to come.

Samuel was an inquisitive boy who was hard-pressed to sit still for even a minute. He'd hardly ever listen to a story all the way through, preferring to act out his own adventures, and he would squirm and wiggle at bedtime every night until the very moment he dropped off to sleep.

Samuel loved to go with me whenever I ventured outside the fort, but I only took him when I knew I could keep an eye on him. There were too many things that could go wrong in this untamed wilderness. We had to deal with wild animals, Indians, creeks, cliffs, and rattlesnakes, which were all potentially dangerous to a little boy.

One day when I was going out hunting, Samuel begged to go with me. I knew I couldn't keep a proper watch on him and hope to bag any game, so I told him that I'd take him to gather wood when I got back. I meant that we would go to gather wood the next day, but Samuel must have been thinking of going the moment I returned. I didn't know his intentions at the time, or I would have told him to go back into the house with his mother instead of allowing him to stand by the gate and watch me ride away from the fort.

I turned around three or four times to wave to Samuel, seeing my boy grow smaller and smaller, but he always lifted his little hand to wave back. Finally, I kicked my horse into a gallop and was soon out of sight.

I was lucky that day—I got a deer. I was feeling mighty happy when I rode back to the fort at dusk. I imagined Mary Caroline sitting at home waiting for me, her hair loose and full around her face, and little Samuel tucked into bed, his cheeks rosy from play. I was mighty content until I rode into the fort and saw Mary Caroline waiting for me, her face streaked with tears. I slid off my horse, the deer forgotten in my concern.

"What's the matter?" I asked.

"Samuel . . ." she said and then broke down crying.

I took my wife by the shoulders and stared into her face. "Where's Samuel?"

"He's gone. An Indian took him." Mary covered her face with her hands and wept.

The image of my little boy waving from beside the open gate of the fort twisted my stomach into a hard knot. Why had I thought he'd be safe? Why did I think he'd take himself home once I was out of sight? Why didn't I insist that he go home while I watched? He was just a baby. What had I been thinking?

My chest hurt. How terrified Samuel must be! What must it be like for him—stolen from his family and suffering who-knew-what at the hands of the Indians?

I hugged Mary Caroline, but it wasn't enough comfort to keep the sting of tears from my eyes. "I'll find him," I whispered through gritted teeth. No one was going to keep my son from me. I would find Samuel or die in the attempt.

I felt a hand on my shoulder. "We're with you, Eleazer," said Fred Scow.

"We're assembling a posse that will leave first thing in the morning."

"I don't want to wait."

"We have to. We can't find him in the dark."

I didn't sleep that night—I couldn't. I cleaned my gun, packed my ammunition, and thought of Samuel.

At first light I was mounted and ready. A dozen men were with me, leaving their fields unworked and their animals untended just to help me search for my son, but there was no room in my heart for gratitude yet. We had to find Samuel first—that's all I cared about.

The gate swung open and I kicked my horse into a trot. Almost immediately, I slowed, and then stopped when I saw Ayusta stumbling toward me, clutching a blanket in her arms. Her face was ruddy from exertion, and her mouth hung open as she breathed in large gulps of air.

"'Leazer," she called. "Here Samuel." She stopped and squatted down, peeling back the blanket to reveal the face of my son. His eyes were closed and his face was pale. For one heart-stopping moment, I thought he was dead. Then Samuel yawned and stretched.

I leapt off my horse and dashed over to scoop him up into my arms.

"Samuel! Samuel! Oh, my son," I cried.

"Papa!" Samuel said, and wrapped both of his little arms around my neck.

I stared at Ayusta, unashamed of the tears that ran down my face. "Thank you, thank you." I whispered.

"How'd she do that?" Fred asked.

"I don't know," I said.

Ayusta started speaking rapidly in her tongue. I didn't care what she had to say. All I cared about was that I had Samuel back.

At last Fred nodded and smiled. Then he turned to me.

"Samuel must have gone out chasing rabbits while he waited for you to come back to take him wood gathering. Seems that the brave who took Samuel is part of her tribe. The Indian rode into camp with him yesterday, and Samuel cried himself to sleep last night. When Ayusta was sure that everyone in camp was asleep, she snuck into the tepee where Samuel slept and rescued him. She's walked most of the night to bring him back to you."

My eyes filled with tears even as my heart swelled with gratitude. "Thank you, Ayusta. Come with me." I motioned with my hand for her to follow. "We'll see Mary Caroline, get some food, and let you rest."

Ayusta grinned. "T'ank you," she said, following me into the fort.

In 1855, Eleazer King found an Indian woman in the foothills where she'd been left to die. He took her back to the fort, where his wife, Mary Caroline, was instrumental in nursing her back to health. The squaw became especially fond of three-year-old Samuel King.

When the Indian was well again, she returned to her tribe. One day not long after, Samuel chased rabbits outside the fort until he was far enough away that an Indian brave swooped down on his horse and stole the child, carrying the screaming toddler back to his camp.

In the dark of night, the Indian woman who'd been cared for by Mary Caroline King stole Samuel from the tepee where he'd cried himself to sleep and carried him back to the fort to return him to his grateful parents.

Sources: Guy Wetzel, "Samuel Eleazor King History," *Saga of the Sanpitch,* vol. 12 (1980), 1. (Author's oral account of his ancestor Sarah Ellen Jones Cox who saved Chief Walker's mother after the chief stabbed her seven times.)

TOPADDIE'S TREASURE

I was the first one to see the Indian stalking down the road. My heart leaped up in my chest, even though I knew that the Indians weren't always looking for a fight. He had no bow and arrow that I could see, nor was his face painted with war paint.

When the Indian drew closer, I recognized him as someone my father knew, even though I couldn't remember his name. They all looked pretty much alike to me. They sounded alike too—all gibberish. Pa could communicate with them, though, a fact that made me proud.

When the Indian reached me, he stooped down and rested on his haunches like a grasshopper settling down in the weeds. "Where Cox?" he asked in his guttural English.

"Uh, do you mean Will?" I stuttered. I had several older brothers and my father who were all Cox. I was Cox, for that matter, but I didn't think that this Indian would have any business with a nine-year-old boy—I gulped—at least I hoped he didn't. Indians were known to kidnap children and take them either to their tepees to raise as their own or else to sell in the slave trade. Surely he would know better than to try to take a child of Orville Cox. Dad was always fair with the Indians and generous to boot. He was nicer to them than a lot of folks thought he ought to be, but Papa didn't care what other people thought.

"Me see Father Cox," the Indian said.

I jumped up and went running into the house to get my Pa. He heard my feet before he saw me. "Walter, running is for outside, not in."

"But there's an Indian to see you, Pa."

Pa's gaze went past me, although he couldn't see the Indian from there. "All right, let's go see what he wants."

I followed Pa out to the yard and heard him say, "Hello, Topaddie." Topaddie sniffed the air loudly, and then placed a hand over his stomach.

"Come and eat with us," Pa said.

Topaddie started for the house, but Pa called him back and led the way toward the stream. "First, we wash," Pa said.

I knelt by the stream next to Pa and watched him work a hard bar of yellow soap around and around his hands in the water. Then he handed the bar to Topaddie. The Indian looked from the soap to Pa and back again. He sniffed the soap. It was obvious that he didn't know what to do with it.

"Here," I said, holding out my hand. "I wash, too." Topaddie surrendered the soap. I showed him how I washed my hands, and then gave it back to him.

Topaddie dipped the soap down into the water and worked it around inside his hands in an awkward imitation of what Pa and I had done.

"That's fine," Pa said, smiling his approval.

We went inside and sat around the table with the family. Pa set an example by folding his arms and bowing his head. Topaddie looked around at all of our bowed heads before he lowered his own.

Pa began one of his prayers where he thanked Heavenly Father for everything and asked a blessing on everyone. I knew I was supposed to keep my eyes closed, but I couldn't help peeking at Topaddie. I saw him glance up at the food on the table more than once and then turn a questioning eye on Pa before he bowed his head again. I nearly laughed out loud when Topaddie's stomach growled loud enough to nearly drown out Pa's words.

At last Pa finished his prayer, and we passed the bowls around. Soon there was not a crumb left, except for the heel of bread that Topaddie held in his hand. He grabbed the soup pot from the middle of the table and swiped the bread around the inside. We all gasped at his bad manners and threw a glance at Ma. She turned her head away.

Topaddie stuffed the bread in his mouth all at once, and then chewed and swallowed. He let a belch rumble out of his throat, and then grinned at Ma. My sisters gasped, and Ma stood up and moved over to stand at the stove.

"Plenty good," Topaddie said.

"Come on, Topaddie, let's talk." Pa pushed away from the table, and Topaddie stood up with the awkward movement of one who is not used to sitting on a chair. The chair toppled over behind him, and Topaddie jumped away from it, startled.

"I'll get it." I got up and lifted the fallen chair back to its place. Then, when the rest of the children were clearing the table, I snuck out the door and went in search of Pa and the Indian.

Pa sat on a porch chair, and Topaddie seated himself on the floor beside him. Pa didn't seem to find this strange at all.

"I find wagons, left from white man in hats with long sticks that spit fire," Topaddie said.

Pa sat up straighter. "Johnston's Army?"

"Yes, army. You come with me, I show you."

"They still have their wheels?"

Topaddie nodded, a pleased grin on his face. "Yes."

"Where are they?"

"Green River."

"How many?"

Topaddie held up two fingers.

"Hmm. That's a pretty far piece, near 200 miles. I need to think this over. Come tomorrow and I'll give you my answer."

Topaddie shot a look at the kitchen door and grinned. "I come tomorrow, same time," he said. The Indian rose to his feet and rubbed his distended belly.

"Good-bye," Pa said before he went back inside in search of Ma. I followed him.

"Topaddie told me of some wagons that the army left behind out by Green River," Pa said.

"You're not going after them alone, are you?" Ma asked.

"I'll go with him," I said, my heart beating hard with anticipation.

Ma looked at me, her eyes round with disbelief. "It might be dangerous," she said.

"I think that if I can find someone else to go along and help me out that Walter might as well come along too," Pa said.

Ma stared at him, her mouth open as though she was trying to catch a fly.

"After all, Walt is nearly a man," Pa said, ignoring Ma's expression.

Pa ended up talking Archie Buchanan into going with him to fetch the wagons. "There ought to be lots of valuable iron left on those wagons," Brother Buchanan said.

"I wouldn't go if I didn't think it was worth it," Pa said.

It was hard to wait for Topaddie to come back the next evening. I was ready to go right now. I was so excited that I almost couldn't stand it.

Topaddie finally came into sight along the road, his smile visible from several yards away.

"Cox here?" he asked. I ran to get Pa.

"Topaddie, welcome," Pa said. "Come and eat with us." This time, Topaddie headed for the stream without any prompting from Pa. Either he was a fast learner of the white man's ways or he was mighty hungry.

Supper went much like the night before, with Topaddie soaking up the leftovers again. I wondered if he ate this much back at his own camp.

Since we'd already decided to go, it was mighty disappointing to me to find out that it would take a few days to get provisioned for the trip. We had to pack food, water, and round up a couple of teams of horses to pull the wagons back to town. More than once, I heard Ma question Pa about taking me. She said he ought to take one of the older boys instead.

"No, Elvira, I'm going to take Walter. Will and the other boys need to keep the place running while I'm gone. Walt's just the right age for an adventure."

At last we set out on our journey, riding the horses that would pull the wagons back home. We had a team from our farm, and one that belonged to Archie Buchanan. There was a horse for each of us, and Topaddie sat proudly on his. Mine had the most provisions. Since there would be stretches without any readily available water, we had to pack some of that too. I wondered if my horse even knew I was up here on his back because I surely didn't weigh as much as the gear he was carrying.

After a day or two of traveling, I couldn't sit still but not because I was excited. It was because my backside was sore! I'd ridden horses around the farm plenty of times before but never for this long in one stretch.

I was grateful for the evenings when we stopped to camp and I could get off my horse and walk around for a bit.

After riding for so long that I wondered if we'd ever get there, Topaddie stopped and looked around, a frown of puzzlement plain on his face.

Pa sat forward on his horse and asked, "What's wrong?"

"The wagons," Topaddie said. "They're gone."

Pa's eyebrows shot up and he scanned the ground. "Are you sure?" he asked. "They were right here?"

"Sure," Topaddie said, his answer sounding more like a question.

We searched for those wagons for two days. Finally, we spotted them in the distance, under a tree.

Topaddie whooped. "Here they are! Under tree, by big rock, just where I left them!"

The wagons were big, heavy things, typical of the United States Army. I'd never seen any before, but I'd heard stories. The army had left Utah and gone back to some war they were having in the east. Dragging these wagons, empty of provisions, must have seemed like too much effort for horses and oxen that still had a fair piece to go.

Pa examined the wheels and axles. One wheel had broken spokes, and it took three days to get the wagons road-worthy. Finally, we headed back toward home.

Pa said that the unexpected delay had depleted our food supply. I thought it was more Topaddie's fault, since he ate so much. Even though we had half of what we started out with, Pa explained that pulling the heavy wagons home would take longer than our ride out to find them. As soon as I heard that Pa was planning on rationing our food to one meal a day, I checked underneath the canvas wagon covers, hoping to find some left-behind Army food or provisions. There weren't any. The canvas covers flapped their tattered edges at me in derision.

My stomach rebelled against having only one meal a day, biting at my belly with sharp pains of protest, but there wasn't anything I could do about it. I rode on the wagon seat beside Pa, my bones jolting with each thump of the metal-rimmed wheels over rocks and ruts.

Topaddie often ranged far a field on foot. It's a good thing he was used to getting around that way because with the horses pulling the wagons, they were no longer available for side trips.

One evening when we got close to a camping place, we noticed Topaddie crouched down in the distance. When we drew near, I caught the welcome scent of fresh roasting meat.

As soon as Pa pulled to a halt, I scrambled down from the wagon seat. Topaddie grinned up at me. Lying before him in a small bed of hot coals was the carcass of a rabbit. Even though it didn't look like much, I grinned back at him. Some was better than none.

After the horses were taken care of, Topaddie divided the rabbit between us. I noticed that he gave us the meat and kept the entrails for himself. I didn't watch him eat but rather turned away and chewed and swallowed my portion with a grateful heart.

There were some steep spots in the trail that we'd ridden over on our journey out without a second thought, but on the way back, we had to double the horses so they could pull a single wagon up the incline. We'd have to put rocks behind the wagon's wheels once it reached the top, and then walk the horses back down the hill and hook them up to the next wagon. In a way, it was a good thing that the wagons were empty, or else our four tired horses wouldn't have been enough to get them up and over the steep inclines.

I was glad that Topaddie continued to find game from time to time, trotting out to where I couldn't even see him and catching up to us later in the day. I especially liked it when he got some animal for us to eat, but even the roots and berries he brought us were welcome. I was sorely missing Mama's flour biscuits, but I would never say that to Topaddie. He was keeping me alive, and I was grateful.

When we finally rolled into town, I was never more glad to see my family. I hopped off the wagon, intent on heading for the house and some of Mama's real food, when Pa stopped me. "We've got to see to the animals, son."

At first, I thought Pa was being awfully hard on me, but then I realized that Pa would expect the same of my big brothers. So I squared my shoulders, took one of the horses, and led it into the barn.

When the animals were settled, we washed our hands and went in to dinner. Topaddie was there, of course, having been the instrument of our family's good fortune. He was the most talkative, speaking around mouthfuls of food while Pa and I just kept shoveling it in.

When Mama asked how the trip was, Topaddie was the one who answered. "Good," he said. "But Cox no wash much."

An Indian named Topaddie came to the Orville Cox house in 1862 with news that he'd found two wagons abandoned by Johnston's Army on its way to the Civil War. They were near Green River, a distance of about 180 miles. Cox invited his friend Archie Buchanan to help him bring in the bounty. Although Orville Cox had a son named Walter, he didn't really go on the wagon rescue mission. I added him so that he could take us along on the adventure.

Sources: Milton R. Hunter, *Utah Indian Stories* (Springville, Utah: Art City Publishing, 1946).

SICK, SICK, SICK

"Lena, the wheel came off my buggy again," Florence whined.

Despite my promise to Mama, I was growing impatient. "Well, then, just carry your doll," I said.

Honestly, sometimes I wondered how Florence could be my real sister. She was so dumb. I was embarrassed to be related to her.

"But I want my buggy!" she cried, the word "buggy" rising up into a teeth-rattling wail.

"Oh, for Pete's sake. I'll fix your buggy," Dorothy snapped.

My eyebrows went up in surprise at her harsh tone of voice. Usually Dorothy was the quiet one—the peacemaker who got in between Florence and me and begged us to get along.

I wiped my face with the back of my hand. It came away wet with sweat and dirty with dust from the road. I didn't figure that Mama would approve if she had been here to see me. But she and Pa had gone to the mill, and I had promised her that I would take good care of Florence and Dorothy. That meant playing, as far as I was concerned. I knew that there were plenty of chores to do, but I reasoned that they would still be there when Mama got back and insisted that we get to work.

Right now, we were playing mommies out in the yard, and we each had our own doll to mother. Mine was the prettiest, of course. Dorothy's was next prettiest, and Florence's was downright ugly. When I really wanted to get her goat, I would tell her how ugly it was. I would never resort to such tactics unless I was mad enough that I didn't care about hearing her whine.

Dorothy picked up the buggy wheel. Florence watched her with a scowl on her face. When Dorothy pulled the buggy up on one side to inspect the axel, Florence shrieked, "You'll dump Maybelle out!"

I was irritated, I'll own up to it. That was the reason I said, "Well, if she hits the ground with her face, it might improve her looks."

Florence really opened up at that, the tears pouring down her face as her mouth opened wide enough to fit both of her fists inside. She screamed and cried as though an ox had just stepped on her foot. I would have liked to step on her tongue. Instead, I plugged my ears and then pulled my fingers out partway before pushing them in again.

I pulled them out and pushed them in as rapidly as I could. It gave Florence's cry a wobble that was rather amusing. It was even better when I closed my eyes so that I didn't have to look at her.

I thought I heard Dorothy say something like, "Hush, now!" but it was indistinct in the warble of Florence's screams.

After a moment, someone pushed on my shoulder. I dropped my hands from my ears and my eyes flew open to see Dorothy standing in front of me, her face the picture of horror.

I'm the first to admit that Florence's crying is bad, but I thought Dorothy was exaggerating a bit. Her expression was positively unnerving.

"Stop it!" I snapped.

"Look!" Dorothy said, pointing to something over my shoulder. When I turned around to see, I started screaming myself. A half dozen Indians walked toward us from the foothills. By their bare chests I knew they were men, and from the weapons they carried I knew that I'd better be scared.

Indians stole kids like us. They killed kids too. One time an Indian had tried to sell a little Indian slave child to Brother Morley, and Brother Morley said he didn't want to buy a child. So the Indian picked the child up by the feet, swung him up over his head, and dashed the kid's head on the ground, killing him just like that.

I didn't want to be any Indian's sledgehammer, so I turned and ran for the house, grabbing Florence's hand along the way. After all, I had promised Mama I'd take good care of her. Dorothy's footsteps sounded right behind me, her heavy breathing hot on my neck. We stumbled inside the house and slammed the door shut.

"Hush your mouth!" I snapped at Florence. "Stop screaming or they'll find us! Do you want to have your brains dashed out? Not that it would make that much of a mess."

Florence clutched my hand tighter and quieted some, but she still caught little sobs between breaths.

The sound irritated me. I knew we weren't safe yet. If you didn't answer your door when the Indians knocked, they just went ahead and let themselves in. Sometimes they didn't bother knocking at all. They had no respect for property or privacy. They figured that a thing belonged to whoever had it, or whoever could steal it—and kids were things.

"Shut up, Florence, you're making me sick!" I hissed.

Actually, it was knowing that the Indians were getting closer and closer with each passing moment that was twisting my guts up in fear.

Dorothy tapped my shoulder.

"Stop that!" I screamed.

"I have an idea," Dorothy said. "Let's get in bed and pull the covers up."

"That is so stupid," I said. "You think they won't look under the covers for us?"

"No," Dorothy said. "That's not what I mean. We should pretend to be sick. I heard Pa say that the Indians think our sickness is bad medicine. Evelyn Carlson's mother told her to put red spots on her face if she ever saw an Indian coming to their house. They won't get close to sick white people. If we're sick, they'll be scared of us and leave us alone."

I looked down at my two little sisters. Imagining that the Indians could possibly be scared of them was difficult, but what else could we do?

"Okay," I said. "Let's be sick."

I made a dash for the big bed just off the front room that Mama and Papa slept in. I didn't even bother to take off my shoes. I just jumped into that bed and pulled the covers up to my chin.

Dorothy followed, dragging Florence with her. Florence was crying again.

I scooted to the middle so that my sisters would have to get in on either side. If Dorothy's plan didn't work and one of us got snatched, I wanted to make darn sure it wasn't me.

"Quit crying, Florence. Start coughing," I said.

Florence muffled her face in Pa's pillow and tried a cough or two. They weren't very convincing.

Dorothy did a better job of it. Her coughs shook the bed.

I gave it a try and found that coughing too hard hurt my throat. So, I did my part by letting out a dry, whispery cough that sounded like it belonged to someone's old grandma.

It seemed like forever before a knock sounded on the door. My heart rattled in fear, and I coughed all the harder. I'd rather have a sore throat than end up missing my brains through a hole in my head.

I shivered for real when I heard the door squeak open. I wanted to look but didn't dare.

Florence wasn't doing her share of the coughing, so I nudged her with my elbow. She squealed in fear and buried her face in Pa's pillow again. Her cry could have been mistaken for a cough—if you had a real good imagination.

Deep, guttural voices raised in argument before the door shut with a blessed *bang!*

Still, I didn't dare look. What if the Indians had come inside and shut the door behind them? What if they knew we were faking? Maybe they were standing on either side of the bed right now, knives drawn, ready to collect our scalps because we weren't any good to them alive if we were sick.

Dorothy grabbed my shoulder and I nearly died of fright. "They're gone," she said. "We can get up now."

I collapsed into the mattress tick and stopped coughing. My throat thanked me.

"I don't want to get up," I said. "I feel sick."

McKay Andreason told me the story of how his grandmother Anne Lena Frandsen Andreason pretended to be sick in bed with her two sisters when they were home alone and saw Indians coming down out of the mountains.

Merilyn Jorgensen told me the story of her mother, Evelyn Carlson Anderson, who was instructed to always check to see who was knocking. If it was an Indian, she had to dot her face with red lip rouge before she opened the door because the Indians were so afraid of white men's diseases that they wouldn't bother her if she was sick.

BOUGHT AND PAID FOR

The Indian boy stood with his head down, his greasy hair hanging around his shoulders in hopeless, black tangles. His face was so dark that I couldn't tell if it was his natural skin color or if it was from the dirt that streaked his body.

His captor prodded him forward, and the boy stumbled. It was then that I noticed his ribs showing plainly through his dusky skin. A rope circled the boy's chest, pinning his upper arms to his sides. I wondered when he'd last had anything to eat.

"You buy," the Indian said to Pa, lifting the other end of the rope while his horse waited, one hoof tipped forward to rest.

I glanced up at the warrior and wondered if he'd made the boy walk at the end of the rope for miles and miles while he rode the horse and pulled him along. I wondered what it would be like to be stolen and forced to go to a strange place, never to see my family again. I took a step closer to Pa. Even though I was twelve years old and could do a man's work out in the fields, I knew I was no match for a full grown Indian.

"Where is he from?" Pa asked.

The Indian stuck his arm out toward the south. "Paiute," he said.

I knew enough about the Paiutes to know that they were gatherers—a peaceful people who did their best to live off the land. They didn't even have horses, so they couldn't put up much of a fight when the stronger tribes came riding down on them to take their children or anything else away from them. Thinking about it made me scared and mad at the same time.

This was the first time Pa had been approached about buying an Indian child. It was pretty common to have Indians sell children from other tribes to the whites. At first, the settlers were horrified at the idea and refused to buy them, but when the slave children were killed right before their eyes, the whites relented and the Indians knew they had a lucrative market with the palefaces.

The boy for sale looked about my age. I wondered if he ate raw meat. He sure didn't wear much. If he was going to live at our house, he'd have to get dressed or Ma wouldn't let him in. Maybe Pa would just buy him and let him go. Then he could go back to his family, and maybe he'd know better than to get caught next time.

I looked up at Pa and saw his eyes fixed on the boy. There was a softness there that I recognized from times when he was feeling proud or sorry for one of us kids. He had looked like that after my baby brother John died just one month past. I knew that Mama's heart was aching for her little boy, and I missed him too, but I sure hoped that Pa wasn't thinking that he could fill the hole John's death left in our hearts by bringing this scruffy Indian into our family.

It seemed to me that Pa was fixing to buy this boy.

"So, Pa," I said. "Don't you think the Larsens would like to buy themselves an Indian?"

Pa didn't even look at me. "No," he said. "I think that I would like to."

Maybe Pa was thinking that he had to restock the Brown family's store of boys in general, since there were only two of us left, and Neuman was a grown man of twenty who had moved out of the house.

I barely remembered my other brothers who had met untimely deaths. Fred died when I was only six years old. He'd been almost three times as old as me, so my memories of him weren't clear. Then there was William, who had been dead for going on four years. He was eighteen when he died, and as much a man in my eyes as Papa was. I remembered Mama crying her eyes out, but she got over it.

I was sorry that this skinny boy had been kidnapped and all, but it wasn't my doing. I didn't know why we had to put up with him just because he was in the wrong place at the wrong time.

"Pa?"

"Robert." Pa's voice carried a warning that there was to be no more argument from me. Even though I wanted to tell him not to buy this boy on my account, because I didn't mind being the only boy left at home, I closed my mouth and watched Pa pull out his money pouch. It was heavy from the pay he'd just gotten for serving in the Mormon Battalion. He opened the bag and pulled out a gold coin. It was stamped with a shield on one side and a cross on the other. I couldn't read the words on it, on account of them being written in Spanish. I groaned inwardly at the thought of all the licorice whips that gold would buy—enough to last my lifetime. And Pa was going to waste it on an Indian.

Pa handed the Indian captor the gold piece. The Indian took it but didn't even bother to look at it. "More," he said, holding out his other hand.

Indians didn't have any use for money itself. You couldn't eat it, you couldn't wear it, and you couldn't trap an animal with it. But they had soon learned that white men would trade valuable things for the yellow metal—things that the Indians could use. They thought whites were crazy to value the small, hard pieces of gold and silver, but they were willing to take them to trade for things they wanted.

To my horror, Pa pulled out two more pieces of gold and handed them over.

"More," the Indian said.

I wanted to grab the money bag and run, to save what was left, but I knew I'd be in trouble if I did. It was Pa's money. He moved his hand to the money bag again. To my relief, he pulled the drawstring and closed it up tight. "No," Pa said. "Twenty-five dollars is enough."

The Indian looked from Pa to his captive and back again, trying to gauge if he could push for any more. Pa stared him straight in the eye.

The Indian must have figured that some was better than none because he handed Pa the loose end of the rope and mounted his horse. He rode away without a single backward look.

The first thing Pa did was untie the rope and lift it off the boy. My stomach turned over in revulsion when I saw the places where the rope had rubbed the skin off, making bloody stripes around the boy's arms. I shivered, wondering if the boy would run now that he was free, but he didn't. He stood with his head down and his shoulders slumped.

"Come with me," Pa said, his voice as gentle as when he'd spoken to my sick little brother before he died.

The Indian boy shuffled forward on his bare feet and followed us home.

Mama turned into a regular mother hen when she saw the boy. "James, the poor child is filthy," she said. "Help me get him washed."

"First things first," Pa said. "He needs feeding worse than he needs cleaning."

Mama hurried around the kitchen getting food ready, speaking kindly to the Indian boy the whole time. After he was fed, Mama got Pa to help her fill the washtub. Pa managed to get the boy into the bath, but it was plain to see that he didn't like it any. He sat and shivered and held his arms in close to his body. Mama had Pa wash his hair, and she stood ready with a pair of scissors. When she started snipping, the Indian boy gripped his head in his hands and cried out.

"It won't hurt," Pa assured him.

At last, Mama got enough black hair cut off to satisfy herself. She told me to run get some of my clothes for the boy. I went, grumbling the whole way. When I got back, I saw Mama wrapping clean white bandages around the boy's bloody arms.

That night when we gathered for scripture reading and prayers, the Indian sat apart from us, his eyes on the floor. He was a strange sight wearing my shirt and trousers with his short hair. My sisters couldn't stop looking back and forth between us. I wanted to shout at them and say, "Stop looking at me!" but I didn't.

Pa opened the scriptures and then he paused. "We want to welcome the newest member of our family," he said. "We need to call him something. Any ideas for a name?"

"How about John?" my sister Mary Ann said.

"No!" I said, my back stiffening in protest. "Not John." John was my brother's name, and this Indian was no brother of mine.

Pa turned to me. "What do you suggest?"

I looked around the room and my eyes fell on the scriptures. We'd been reading about Alma in the court of wicked King Noah from the Book of Mormon. Maybe because this Indian boy had so recently been hunted, just like King Noah's men were doing to Alma, I said, "Alma. Call him Alma."

"That's a fine name, son," Pa said.

Mama turned to the Indian and said, "Your name is Alma."

The boy shook his head. He said one word, "Shock," the first thing I'd ever heard him say.

My older sister Sarah said, "Shock? That must be his name."

Mama frowned. "I'm not going to call him Shock." The Indian looked up at her with recognition in his eyes.

"Alma Shock Brown," Pa said, his voice firm with authority.

Alma Shock was sent to school with me, although I didn't see what good it did. He just sat there and didn't say anything.

Over time, however, Alma Shock warmed up to us. He even quit flinching any time Mama or Pa reached for him. He learned to speak our language, and he taught me Indian words. I was pretty proud of being able to speak Indian, although I didn't learn Alma's language as well as he learned English.

Alma liked living with us—I knew because he told me so. He didn't ever want to go back to digging for worms to eat and going hungry most of the winter. He liked licorice whips as much as I did, maybe even more. He didn't care for peppermints, though; he was more partial to horehound candy.

As the years passed, it seemed as though Alma had always been part of our family. He grew to manhood, and in 1861 he married Betsy Peacock, the adopted Indian daughter of Judge George Peacock.

Alma was handy to have around when it came to Indian communication. He would often act as a go-between, trying for peace that was long in coming. Most Indian children were sold to the whites at a very young age and didn't have much memory of their birthplace, but Alma was half grown when he was captured, so he remembered his language and his life among the Indians. When the Black Hawk War broke out a couple of years later, Alma used his unique position of being an Indian raised by whites to work between the warring factions.

There was that memorable day when Alma Shock learned that Christian Anderson had been captured from where he'd been working in his field. The other men with him had been killed outright.

Alma didn't hesitate to ride his pony up the mountain, hot on the trail of the marauding Indians. He found Christian Anderson tied to a post. The Indians were preparing to torture and kill him, to make him suffer for all of the Indians who had been slain during the war.

Alma Shock managed to convince the Indians that Christian was a good man, and not one of those who had raided and killed Indian women and children. The Indians set their captive free.

It turned out that twenty-five dollars was a real bargain for my brother Alma Shock Brown.

Ruth Davenport Scow's great-grandparents James "Polly" and Eunice Reasor Brown paid $25 for an Indian youth in the 1850s. They treated the boy, named Alma Shock Brown, like a son. He grew and married another adopted Indian named Betsy Peacock. Alma Shock Brown acted as a go-between for whites and Indians during the Black Hawk War. He rescued Christian Anderson from certain death when he convinced Christian's captors that he was a good man, and the Indians let him go.

Source: *Saga of the Sanpitch*, vol. 27 (1995), 23.

A FAIR TRADE

I was brushing my best horse, a fine three-year-old stallion, when I heard footsteps behind me.

I turned to see an Indian brave move up to the rail fence that surrounded the paddock where I stood. I kept a hold on the stallion's lead rope and gave my visitor a friendly nod. "Hello," I said.

I wasn't alarmed. I didn't feel I had any need to be. Indians were a common sight, and we generally got along.

An Indian woman, who I assumed was the brave's wife, trailed behind him with a young child cradled in her arms. She halted when she was a respectful distance behind the Indian brave. She boosted her child up on her hip and pointed to my horse with a slender brown finger. She whispered something into her baby's ear.

The child grinned, its dark eyes squinting in sheer delight. The mother smiled at her baby with such tenderness that it lifted my heart and spread a smile across my face.

The Indian grunted. "Fine horse," he said.

"Yes," I agreed, turning back to admire my stallion's glossy brown coat. He was a beauty—full of heart and stamina, with a good disposition too. It seemed that everyone who saw him, whites and Indians alike, had something good to say. I'd already had several handsome offers for him and turned them all down. I'd also refused a couple of generous trades from Indians who had hoped to make him theirs. I kept him locked in the barn at night because I wasn't interested in parting with him.

The baby laughed out loud, and the Indian's brow lowered in anger before he whipped his head around to glare at his family. The woman curved her arm around the baby and turned her shoulder toward the brave, as though to shield the child from harm.

The Indian turned back to me while the woman bounced the baby in her arms, her eyes flitting between the brave and the child. I saw her pull out a ball of red cloth and hold it out for her child to take. The child grabbed the ball in one hand and then raised its face toward its mother. The baby grinned, its dark eyes dancing, and then it lifted its little hand and patted the woman's cheek.

"Fine horse," the brave said again. "You trade?"

My eyes still watching the child's antics, I thought I would honor the Indian by paying his family a compliment. "I'll trade for that baby," I said.

The Indian gave a single nod of his head. "Good," he said. "Fair trade." He turned and strode away from me, toward the woman, who shrank back from him, clutching the baby to her chest.

"No," I called. "I didn't mean it."

The Indian ignored me. He grabbed the child around its middle and pulled it away from its mother.

The cry that rose from the woman's throat cut my heart in two and made my blood run cold. The Indian was on his way back to the fence, dangling the baby in front of him.

"You take," the Indian said, holding the baby out.

I put my hands up to ward off the child. "No. I don't want to take the baby."

The Indian's face grew dark with anger.

I could see that I had made a terrible mistake in thinking that the Indian could take a joke, and I couldn't think of any way out of it. I didn't know how to tell the man that I had only been teasing, but my attempt at a compliment had broken a mother's heart and made me feel sick clear down through my soul.

I'd had this awful feeling once before, when I had let Jake Anders finally talk me into selling him my big black stallion for a handsome sum. For two nights I couldn't sleep worth a pan of beans. The money was no comfort because all I could think about was my horse. Finally, I approached Jake and told him that I'd made a terrible mistake. It took twice the purchase price to get my stallion back, but he was worth every penny.

Well, because I had made this blunder with the Indian, albeit unwittingly, I had to set it right. Even though I figured my horse was lost for good—a fact that made my heart sink like a stone in a cold-water pond—at least I could make amends to the baby's mother.

"You," I began, swallowing the lump in my throat. "You can have the horse."

The Indian's face cleared, and he pushed the child up against my chest with such force that I nearly stumbled backward. I instinctively grabbed the child to keep my balance and to keep it from falling. The chilling wails of the baby's mother sent shivers up my spine, even though it was a warm day.

The Indian let himself into the corral and pulled the lead rope out of my hand, his eyes shining as he looked over his new possession. My insides caved when I saw the Indian with my young stallion, but worse than that was the torture of having to listen to the mother weep for her baby.

"Take the stallion," I said. The Indian headed for the open gate.

"And take the baby," I called, holding the child out toward him. "You can have them both."

The Indian stopped short, forcing the stallion to dig his hooves into the dirt in order to keep from running his new master down. The Indian glared at me. "Girl child yours," he spat in a voice so venomous that it stopped me cold. Something in his eyes sealed up my mouth and curbed any further protests. It would be a mistake to invoke this man's wrath. I was sure there would be a fierce price to pay, one that might be taken out on my family or even his own. I feared that the child in my arms would suffer if I insisted that she return home with her parents.

I couldn't understand the Indian's attitude. I knew that sons were more highly valued in Indian camps than daughters, but she was his child, after all. Perhaps he would lose respect in his tribe if he did not honor the terms of the trade that he had agreed to.

The Indian drew himself up to his full height and said, "When me trade, me trade."

Then he turned and stalked toward his woman. He gave her a sharp command, and she fell into step behind him, her face buried in her hands and her shoulders shaking with sobs.

I wished I could tell her that I would take good care of her baby. I wished with all my heart that I could let her know that we would treat her like one of our own.

I stared after the retreating couple, paralyzed, until a touch as soft as a butterfly wing brushed against my chin. Startled, I looked down to find a little pair of black eyes staring up at me, a little brown hand patting my face. Then the baby turned her little pink mouth up into a grin.

I smiled back, even though my heart ached for the child's mother. Then I turned toward the house. It was time to introduce my wife to our new daughter.

Somewhere around 1860, Daniel Henrie had a promising young horse that was envied by white men and Indians alike. One day an Indian and his wife came to the Henrie house and asked about trading for the horse. Daniel was in a jovial mood and teased that he would trade his horse for the Indian baby the woman held in her arms. He was horrified when the

Indian brave pulled the baby away from her mother and placed her in Daniel's arms.

Daniel tried to give the baby back, insisting that the Indian could keep both the horse and the baby, but it's reported that the Indian refused with the words, "When me trade, me trade." The Indian left with the horse, his weeping wife at his side.

Earlier in his life, Daniel Henrie had let a friend of his talk him into selling his favorite black stallion. Afterward, Daniel was so distraught that he couldn't sleep. He ended up buying the stallion back for twice the amount he'd sold it for.

Source: *Saga of the Sanpitch*, vol. 7 (1975), 1.

A RUDE WELCOME

I cut the dough with a floured glass, and then laid the circles out on a tin sheet. I peeked inside the oven to see a pan full of biscuits browned to perfection. I pulled them out and set the hot pan onto the wooden sideboard. Then I slipped the last pan of doughy biscuits inside and closed the oven door.

Even though there were far too many biscuits for me to eat myself, I liked to bake ahead. The oven made the house so hot, that unless it was the dead of winter, I tried to get as much baking done in one day as I could.

I shot a calculating look at the overflowing cookie jar—enough cookies. Maybe I should mix and bake a cake too. I debated about the extra work it would take as I lifted the lid off the big pot of stew on the stove. Earl wasn't going to be back from his coal run tonight. I'd be lucky if he even showed up by tomorrow, though I certainly hoped he would. The big pot of stew would take care of our supper for a couple of days at least, and it was always better the day after I made it.

With the last of the biscuit dough in the oven, I swept the table clean of flour, and wiped my hands on my apron. They were still sticky with dough so I dipped them into the tin pan of wash water. I'd used the same water all day long to wash up the dishes, and it had turned cold. Since it left a greasy sheen on my hands when I pulled them out, I decided it was useless to try to clean anything else with it.

I wiped my hands on my apron and picked up the wash pan. I knew that I really should carry it out into the yard and pour the used water on the garden, but I was too impatient to walk clear out there. My mind was fixed on mixing a cake before the oven cooled down too much to get it baked.

I carried wash water across the room, pulled the door open, and flung the water out. Before it had even left the pan, I desperately wished I could call it back. But it was too late; I could only stare in horror as the water flew smack into the face of a broad-shouldered Indian man. His eyes widened in shocked surprise and then narrowed with anger as he glared at me.

"Oh, oh, I'm so sorry," I gasped.

The Indian spat some words at me that I didn't understand, but I didn't need an interpreter to be certain that what he was saying was uncomplimentary. He raised a dark hand and rubbed it across his forehead.

"I didn't know you were there," I said. I couldn't tell whether he understood English or not, but I had to at least try to explain that I hadn't seen him coming, and that I didn't mean any disrespect.

"Please, come in and get dry," I said.

I wouldn't normally invite an Indian inside with my husband gone, but this was not a normal circumstance. I had to appease this Indian before he got angry enough to retaliate. I was just glad that my children were having their afternoon naps in the other room and that the door was closed.

The Indian strode inside. I had intended for my invitation to put him in a better frame of mind, but instead his scowl deepened.

I pulled out a chair. "Sit down," I said. I turned to the wooden towel bar next to the sink and pulled a towel off it. I spun around to pat the man's face with the towel, trying to dry him off. He snatched the towel from me and wiped it across his face himself, but his scowl remained.

What else could I do? I spied the pan of biscuits cooling on the sideboard. Perhaps some bread would help his mood. I stacked some biscuits in my hand and slid them onto a plate.

"Here," I said, setting the plate on the table. He looked down at the biscuits and then up at me. He grunted, picked up a biscuit, and bit into it. His frown remained.

Maybe the biscuits were too dry. I'd made them to go with soup, and I hadn't given him any butter. If I did, would he even know what to do with it? Maybe he'd eat it plain.

I turned, lifted the coffeepot, poured a cup, and set it on the table before him. The Indian picked up the cup and raised it to his mouth. I hoped it wasn't too hot. He drank the coffee with his scowl firmly in place, so I pulled a handful of cookies out of the cookie jar and laid them next to the biscuits on his plate for good measure.

The Indian picked up a cookie and turned it over and over in his hand. Then he sniffed it and took a bite, his eyes on me. He chewed, and his brow cleared for the first time since I'd laid eyes on him. He stuffed the rest of the cookie in his mouth and grabbed another.

By the time the Indian was satisfied, the cookie jar was half empty, but it was a small price to pay for my family's safety.

Without a word, the Indian stood up. He grabbed a handful of cookies and strode out the door. I collapsed against the table. I hadn't realized how tense I'd been until he was gone.

"Mama?" Leo stood in the bedroom doorway, his hair sticking up on one side.

"Leo!" I hurried over to my little boy. "Are you all right?"

Leo looked up at me with heavy-lidded eyes. "Can I have a cookie?"

I laughed in relief. "Of course! You can have two! Just eat your supper first."

Amy called out from inside the bedroom. "Mama?"

I brought my daughter to the table and fed my children biscuits and stew. After they finished, I let them have as many cookies as they wanted.

Little Amy crumbled a cookie in her small fist and tried to push the crumbs in her mouth. I laughed and picked her up in my arms. I carried her out to do chores and Leo followed along behind.

A bay horse trotted over to the fence to meet us.

"Hi, Donkey!" Leo called out to the old horse.

I wondered if my children would forever be confused about donkeys and horses because when I was a child I couldn't tell the difference between any animals with four legs, hooves, and a tail. The first time I called our new colt a donkey, my older brother thought it was hilarious, and the name stuck. When I got married and moved out of the house, Donkey came with me.

I stepped into the paddock and lifted Amy onto Donkey's back. Leo clamored for his turn. It felt good to stand next to the warm comfort of my old horse. Donkey followed us inside the barn and waited while we milked the cow. He watched us scatter grain for the chickens, and I pretended not to see Leo give Donkey a handful of chicken feed to eat. Even though we stayed out in the paddock for longer than usual, Donkey didn't want us to leave. He must have been missing the horses that Earl had taken with him to pull the coal wagon.

"I'm lonely too," I said, rubbing Donkey's forehead. "But don't worry. They should all be back tomorrow."

Finally the sun lowered enough that I had to tell the children that it was time to tell Donkey good night. We made sure he had plenty of hay and water before we made our way back to the house.

I locked the door and got the children ready for bed.

"When's Papa coming home?" Leo asked.

"He should be back tomorrow, I hope."

"He's been gone a long time," Leo said, looking out the window.

"Only two days."

"Why did he have to go?"

"To get coal for us to burn in the winter to keep warm."

"So after I sleep and wake up he'll be here?"

"No, it will be later in the day—at nighttime," I said. *Unless he has a broken wagon wheel, or a lame horse, or runs into unfriendly Indians.* I kept my thoughts to myself, but I couldn't keep from shuddering.

"Mama, are you cold?" Leo asked. "Should I build you a fire?"

"No, thank you, Leo!"

The house was still plenty warm from the baking earlier in the day. I hoped that I'd fed the Indian enough cookies to make him forget my accidental insult of splashing dirty water on him. An Indian with a grudge was a dangerous thing; they tended to strike first and never ask questions later.

"Tell me a story," Leo begged.

I told my children stories until they drifted off to sleep—Leo with his ruddy cheek pressed into the pillow and Amy with her thumb in her mouth.

I got up from beside my sleeping children and moved into the kitchen, ready to put myself to bed too. Once I was asleep, the time would pass more quickly and it would be that much closer to the time when Earl would be home.

As soon as I stepped out of the bedroom, the front doorknob rattled. Fear shot up my spine. I whipped my head around to stare at the door, grabbing the back of a chair so that my knees wouldn't collapse. The knob was quiet and still.

Had I really heard something? My heart pounded hard enough to assure me that I had. It wasn't my imagination; someone was trying to get in.

With my eyes still fixed on the knob, it rattled again. I jumped as if it were a striking snake. I threw an anxious glance toward the room where my children lay sleeping. Knowing that I was their sole source of protection forced my courage to the surface.

My eyes darted around the room, looking for something—anything—that I could use as a weapon. The knob rattled again with such force that the door thumped inside its casing. I clutched at my throat, trying to keep my fear from erupting into a scream. My eyes fell on the poker standing by the fireplace. I dashed across the floor and grabbed it. I wished that it were red-hot, but I had to settle for room temperature.

I flattened myself against the wall and walked on cat feet toward the door. I wondered if the sound of my voice would frighten whoever was on the other side of the door away.

Impatient feet stamped outside, and the doorknob shook again. This time I was so close that I was startled into nearly dropping the poker.

"Who's there?" I called. My throat was so dry that the words got stuck and came out as a whisper.

In reply, there was more stamping and a low chuckle. What if there was a drunken Indian waiting outside? How could I possibly reason with him?

The door rattled in its frame again. Whoever was out there wasn't going to give up and go away.

"I have a weapon," I called out.

The doorknob rattled.

I had to get rid of whoever it was before they thought of setting the house on fire or something equally horrifying. I reached out toward the knob, my fear as sharp as an axe. I worked the lock loose with quiet fingers and gripped the doorknob as I hefted the poker in my other hand. I would wait for the next rattle—wait for whoever it was to try the door again—so that they wouldn't be expecting me to fling the door open and smack them with the poker.

The doorknob jiggled. I gave it a fierce twist, pulling the door open and raising the poker at the same time.

Donkey gave a snort of surprise and stepped back, his eyes wide.

"Donkey!" I cried, my voice coming out in a sob. I lowered the poker and sagged in relief against the horse's side. "Oh, Donkey, I thought you were an Indian coming to murder me!"

Donkey chuckled a soft whinny and nuzzled my shoulder.

"How did you get out of your pen?" I asked with mock severity. "You're not allowed to sleep in the house, you know, but I'm awfully glad you're here, just the same."

I stroked Donkey's nose. "Come on, I'll go tuck you in next to the cow so you won't be lonely." I pulled Donkey toward the barn and he followed willingly. "I'll even tell you a bedtime story about a lady who accidentally threw her wash water onto an Indian."

Sometime in the 1880s, Elizabeth finished mixing bread and set it to raise. She washed her hands in the tin washbasin and tossed the water out the door, right into the face of an Indian brave. He was very angry and was only pacified when Elizabeth's sister Johanna offered him a plate of cookies and coffee.

Ann was home alone with her children while her husband was gone overnight to get a load of coal. In the evening, the doorknob rattled, and Ann was afraid it might be hostile Indians. She armed herself with a poker, just in case, and opened the door to find the lone horse that had been left behind (which I named Donkey), looking for company.

In none of my research did I come up with last names for any of these ladies. In the interest of storytelling, I combined the stories into one.

Source: *Saga of the Sanpitch*, vol. 17 (1985), 98.

ONE AGAINST

"They can't get away with it," To-ko-witz growled. "We must not let them think that the battle is won."

"I agree," said Mon-dats. "We need white blood."

I didn't say anything, even though I wanted to remind Mon-dats that the blood of the white-skinned people had proven to run as red as ours when it spilled from their bodies. It's true that it made a brighter contrast against their pale skin, especially if their hair was the strange, ghost color of many spiderwebs strung together over their heads. It was fascinating, this light color that made me think they already had half of their spirit in the grave. The spider hair made them look old, even if their faces were young. I wondered if these light-hairs felt the wounds of death as keenly as those of us with the solid skin color of earth. I had killed my share of the pale skins, but I hadn't known how to ask them how it felt to die.

"We'll lie in ambush," To-ko-witz said. "Many of the pale skins are coming into the canyon to cut wood."

"Bah," said Orro-kani with disgust. "They build their shelters thick and solid, and they don't move them with the seasons. They squat together like ants crawling over a carcass, and their dwellings are as ugly as a pile of moose turds."

This made me laugh. It was so like Orro-kani to speak his mind. Even though he was one who liked to laugh, I would not want to be on the wrong end of the spear if Orro-kani were my enemy. There would be nothing left of me if he truly wanted to be rid of me. He was the fiercest warrior I knew.

"They make good bread," I mumbled. My stomach growled in agreement. The others stared at me, their eyes narrowed.

"What?" I asked.

"You would trade a loaf of bread for the lands of your forefathers?" To-ko-witz demanded.

"No, of course not." I set my jaw so they would not ask me any more questions. Was I the only one who missed the days when the white settlers first came to our valley? They had come here during a time of first cold, bringing their fat cattle, who were so tame that they stood and watched while you notched your arrow and let it fly toward their hearts.

Then they would fall over dead. They were more accommodating than deer or elk. As the winter wore on and the snow piled deep, the cattle began to die of their own accord. We would drag off their carcasses and feast in our camp.

More settlers came the next year, bringing more cattle. We found it to be much more convenient to drive the cattle into the mountains before slaughtering them because some of the settlers didn't like us to help ourselves. They had a strange word—stealing. We didn't have such a word in our language. We saw things very differently from the whites, with their pale eyes. We took what we needed, and we took what we wanted. If anyone could take it back from us, then it was theirs by rights and they deserved to have it more than we did.

We soon discovered that some of the cows gave milk and cream, and the that whites had magical machines that turned cream into butter and buttermilk. I had even been to Walter Cox's house on some occasions when they had made ice cream. They shared it with me, as they did their other food. When I lifted a spoonful of ice cream to my tongue, it hurt. I yanked the spoon away, thinking I'd been burned. But the little Cox children were putting spoonful after spoonful into their mouths. The bit of ice cream on my tongue melted and I caught the flavor. I had never had anything like it before. I thought that it must be the food of the Gods. I scooped the rest of my ice cream into my mouth as quickly as the awkward spoon would allow. When Walter's missus saw my empty bowl, she looked into my eyes, smiled, and served me more ice cream.

"Mama," said one of her daughters, called E-mi-lee. "May I have more?"

"No, I'm sorry. There is no more."

E-mi-lee stuck out her bottom lip. "Then why does he get more?" She pointed her spoon at me, and I began to scoop the ice cream into my mouth faster.

"He's our guest," said Missus Cox.

I grinned at E-mi-lee and opened my mouth wide to take in the last bite of ice cream, delighting in the shock of cold that melted into sweetness that surpassed any of the berries or honey that I'd ever found in the forest.

E-mi-lee wasn't a spiderweb hair but her sister Sarah was. When Sarah saw that my bowl was empty, she leaned over to take it from me. I reached up to touch her hair. She jerked away, a look of surprise in her strange round eyes, which were as blue as the sky in summer. I wondered if everything looked blue through her sky eyes.

"It's all right, Sarah," said Cox. "He's not used to blonde hair, that's all."

Sarah gave me a thin smile and hurried into the kitchen with my bowl.

I burped as loudly as I could so that Missus Cox would know how much I liked the food she'd given me, especially the ice cream. E-mi-lee gasped and put her hand over her mouth as though she'd burned her tongue on a roasted cricket. One of the little Cox boys laughed out loud, and I grinned at him.

Nearly all of the whites would give us food when we asked. Most of them handed it to us through half-opened doors, which they then shut in our faces instead of inviting us to eat with them like Cox did.

There was one white woman, the crazy Yew-nees Warner, who held no good will toward us, even though her husband had honor in death by killing an Indian before he'd been killed. It was an even exchange—a trade that balanced the numbers in the best possible proportions. Yet Yew-nees didn't seem satisfied that her husband had died a noble warrior's death and gone to the best afterlife—one far better than if he'd died an old man in his wigwam.

I had gone along when we'd been to visit Yew-nees at the dwelling of her parents after we'd made peace from the killings. Her father was a white leader, a man we called "Captain." He was reasonable about war. He knew that it was simply a way of life; once their deaths were avenged, there was no sense in hanging onto the dead with a heavy heart.

One of those who had killed Warner claimed his strange neck cloth, although he didn't tie it in the same fashion as Warner had, with a knot that slid magically along the length of fabric. Warner also had some curious talismans with him, including a metal cylinder from which folded out some of the most wondrous tools that we had ever seen. None of us had been selfish; we broke several of the tools off so that we might all share in the new and wonderful things that the pale skins brought with them. Yet, when we visited as guests in Yew-nees's home, she glared at us as if we were demons. My fellow warrior adjusted his neck cloth and smiled at her, thinking that if she saw how we honored her husband's belongings, it would prove to her that we held him in the highest regard.

We all pulled out the pieces of metal that we had divided between us and laid them out on the table for her to see with what honor we esteemed the brave Warner.

As soon as she saw the items, a most wondrous change occurred in Yew-nees's face—it drained of what little color it had until she truly appeared as one dead. Her eyes narrowed and her mouth compressed into a thin line. She hardly looked human anymore. Even though she was obviously with child, she wasn't slow to grab up a knife and start toward us. If she had reached us, I have no doubt that she would have done her best to plunge the blade into at least one of us, possibly more, since we were so surprised at her actions. Yet she didn't get the chance to kill even one of us. Instead, her father grabbed her by the shoulders and pulled her from the room. A sound escaped her mouth—a strangled cry that didn't even sound human.

We laughed in amazement at her power and determination. She would have a strong papoose, of that we were all in complete agreement.

Captain returned alone. If he had beaten her while in the other room in order to teach her to keep her place, she hadn't cried out—not even once. Our admiration for her grew, as well as our conviction that she was possessed of an unusual spirit.

It was after she had her papoose that one of our young men, Enapay, who had heard our stories of Yew-nees decided to go and ask for bread from her household. He said he wanted to see this pale devil woman. He would have to go without me because I remembered, all too well, the knife that had come for me faster than I had thought possible.

We could see the fort from our Indian camp. We watched Enapay go in and, later, we saw him come running out, screaming and crying that the devil woman had beaten him nearly dead. When he calmed down enough to make sense, he said that he had found her alone with her papoose. He asked for bread.

"No," she said. "Go away."

She was not a large woman, or tall. Enapay closed the door and leaned against it. "Give me bread," he said. He was determined not to be put off by this small white woman. He would make her do as he commanded, as a woman should.

Yew-neese laid her papoose down on the bed. "That baby stared at me with its strange, pale eyes," Enapay said, his own eyes growing wide with the memory. "He bewitched me and fixed me to my spot. I couldn't move. Then Yew-nees pulled a stick from where it propped up one of their glass walls. The pane of glass crashed down, sounding just like rifle fire. I thought that someone was shooting outside, so my attention was distracted. Then she came at me with her stick, swinging it with such ferocity that I didn't even have time to pull my blanket up around my shoulders to protect myself. She beat me until I had to cry for mercy or die. At last that devil-woman opened her door and told me to get out."

Enapay showed us the bruises and bloody cuts on his back and shoulders.

When Chief Arropeen heard his tale, he told Enapay that he deserved just what he got.

"I was bewitched!" Enapay declared.

"Squaw," Arropeen said.

Ever since that exchange, Enapay had been "Squaw," and not one of us would ever ask Yew-neese for anything. Sometimes the children of our tribe would dare each other to approach her and touch her skirt, but it was a rare child who would even take up the challenge, and none followed through. Yew-neese was possessed of a devil spirit, there was no doubt about that, but we still called Enapay "Squaw."

The Cox family was as opposite of Yew-nees as it was possible to be. They would always smile when they saw that it was me at their door. They invited me in, cut the bread thick, and spread it with some of their good, sweet butter before handing over it to me. Sometimes it had golden honey poured over it, if they had any. They would ask me to sit at their own table to eat, bringing a cold glass of milk for me to drink with the bread. I felt as though I was one of their tribe.

If all whites had been like that, more of them would have kept their hair. Yet some whites called us names, cheated us in trading, and taught their children to throw rocks at our children.

Recently, some of our tribe had been killed in a skirmish a day's ride south. We had to avenge our tribesmen, and we now sought enemy blood.

"We will kill some of the men who are cutting down our trees in the canyon," Mon-dats declared.

"They always have some of their numbers stand guard with fire sticks," said To-ko-witz.

"We'll get them first," said Orro-kani. "We'll gather enough of us to kill the fire-stick holders, and then we'll kill the rest." His eyes shone with eagerness.

"Or we could lie in wait and ambush anyone going into the canyon," I said. "They won't be expecting us to wait patiently. They think we're blood-thirsty barbarians."

Orro-kani turned his eyes to me. "We could be as sneaky as rabbits in a burrow," he said. I thought he was poking fun at me, until he said, "We could be rabbits hiding the teeth of a bear in our mouths and the claws of a cougar in our paws!" He grinned, and I grinned back.

"Are we all agreed to this plan?" To-ko-witz asked. He looked at each of us in turn, and we all gave him a nod of assent.

"All agree," he announced. "Let's go spill some paleface blood and avenge our brothers."

"The first ones to come along," Mon-dats said. "We'll kill them before they can even scream."

My heart pounded with anticipation as we grabbed our weapons and headed for the canyon mouth. I even let myself hope that maybe there would be a flame-hair among those who would fall into our trap. I had seen only two flame-hairs in my life, and I would be proud to own a scalp like that. It couldn't help but bring me luck, to have a scalp with such powerful magic as to be the color of fire.

We made our way through the trees along the river that ran along the bottom of the canyon. When I spotted the white man's bridge, I had an idea. "Wait!" I said. "Let's hide under the bridge. It will be the perfect place to wait for our victims. After they've crossed, we'll attack from behind and they won't even see us coming."

Orro-kani placed a firm hand on my shoulder. "Good thinking," he said. "I say we make our burrow under the path that spans the river."

Again, To-ko-witz checked that we were all in agreement, and then he led the way to the bridge. We hunkered beneath it, weapons in hand, our heads tilted upward to listen for any sound of feet on the planks of wood that stretched out into a shelter over our heads.

We were patient. After a time, we heard the sounds of female voices and laughter.

It was difficult to keep my heart calm as the voices grew louder and the sound of feet rattled the boards over our heads. Females had long hair, and long hair made the best scalps. It sounded as if there could be one for each of us. I strained to hear the sound of a male voice, but none came to my ears. It was rare to have women pale-skins out alone—stupid women. Even if they had a firestick, we would be upon them before they could raise it toward us.

After the feet left the bridge, To-ko-witz signaled to us. We slid like shadows into the brush beside the road to make our attack.

Six white women walked along the road ahead, baskets in their hands. I grinned. After the massacre, we could take the baskets, which surely carried food for the pale men cutting trees in our mountains.

So much the better. If we took the lives of women who belonged to the men, they would be wounded in their hearts as well. Even better than that, we would get some white men's food to eat.

I was suddenly hungry. Their bread was so fine compared to the fry cakes made from coarse flour that our women ground with rocks. Too bad for the pale men gathering wood. They would now have to do without food and without women.

Then my eyes stopped on a head of hair the color of spiderwebs. Many whites had light hair of different shades, but something about this hair struck a memory in me. When the smaller woman beside her turned to say something to spider-silk hair, I nearly gasped out loud—it was the face of E-mi-lee, Cox's daughter. And spiderweb hair was Sarah. I knew it without having to see her face.

"Stop!" I hissed.

Orro-kani spun around and scowled at me.

"We cannot do this," I said.

"Why?" Orro-kani demanded. His eyes narrowed into angry slits, his fist wrapped around the shaft of his bow, and his fingers worked the fletching on his arrow.

"I know those women," I said.

"Then you get to kill the ones you know," Orro-kani said.

"No. I cannot kill them. They are daughters of my friend."

"Whites are not our friends," Orro-kani spat. "That's why we're doing this." He shook his head as though despairing of my sanity.

"We must vote," To-ko-witz said. "Who is ready to kill these white maggots and get them off our land?"

Orro-kani nodded his head, and so did the others. I shook my head no.

Orro-kani looked at me as if he would like to kill me.

"We have one against," To-ko-witz announced, not sounding the least bit happy about it. "It is over."

Orro-kani gave a gasp of disappointment loud enough that I was sure the women would hear him. I glanced down the road where the white women were disappearing around the bend. Not one of them looked back.

"You rabbit!" Orro-kani snapped. He stomped off through the forest. I knew his feet were heavier than they needed to be.

A couple of weeks later, I went looking for Cox and found him in his field. As soon as he saw me, his face broke into a smile as broad as the yoke he had on his oxen's shoulders. He showed no sign of fear, even though I had my bow in my hand and a quiver full of arrows slung across my back. "Are you hungry?" Cox asked. "Come, share my lunch," he said. He didn't even hesitate, and I knew I had done right in sparing his daughter's lives, even though I was about as popular in camp as a bloated buzzard.

Cox opened his cloth bag and pulled out some bread and a lump of yellow that he called cheese. It was soft, chewy, and salty, and it tasted delicious.

"Cox," I said, "Don't let your E-mi-lee and Sarah go in the mountains alone any more."

His eyes opened wide in surprise. "Why? What's wrong?"

"They could get dead."

Cox's face darkened. "Is this a threat? Haven't I always been your friend?"

I held up one hand to ward off his sudden anger. I had enough people mad at me back in camp. "It is because you are my friend that your daughters are alive," I said. I told him of our plans, and how I had voted against the massacre.

Cox's eyes got wet, just like a woman's. I looked away so I wouldn't have to see his loss of manhood dripping down his face.

"You are a true friend," he said, his voice tight and garbled with women's water. I was feeling sorry that I had told him anything. Certainly women were valuable property but not worth crying over. Cox's next words redeemed him in my eyes.

"Come to my house tonight," he said. "Come and have all the ice cream you can eat."

Around 1864, Jane Reid, Christena Anderson, Susan Henrie, Liz Johnson, and Sarah and Emily Cox wanted to visit their sweethearts, who were spending the summer cutting timber up in the mountains. Since there had been a month with no hostile Indian activity, their parents agreed to let the girls go. The visit to the timber camp and back was accomplished without any problems.

A few days later, it was learned that a group if Indians had been hiding under a bridge in the canyon on the day the girls made their journey, intent on killing the first whites they saw. The only reason the girls were spared is that one of the Indians in the group was friends with Sarah and Emily's father, Frederick Walter Cox, and recognized the girls. All Indians had to be in agreement for a massacre to be carried out, but this Indian voted no.

Eunice Warner Snow wrote a firsthand account of her troubles with the Indians. On October 4, 1853, she was pregnant with her first child when her husband, John, and his companion, William Mills, were killed by Indians while tending the grist mill at the mouth of Manti Canyon. After the Indians made peace, they said that Eunice's husband had fought desperately, managing to kill an Indian. One wore her husband's necktie on his bare neck, and they showed her his slide rule and penknife, from which they had broken off the ear spoon and button hook.

Once an Indian man came asking Eunice for bread. He wouldn't leave when she told him to, so she beat him with a stick until he cried like a baby. Arropeen said it served him right, and all the Indians called him "squaw" after that. "Squaw" was a more derogatory term than simply calling him a woman.

Sources: Eunice Warner Snow, "A Short Accounting of Troubles and Trials with the Indians," in *Saga of the Sanpitch*, vol. 16 (1984), 30; vol. 29 (1997), 41.

IS THE DOCTOR IN?

An urgent knock sounded at the door. I pushed the cork into a newly filled bottle of cough medicine, set it down, and then hurried to the door, hoping that whoever was on the other side wasn't seriously ill or hurt. My husband was the doctor, not me. Whoever was waiting would have to come back later. Babies have their own timetable, and because my husband was out on a birthing call, I couldn't guess when he'd be home.

I grabbed the handle and pulled the door open. It was worse than I thought. I gasped and took a step back, my eyes widening at the sight of a tall Indian named Brockley standing in the doorway. He didn't smile; in fact, he didn't seem pleased to see me at all. His eyes darted around the interior of the clinic before he jabbed a dark finger at the sign hanging outside. It read, "Teeth extracted with pleasure, without pain, without price."

My heart did a little hop-skip of dread. I hoped against hope that Brockley hadn't come for a tooth extraction. If my husband tried to pull a tooth from this Indian's mouth, I was afraid that Brockley would bite down hard enough to take off one of Joe's fingers. "Dr. Nine-fingers" didn't sound nearly as good as "Dr. Richards."

"White medicine here?" Brockley asked, taking two steps inside but leaving the door open.

I was pretty sure that he meant the white medicine man, so I answered, "No."

"My baby sick," Brockley said. He folded his arms and scowled. "My son need white medicine now. Medicine man no good."

"What's wrong with him?"

"He call on spirits, he shake sacred rattles, and they not listen. Spirits angry."

I nodded as though I'd meant that my question was about the tribal medicine man all along. I wasn't going to be the one to tell Brockley that I'd really been asking about his son.

"And what seems to be the matter with your son?" I asked, making sure there would be no misunderstanding this time.

There was a shift in Brockley's countenance—a hardening around his eyes.

"What illness does he have?" I asked, hoping to correct any faux pas I may have committed.

Brockley folded his arms and narrowed his eyes at me. "He cough all time, *kugh, kugh.*" He demonstrated with a fake cough of his own.

I nodded. "Anything else?"

"He no breathe nose." Brockley shoved two fingers up his nostrils. "Clogged."

I nodded again.

"Him spot here, there, all place." Brockley tapped his fingers in various places all over his cheeks and forehead.

"I think I have something that will help," I said. I stepped over to the bottles lined up in the cupboard and scanned the labels before selecting one. I turned and held it out toward Brockley. "Here."

When he reached for it, I instinctively pulled back a little. I slipped the bottle through my fingers until I held it by the neck in between my thumb and forefinger.

Brockley snatched the bottle with a "humph" of disgust. I could have shown more disgust than that at the fingers he'd had up his nose, but I practiced restraint.

"What is?" Brockley asked, holding the bottle close to his eyes, trying to see through the brown glass.

"Medicine."

Brockley gave me a blank look.

"Give some to your son," I said, and pointed my finger into my mouth.

"Eat?" he asked.

"Yes." I pointed my finger into my mouth again. "He eat medicine." I pointed to the bottle.

Brockley nodded, turned away from me, and headed toward the Indian camp that was a short distance from the fort.

I went back to my task of pouring cough syrup into bottles. I was nearly done when I heard a shout from outside. It sounded as though someone was quite upset about something.

I stepped to the front of the clinic and glanced out the window. What I saw sent a ripple of terror from my head to my feet. Brockley charged straight toward me, a large knife in his hand and murder in his eyes. Something was terribly wrong.

He would be certain to blame me if his child happened to die right after he gave him the medicine I'd put in his hand. He wouldn't wait for explanations either, and I wasn't going to stay and hope that he might ask for one.

I dropped the medicine bottle that I held, heedless of the dark syrup the spilled out onto the floor. My life was worth more than a bottle of cough medicine.

I picked up my skirts and dashed for the back door. I flung it open and darted outside. As I sped down the alley, I heard the front door of the clinic bang open. A crash of glass only served to spur my feet to greater speed. A roar from Brockley's throat sent me flying even faster, my skirt flapping like wings.

I had to get off the street, or else Brockley would spot me and get me for sure. Even while I was running for my life, I had no doubt that Brockley could throw his knife with enough accuracy to hit me squarely in the back. The muscles around my spine tensed and twitched at the very thought. As much as he might love me, my husband didn't possess enough medical magic to repair what would surely be a mortal wound at the hand of a well-muscled Indian fueled by rage. Even if Brockley didn't manage to hit any vital organs, a wound with the knife gripped in his fist would surely cause me to bleed to death in a matter of minutes.

Without stopping to knock, I wrenched open Eunice Brown's door and ducked inside. A bellow of primitive fury sounded from the street outside. I slammed the door shut. Eunice looked up from her potato peeling, her eyes wide with amazement. If Brockley had seen me come in here, I was dead. Perhaps Eunice was too.

"Help me," I begged, my eyes filling with tears. "Please, for the love of God, hide me!"

Without wasting time on questions, Eunice's eyes darted to the spot where the quilt on her bed touched the floor. Then she swept her gaze across the row of clothes hanging on pegs along the wall. She stabbed the potato she held with her paring knife—an uncomfortable reminder of what Brockley intended to do to me. Then Eunice stood and crossed the room, opening the door that led to the lean-to built on the back of her house. "In here."

I darted toward Eunice like a moth to a lantern. As I ran past her, she grabbed my arm and flung me into the space behind the door.

"Stand here," she said, her forehead creased with intensity. "Stay here." She stared at me, and I nodded.

Eunice pushed the door against the wall, trapping me in the little triangle of space next to the door's hinges. She swung a chair up against the edge of the door, a fragile lock to my prison. I watched through the small crack between the door and the wall as Eunice sat down on her stool again and took up her potato and paring knife. She had just pulled the knife out of the partially skinned potato when Brockley burst in through the door.

My knees nearly gave out under me, and I had to clamp my hand over my mouth to keep from screaming with fear.

Brockley ignored Eunice and yanked the cover off the mattress. He bent over and slashed his knife in the space underneath the bed. Then he straightened and glared around the room. I was sure that he could see me and hear my heart banging against my ribs—but his glittering black eyes swept past my hiding place and fastened on the row of clothes hanging against the wall. He strode over to them and slid the flat of his knife against the entire length of clothing. Then he turned and addressed Eunice.

"Where white woman?" he roared. I was trembling so badly that I feared that he would hear my knees knock and stab me right through the narrow gap that I stared through. *This is a stupid hiding place; I'm practically in plain sight. Why did Eunice put me here? I should have run out of the lean-to when I had the chance.*

I was frightened enough when Brockley asked Eunice my whereabouts, but I was struck nearly numb with terror when I saw her lift her hand with the paring knife extended and point straight to my hiding place. She didn't say a word, but her gaze was on me as she betrayed me to certain death.

My eyes rolled back, and I leaned my head against the wall, sagging against the rough logs, heedless of the bark snagging my dress. I recognized my own symptoms—I was going to faint. Then I was going to die.

I could hear Brockley's heavy breathing as he moved toward me. I prayed that the blackness teasing the edges of my mind would close in swiftly enough that I would be oblivious to the hard bite of the steel blade that was coming for me.

Then a horrible thought struck me: *Oh, please, God, no. Don't let him scalp me before he kills me.*

Brockley's tread was so heavy that I could feel the floorboards bend beneath my feet when he reached the door that separated us. I had no doubt that he was strong enough to plunge the knife right through the wooden door and kill me.

Tears burned my eyes, and I squeezed them shut, not wanting to see my death coming. I waited, trembling, stifling the sobs, although I didn't know why I should bother. It was pure instinct, like an animal hiding in its hole, waiting helplessly as the predator digs ever closer at an alarming rate. I waited to die.

It seemed like years before the door moved away from me. I shrank back against the wall. "No, no, it was an accident," I cried. "It wasn't the medicine, it wasn't my fault. Oh, please, don't kill me."

"He's gone," Eunice said, touching my shoulder.

I jumped at her touch, and my eyes flew open. I glanced from side to side, searching for my killer. I couldn't see him anywhere.

I stared at Eunice with wide eyes. "Where'd he go?" I whispered.

"He ran right through," she said. "He's outside somewhere."

I grabbed her by both shoulders. "Why did you tell him where I was?" I demanded, shaking her. "Why?"

Eunice's gaze was steady on mine. "I'm an honest woman," she declared. "I answered his question with a gesture. It's not my fault if he misinterpreted it to believe that you had escaped outside through my lean-to."

I didn't know whether I should hug her or hit her.

She made me sit down and gave me some tea to drink. I stayed in hiding at Eunice's until my husband returned. He'd heard all about what happened between me and the disgruntled Brockley. He'd even stopped in to check on Brockley's baby and found him to be sleeping peacefully. The crisis over, Brockley greeted my husband with great cheer. He explained with a laugh that when he first gave his son some of the medicine, the little boy's toes had curled up and changed color. Certain that he was dying, he'd gone after the murderer—me. He wasn't the least apologetic for his behavior. He thought it was great sport. When he couldn't find me anywhere in the settlement, the brush, or the willows along the creek, he'd returned home and found his son much improved.

Even after that, Brockley never thanked me. Whenever I encountered him, he acted as though I didn't even exist. That suited me just fine.

Doctor Richards covered a spectrum of medical ills, and in the 1850s hung up a shingle that read, "Teeth extracted with pleasure, without pain, and without price." He explained that the pleasure was his, the pain was the patient's, and he would perform the operation for free.

One day, Brockley the Indian was disappointed to find the white medicine man out when he came seeking relief for his baby boy, who apparently suffered from measles. Mrs. Richards gave Brockley medicine that turned the boy's toes up. Certain that his son was dying, the enraged Brockley went after Mrs. Richards with a knife. She ran into Eunice Brown's house, where Mrs. Brown hid her behind the lean-to door before resuming her potato peeling.

When Brockley appeared and demanded Mrs. Richard's whereabouts, Mrs. Brown couldn't bring herself to lie. She gestured toward the lean-to door, and Brockley ran through. Eventually he returned home and found his son much improved.

Sources: Ruth Scow (Mrs. Brown's great-granddaughter), *Song of a Century* (Manti, Utah: Utah Centennial Committee, 1949).

A TOKEN OF LOVE

I glanced around the circle of faces surrounding the campfire. Josiah was still not there, and by now, I was fairly sure he wasn't going to show up.

I tried not to care. After all, he was just a trail hand.

I hid a yawn and then pushed myself to my feet. I felt eyes on me, and glanced down to see the Holman brothers staring up at me with undisguised adoration. I tucked a strand of my fox-red hair behind one ear and favored them with a smile. Then my smile slipped and I turned away. I'd trade every stare I ever got from every man for a single kiss from Josiah.

Oh, why did I have to feel this way? My cheeks warmed as my mind filled with thoughts of him. I'd caught his dark eyes on me enough times to know that he was interested. I admit that I'd flirted with him, and found his confident replies, playful banter, and proud bearing to be downright intriguing.

I headed for the wagon that I had been assigned to share with the Carson family. Their four little boys looked so much alike that I never could keep their names straight, and Emily Carson, the mother of the brood, was in constant need of my help. If I'd wanted to be a mother, I'd had plenty of marriage offers already. I turned them all down for good reasons. Those men were the same bratty boys who'd teased me mercilessly when I was a skinny, pale-as-milk girl with bright red hair. Now it was my turn to tease them with porcelain skin, green eyes, and dark red tresses that drew them like a siren's song.

I looked up at the crescent moon hanging low in the sky. Josiah's earlier warning that no one should ever leave the circle of wagons at night without a guard was positively suffocating. I wanted to walk out into the moonlit night and be by myself.

A strong hand took hold of my arm. I whirled to face my attacker. Josiah grinned down at me, his bronze skin even darker in the night—a perfect backdrop for his arresting white smile. My heart melted, but I didn't let on. I planted one fist on my hip, tilted my chin up, and said, "Unhand me."

Josiah's grin faded, and he let go of my arm. Had I sounded too harsh? He had startled me, but I didn't intend to put him off.

"Sorry, Olivia, but you know you aren't allowed out beyond the wagons after dark without a guard."

I raised one hand to twist a strand of sunset-red hair around my finger. I looked up into Josiah's eyes and asked, "What if I was just wishing on a star?"

"You can do that inside the circle of wagons."

"Well, now that I'm out here, who's going to guard me from the guard?" I nearly laughed out loud at the look on Josiah's face. His eyebrows dipped over his dark eyes and his full mouth twisted ever so slightly underneath his straight nose as he pondered my words. He glanced back over his shoulder, and my heart thudded in appreciation of the sight of his square jaw against the night sky. When he turned back toward me, I glimpsed the dimple in his chin.

Josiah lowered his head, placing it close to mine. "Now, ma'am, that would depend on whether the lady in question wanted guarding or not."

Even in the dim light, I could see Josiah's eyes roving over my face. I hoped he liked what he saw. I turned up the corners of my mouth to make the scenery more pleasant.

"I like to see you smile," Josiah said, his voice husky. "And I'd like to show you something."

My heart caught. "Something I've never seen before?" I teased.

"Not unless you've been through my things." Josiah led the way to the inside of the circle of wagons. I followed him to where his saddlebags rested on the ground. He bent over them and rummaged inside.

I was intrigued. What could he possibly have in there that would be of any interest to me?

Josiah stood and turned toward me with a small silver box in his hand. "It's prettier in the day," he said. "Then the sun lights the scroll work." He lifted the lid, and music spilled out into the night.

I was enchanted. "Oh, that's lovely!"

"It was my mother's."

"It must be very precious," I said.

I could feel Josiah's eyes fastened on me in the silence before he whispered, "It is." Then he stepped in closer, so that the music box was nearly touching us both. I stayed where I was, my face tipped up to Josiah's, my heart thudding an invitation for him to come closer.

"There's something else that's precious to me too," Josiah mumbled.

"And what would that be?" I whispered. I felt a hot stirring inside and my heart grew warm in anticipation. He was going to kiss me at last.

"You." Josiah's lips were so close to my face that his whispered confession felt like the wings of a butterfly against my cheek. I suddenly realized that if he wasn't going to kiss me, then I would surely kiss him.

"Libby!" a small voice lisped.

Josiah pulled away from me and let the music box lid fall closed. My heart sank, and I turned to see one of the little Carson boys, the one who always called me "Libby" instead of "Livvy," pounding his way toward us.

"Ned said he was gonna bite me and make me bleed!" the little Carson shouted, grabbing my skirt and twisting himself around to make me the shield between him and Ned, who was close on his heels.

"Now, Ned, no more of that," I scolded, shaking my finger as Ned skidded to a stop in front of me.

"But he kicked me in the leg!" Ned said in his own defense. "If he hadn't, I would have caught him by now!"

I turned back to Josiah with an apology on my lips, which was far less satisfying than a kiss. But Josiah had picked up the little Carson and was headed toward our wagon. I followed, herding the grumbling Ned ahead of me. I was grumbling too, but not so anyone could hear.

Josiah deposited the boy into the arms of his father and then moved toward me. I was disappointed that he didn't stop, but he touched my hand as he passed. It was no accident. The brief clasp of his fingers shot sudden warmth up my arm and straight into my heart. "Hope your wish comes true," he said, and then he was gone.

I helped get the boys ready for bed, and fell asleep in my own bedroll beneath the wagon.

I woke up to vibrations in the ground beneath me, drumming a warning through my bones. The distant thunder sounded louder and louder. Was it a stampede?

I raised my head. A storm was headed right for me. The strange thing was, it was coming at me along the ground. When the cloud was so close that I smelled dust, I made out the bodies of horses and riders inside it.

Suddenly, my heart seized my ribs and beat against them so hard that my chest hurt. Dark-skinned men rode those horses, their faces painted in inhuman shades and their straight hair fluttering behind them in black whips that beat against their backs.

I screamed.

One of the smaller Carsons sat up and stared at me with frightened eyes. He scrambled to his feet and tottered away from me, straight toward the Indian riders, his mouth open in a wail that was lost in the thundering hooves and shrieks coming from other wagons.

"No!" I screamed. I untangled myself from my blankets and dashed after the toddler. I scooped him up and turned back to the wagon, bending down to thrust the boy into his mother's outstretched arms.

Then Emily Carson did the strangest thing: her eyes widened in horror and she screamed. Startled, I stepped back. What was wrong with Emily? In the next instant, a strong arm circled my waist and lifted me off my feet.

My mouth opened in angry astonishment. How dare anyone grab me? I gave the arm a hard slap, but it didn't let go. It swung me up and sat me sideways smack in front of an Indian warrior astride his horse.

"Let me go!" I screamed, but the brown arm pulled me in tight, forcing my cheek against a bare brown chest of hot, oily skin stretched over hard muscles. A primitive cry rose from the body, tore the air, and stole my breath away. A shiver of absolute terror ripped through my body.

The brown arm clamped me closer still, so that I could hardly breathe. The horse wheeled and broke into a gallop. The circle of wagons faded into the distance.

"No!" I screamed. I renewed my struggles against the Indian that held me and managed to free one arm. I beat on the Indian's chest with my fist.

The Indian laughed and tightened his grip with his knees on his horse so that both of his hands were free. He grabbed my wrist and laughed again, but there was nothing funny about this to me. His amusement inflamed my anger. I would get free of him now or die trying.

I twisted my face into the Indian's chest, opened my mouth, and stuck my teeth into his muscled torso with such force that I blocked my own breathing. I didn't back off, though, not until I had a good grip with my teeth. I bit down with every bit of strength I had, fueled by fear and anger that pounded through me in rhythm with the thud of horse's hooves.

The Indian let out a scream of pain. He turned my wrist loose and grabbed my hair, pulling with all his strength. It felt as if he might rip my head off, but I wouldn't turn him loose. My vision went blurry and I bit down harder. I hoped I was causing him more pain than he was giving me.

Suddenly, the Indian let go of my hair and gave me a sound thump to my head. It hurt, but I still wouldn't let go. I would never let go until he took me back. He hit me again, and again. A chant began in my head that matched the blows of the Indian's fist—*let me go, let me go, let me go.* Then everything went black.

I woke up with a bad taste in my mouth, my head resting on a pillow made of leather.

I forced my eyes open and bright sunlight stabbed my eyes. The smell of horse was strong. I tried to move my head but something held my cheek and wouldn't let go. Then I remembered.

I yanked my face off of the Indian's chest, tearing away the dried blood that had secured my head to my captor's body. The Indian winced as fresh blood leaked out of the wound I'd given him. I was glad. I hoped he'd never heal.

The Indian moved his hand up toward my head. I pulled away but couldn't go far. He murmured something before taking up a section of my hair, and fingering the gleaming strands with great tenderness.

I couldn't help myself. I started to cry. I wanted to be ugly so he would never have taken me in the first place. I knew now that fighting would do me no good. I had a powerful headache to prove it, but I vowed to find a way to escape soon.

When we came within sight of an Indian settlement, I stared at the animal skins stretched over pole skeletons that stood spread-legged along the edge of a stream. The Indians who moved among the crude shelters turned and stared at me before heading toward us with smiles of welcome on their faces and excited chatter flying between them. My captor stopped his horse and waited until another brave jumped from his mount and stood on the ground beside us. Then he slid me down to the arms of this new Indian.

As soon as my feet touched the ground, I renewed my fight for freedom. I would have used my teeth again, but he twisted me around so that I faced out, and clamped me against him. I screamed, and the Indians who were gathering stared at me. I struggled until the Indian who held me lifted me off the ground. I swung my feet back and kicked him in the shins. He grunted and stepped back, dragging me with him.

A sharp command cut through my pounding headache. My feet touched the ground and I stared up into the face of an Indian with a white smear of paint cutting his face in two. A slash of vermilion scarred his forehead. The effect was startling, as was the raw wound on the man's chest. Trails of dried blood streaked his torso and were lost in the deerskin wrapped around his hips.

I pulled my eyes up from the trail of blood and stared into my captor's face. I hoped he would kill me quickly.

He spoke, but I didn't understand anything he said. His tender voice took me completely by surprise. I stared into his eyes and saw a softness in their depths that didn't fit the savage.

My captor called something over his shoulder. An Indian woman carried a wooden bowl over to him. My captor reached his hand into the bowl. I tensed. He drew out a striped cloth that was heavy with water. He moved it toward my face, and I twisted away from him as far as I could, not wanting to be suffocated.

Instead of pressing the cloth against my mouth and nose, my captor touched it to my cheek. With quick, sure strokes he cleaned away the dried blood.

When he finished, he took me by the arm and the other Indian let go. I pulled away, but I couldn't get free. He anchored me to his side with one arm and guided me through the Indians who gaped at me in open-mouthed amazement. I couldn't tell if they admired my red hair or thought I was a devil woman.

When my captor pushed me inside a tepee, I lost my balance and fell onto a fur robe ingrained with the sharp odors of smoke and sour sweat. I rolled onto my back. My captor gazed down at me with a queer light in his eyes. My stomach churned, and I curled into a ball, tugging my nightdress down as far as it would go.

My captor laughed again and left the tepee. I was momentarily relieved, even though I knew I hadn't seen the last of him.

My limbs felt as weak and heavy as wet laundry. I decided to rest a moment before making my plans to escape.

When I awoke, I was alone. This was my chance. I stood up and took a careful step toward the tepee opening.

Suddenly, my captor stepped into the entrance. Even without his face paint, I recognized him. I stumbled and fell back again, angry at myself for my inability to appear strong before this savage. I noticed that the trail of blood had been washed away, leaving only the distinct print of my teeth on his chest.

I sat up and yanked my nightdress down over my calves and feet. My captor lowered himself to the ground, never taking his eyes off me. The sight of the wide prairie beyond him tormented me.

The Indian put his hand out toward me, and I scuttled backward, my eyes wide. I knew I didn't have the strength to stop him, but I would do anything I could to cause him pain if he tried anything.

"Deche," the Indian said in a voice that was surprisingly kind.

I shook my head. "No." I didn't know what he'd said, but I wasn't agreeing to anything.

My captor leaned forward and lifted his hand toward me.

"No!" I said, clutching at my nightdress.

The Indian dropped his arm, his eyes alight with interest. He spoke again, longer this time, gesturing out of the tepee before touching himself on the chest. Then he held his hand toward me again.

I shook my head, and felt my fiery hair dance around my shoulders. I wished that I had some hair pins.

"Bambipe ainga," the Indian said, his eyes fastened on my hair. His mouth turned up in a grin. I was horrified to be reminded that my most vehement protests only served to amuse the savage. Yet I still had my teeth, and I curled my lips back to remind him of that fact.

Suddenly, my captor tossed an object that he held in his open hand toward me. I dodged some type of black bread that sailed past me, and my captor grabbed the hem of my nightdress. I screamed in protest and kicked out at him. He grabbed my feet and held them firm. I shrieked. He put one of his palms out toward my mouth, speaking rapidly to me in his own tongue, his voice low and soothing.

This was a nightmare, but I stopped screaming and forced my mouth closed for fear that he would actually put his hand over my mouth if I didn't.

He stared down at my feet—dead white against his dark skin. His touch was gentle as he slid his brown hands around my ankles. I stiffened, my body protesting any contact with this savage. He spoke again, his voice deep and soft. "Andahtese." His eyes traveled up from my feet, taking in the line of my legs, lingering on my torso before settling on my face.

He obviously did not see me as a devil. I kept my eyes pinned on him, watching for any sudden moves.

Suddenly he pulled back and let go of me. I yanked my feet away and tucked them inside my nightdress.

My captor brought out a square of buckskin and held it out toward me. The buckskin was tanned to a dull white and had several red beads threaded onto two leather strings dangling from the center. I wondered what it was for. The Indian thrust the talisman toward me.

Something stirred in the camp beyond the tepee, and the Indian turned his head. I strained to look beyond him, but I couldn't see anything except a few Indians running past the opening.

My captor turned back to me. He spoke again, his voice raised with urgency. "Bahambia," he said. He thrust the ornament toward me, his arm stretched out. It was obvious that he wanted me to take it.

I stared at the ornament with swaying red beads. If I took it, would he leave? If so, might I make my escape now? I lifted my hand toward the offering.

"Livvy!" The unexpected bellow of Josiah's voice cut through the wall of the tepee.

A flood of joy pushed me up onto my feet. "Josiah!" I screamed. "I'm in here!"

My captor leapt up and stepped outside the tepee. I followed him. The Indian barred my way and again held the buckskin talisman toward me.

I stood looking up at him. What should I do? If I took the talisman would he let me go to Josiah? I bit my lip and put my hand out toward the red beads.

"Don't touch that!" Josiah's command split the air.

I dropped my hand to my side, and the Indian spun around to face the dozen white men from the wagon train, who sat on their horses with rifles in their hands. My heart swelled with joy when I saw Josiah in the lead.

I glanced around the camp, gauging my chances of making a run for it. Several Indian men armed with bows, spears, and rifles watched the white visitors.

My captor accosted the newcomers with a rapid stream of Indian words. Josiah leaned forward in the saddle, his eyes fastened on me, though his words were directed at the men in the posse. "He says he stole her fair and square," Josiah translated.

I felt like a jackrabbit was fighting to get out of my belly. The Indians couldn't possibly keep me here now.

"Will he trade?" Zebedee Carson asked.

"Indians will always trade," Josiah answered. He tore his eyes away from me and slid off his horse. He faced my captor and spoke rapidly in the Indian tongue. My hope soared. Josiah knew how to talk to these Indians. I studied Josiah, my heart swelling with a curious mixture of pride and longing. Josiah stood tall and unafraid. His features etched themselves deep into my heart as I watched him bargain for my life. I was so close to freedom that I yearned to run to Josiah, wrap my arms around him, and never let go. Yet my captor was between us, and I feared that I might make things worse if I gave in to my wild impulses.

Josiah drew out a pocket watch and held it toward my captor. The Indian took the watch and held it to his ear. His eyes grew wide with wonder. Then my captor looked over at me where the sunlight glinted off my fiery hair. He shook his head and pushed the watch back into Josiah's hand.

Josiah pulled away, refusing to take the watch, and spoke in the Indian language again. My captor kept his eyes on me. Several of the Indians who were gathered around murmured among themselves. My captor looked at the white men who sat on horses with rifles across their laps. Then he spoke.

"He says it will take much to exchange for this woman," Josiah translated.

"We will trade," Zebedee Carson said without pause.

My eyes filled with tears as my rescuers opened up their saddlebags and handed out knives, watches, tobacco, and other trinkets. Finally, Josiah pulled out a silver box decorated with scroll work.

"No," I whispered. My hand pressed against my chest. Josiah opened the lid and the Indians gasped when the music spilled out over the camp. My captor reached for the box. Josiah let him take it.

The Indian closed the lid, and opened it again, a smile of delight spreading across his dark face when the music started up again. He turned away from Josiah.

Josiah held his hand toward me. I ran to him, and he boosted me up onto the back of his horse. Then he pulled himself into the saddle and turned away from the camp.

I flung my arms around Josiah's waist and hung on shamelessly. I determined not to let go until the Indians were out of sight.

Just before Josiah turned his horse, my green eyes caught sight of my captor's face. His dark eyes bored into mine as Josiah kicked his horse into a trot and we left the Indian camp behind.

The wagons stood in the same place they'd been that morning. Josiah had to pry me loose before he could get down from his horse. He turned and caught me around the waist and lifted me down, his hands warm through the fabric of my nightdress.

Emily Carson grabbed me up in a hug, bulbous tears rolling down her face. "Oh, Livvy, I was so scared for you."

As soon as Emily turned me loose, a pack of Carson boys crowded around me, tugging on my skirt and asking questions. "Where did you go?" "You scream loud!" "I got an owie!" "You made Mama cry." "Are you an Indian now?"

Zebedee Carson waded in. "Now, boys, quit pesterin' Livvy. Go get your Mama some firewood."

Josiah took my arm and led me away from the Carson wagon. "You certainly livened things up around here for a bit, but things will soon get back to normal."

I looked up into Josiah's face and felt my heart twist with disappointment. I never wanted things to be the same again.

"Are you all right?" Josiah asked.

I lowered my head and nodded, fighting tears.

Josiah's hand wrapped around one of mine. When he spoke, his voice came out low, "I couldn't have gone on without you."

I lifted my head and looked into Josiah's eyes, which were dark and soft as night.

"Thank you for rescuing me." My heart caught in my throat. "I'm real sorry about your music box."

"Don't be," Josiah said. "I'd give anything for you."

My heart skipped a beat, and I wiped my eyes. "Anything?"

Josiah's voice didn't even waver when he said, "I'd die for you, Olivia."

Tears burned my eyes, blurring Josiah's features. "Well, if you'd died rescuing me, it wouldn't have done me much good."

"It came awfully close."

"What?"

"We were nearly too late."

"Why?"

"The marriage token," Josiah said.

I was taken completely aback. I didn't remember any marriage token.

"That scrap of skin with the beads was an offer of marriage. If you had taken it, you would have been married to the man who offered it to you. We would have had to battle to the death if we were to take you back with us."

"But you were outnumbered." A shiver of dread ran down my spine.

"I'd have fought for you." Josiah's eyes burned the truth of his words into me. He pulled me in against him and wrapped me in his arms. I leaned my head against his chest and felt his heart beat strong and hard beneath my ear. I knew I belonged there.

"Thank goodness you warned me in time," I said. I tipped my head up at him and asked, "How did you know what it was? And how in the world did you learn their language?"

Josiah's eyes wavered for just an instant, before he straightened and said, "My father was Indian."

My stomach swooped the same way it had when I'd been lifted up onto the Indian's horse. "Your father?" I asked, not wanting to believe it. "He stole a white woman?"

"He didn't steal her," Josiah said, his eyes flashing indignation. "My mother went willingly."

I stared into Josiah's hard, black eyes that were alive with passion. Under my gaze, his eyes softened. "It wasn't like what happened to you," Josiah said. "Mama loved my ah-pey—my father."

Josiah took my hands. I looked down at my white hands buried in his brown ones. They looked good together.

"I believe that a woman should have some say in who she spends her life with," Josiah said.

"I'm glad."

"What would you say to spending your life with me?"

I grinned and pulled one hand free, lifting it to Josiah's head. I slid my fingers through his black hair. "I'd say someone's got to watch over the guard."

Josiah grinned and gave in to the pressure of my hand on the back of his neck. Our lips met.

When Josiah pulled away, he slid one finger down my cheek. Then his eyebrows locked together in mock severity. "Here, now. You'd better change."

I had the decency to blush when I realized that I was still clad only in my nightdress. But after what I'd been through today, it seemed a small matter.

"Why?" I asked. "It's going on evening. I'd just have to change again before I go to bed." I looked up at the clear sky—the pinks of sunset beginning to dust the western horizon. "Anyway, I don't want to miss the sunset. It looks like it's going to be a good night for wishing on a star."

This is a compilation of various experiences I've read about from the 1800s in which Indians captured white women and children with the intent of assimilating them into their tribes. Sometimes ransoms were arranged, but sometimes the captives couldn't be found, and the missing white people were left to their new lives. In some instances when the whites were found at a later time, they were happy in their new lives in the Indian camp and chose to stay with the tribe.

Andahtese: another person
Bambipe: hair
Ainga: red
Deche: quiet
Bahambia: wife
Ah-pey: Father

A LIFE FOR A LIFE

Will Probert dashed through my office door, his cheeks as red and shiny as a newly washed apple and his breath coming as hard and heavy as an apple thief running from the orchard owner. "Bishop!" he said, "Black Hawk's kin just got a beating!"

I jumped out of my chair. "Where? Is he hurt bad?"

Will shrugged. "Who knows? He got knocked around some, beaten down. Then he broke free and made it to his horse. He lit out of here on his own power, but he was bleeding pretty bad."

I stared at Will. "What was the provocation?"

"I wasn't there for the first of it," he said. "I just came at the end." Then he raised a warning finger and shook it at me. "But it's not the end, Henry."

My stomach dropped at his warning. I didn't want to hear about any more trouble, even though trouble was all that we seemed to be having lately when it came to Indian matters. This was war.

In nearly every church meeting I'd conducted since before the war began, I'd spoken of our need to show the Indians mercy—to set the example for kindness. What I didn't speak of was Chief Black Hawk's personal promise to me.

I had made the acquaintance of the chief when I'd been called as bishop three years earlier, and we had struck up a friendship. I found him a fascinating study; he was a mix of old traditions and new knowledge, since he had attended a white man's school as a child. I respected the aging Indian, and didn't wish any harm or trouble to come upon him or his people.

Only a few months earlier, the chief had met me on the road. We greeted each other warmly, and then he stopped speaking and fixed me with his eyes—black and solemn. I, too, fell silent, a sudden uneasiness creeping over me.

"You needn't worry," Black Hawk said at last, his deep voice rumbling. "I promise no harm will come to you and your family."

"Well, uh, thank you," I stammered, not sure why the chief figured he needed to make such a promise. We had always gotten along. We shared our food and clothes with the Indians and they shared their knowledge of survival in this wilderness with us.

It was only after my impromptu meeting with Black Hawk that trouble started in earnest between our two cultures. A few Indians tried to help themselves to some cattle that were grazing in the fields, and the owners tried to stop them. Arrows and bullets flew, and several whites were killed. Then word came that several Indians had been killed in another skirmish, then more white men, then both. The news from other settlements was that war was escalating.

"You know it's an eye for an eye to an Indian's way of thinkin,'" Will said, bringing my mind back to the present problem.

I knew.

"When I was staying over by Scipio, an Indian by the name of Panacara got killed," Will said. "It was a terrible mistake. Panacara was a friend to us. He came vistin' at the fort, and turned in his gun just like he was supposed to. But then one of them whites with a chip on his shoulder follered him real sneaky like and shot him."

Will scratched his chin. "It was a terrible loss, just terrible. And if that wasn't bad enough, Panacara's close friend Nun-ka-tots started follerin' me around. I thought at first that maybe he was just lonesome, but he proved otherwise.

"Came a day I was driving a wagon load of wheat past Mud Lake. When I happened to glance down into the water, I caught sight of a mighty strange reflection. I stared at it, ponderin,' before I realized I was lookin' at a rifle barrel stickin' up in the air. I wondered why I couldn't see it from the road 'til I realized that whoever was lyin' in ambush for me was crouched behind a mound of earth up ahead.

"I drew my wagon up short and pulled out my gun. Before I could get into firing position, I heard scrabblin', and then Nun-ka-tots lit out of there fast as he could go.

"After that, he quit follerin' me around. Then it was a long time before he spoke to me. First thing he sez is, 'You tobuck?'" Will tipped his head toward me. "That means 'angry,' in case you didn't know."

"What did you say?" I asked.

Will raised his eyebrows. "I told him I wasn't tobuck, but why'd he try to kill me anyway? That Indian just looked at me and sez that they avenge their dead by killing one of the enemy—doesn't matter who, it's nothing personal, but they've got to kill one of their enemy in order for their tribesmen's spirit to rest."

I felt a chill roll down my spine. "But you said the Indian boy, Black Hawk's kin, got away."

"He was hurt bad, though. Can't tell if he'll make it. You know, some people die from injuries long after the fact."

I knew. With the way things had turned between our people, and Chief Black Hawk's own kin being so brutally treated in our town, how could I hope to hang on to the promise that he'd made to me? And why did I think I deserved special consideration over anyone else in town? Surely the war made everything that had been said earlier null and void.

The next Sunday, we waited and waited for my son William and his wife, Martha, to come over for supper. They came every Sunday for supper. As it grew later and later, I paced the floor until, finally, I could wait no longer. I got on my horse and rode for my son's place. I was too late. I found Martha weeping and William dead—killed by an Indian arrow.

Black Hawk had lied to me. Even though I'd tried to convince myself that his promise couldn't possibly matter anymore, I found myself furious that he hadn't kept his word. His promise was worthless.

I couldn't leave Martha there alone with her grief, so I took her home with me. Because of her, I held back my tears.

When my wife caught sight of our daughter-in-law, she began to cry before she even heard the news. She had already suspected the worst, and Martha's red, tear-splotched face confirmed it. The women fell together, sobbing, and I sank into a chair with my head in my hands.

I didn't feel like I would ever smile again. What a senseless waste of a young man's life. I prayed earnestly, searching for any shred of peace to soothe my aching heart. But the gap of sorrow was just too big to fill with prayer—I wanted revenge.

I knew this was wrong, so I shut myself in my room and begged for forgiveness. A shadow of comfort crept into a corner of my heart, but it vanished when I opened my eyes and stepped out of the seclusion of my room. I tried in my office with the same result. I prayed several times a day, but the core of anger and hurt remained.

If only William had been taken by illness. Then I would know that his death was the Lord's will. His murder was too arbitrary. He was in the wrong place at the wrong time. His life had been stolen from him, from Martha, and from me. It was all so pointless and cruel; I couldn't seem to wrap my heart around it and soften the sorrow.

It was a long and heavy-hearted week later that found me walking toward home with my hands clasped behind my back and my head bowed. A shadow fell across my path, but I didn't look up right away.

I simply couldn't take even one more expression of sympathy from someone who still had their son and had no idea what I was feeling with the loss of mine.

At last, I raised my eyes to see Chief Black Hawk standing before me. His back straight, he fixed his dark eyes on my face. My eyes slid to his hand, which wrapped around the handle of a large knife.

A sudden, fierce anger shot through me. Had the chief come to pick off another of the Kearns family? My fists curled, my jaw clenched, and I stared up into his face, unblinking, to prove that I wasn't afraid.

Chief Black Hawk stared back at me with eyes as deep and black as an open grave at midnight. He regarded me for a solemn moment before lowering his gaze to the ground. A surge of triumph crowded in with the anger in my heart. I had cowed the mighty chief.

"My grandson died," he murmured.

A strange sense of perverse jubilation gripped me. I would not say I was sorry.

"His brother sought vengeance and killed your son." There was no triumph in Black Hawk's voice, only sorrow. I gritted my teeth at the sudden wave of grief that threatened to overtake me at this blunt reminder of my son's death.

Black Hawk gripped the edges of his shirt and ripped them apart, baring his bronze chest. "I am ready to die in exchange for the life of your son." Black Hawk threw his knife at my feet. He dropped his hands and pulled his shoulders back, making his bare chest an easy target.

His words hit me like a mad bull. I stepped back, dizzy at the prospect of striking Black Hawk dead. My stomach turned over, sickened by the thought of stabbing a knife into his old, brown flesh.

At last, the anger fled completely from my heart, and I put my hand up toward Black Hawk. "I do not wish to kill you," I said, and I meant every word. "I do not wish to kill any of your people." I stopped and swallowed the lump in my throat that threatened to break my words into sobs. "I only want us to stop fighting."

Black Hawk relaxed his shoulders, and his eyes found mine again. "We are still friends?" he asked, his eyebrows rising.

I nodded. "Friends."

Black Hawk put his hand out and clasped mine, his grateful smile big enough to wrap around my heart. "Friends."

Before the Black Hawk War began in 1865, Chief Black Hawk struck up a friendship with Bishop Hamilton Henry Kearns of Gunnison, Utah. The Indian chief promised that Kearns and his family would always be safe.

Then one day in 1865, Black Hawk's grandson rode into town and was beaten and driven away. A little while later, perhaps in retaliation, the Bishop's son, William, was killed by an Indian arrow. When Black Hawk heard of the incident, he sought out Bishop Kearns, bared his chest, and declared himself ready to die for the loss of Kearns's son. Instead of killing Black Hawk, Kearns said that he just wanted the fighting to stop.

Before his death, Chief Black Hawk visited all the towns that had received the brunt of warfare during the Black Hawk War and apologized for fighting with them.

William Probert wrote a letter in 1912 in which he described an event that happened to him on the road from Deseret to Scipio in the 1860s after a peaceable Indian named Panacara was murdered by a white man named Ivie.

According to Indian custom, it was a life for a life, and it didn't matter who died in place of the Indian who had been killed. Panacara's friend Nun-ka-tots stalked Probert and then hid along the trail in ambush. Probert saw the reflection of a rifle in Mud Lake and then saw the Indian's reflection. Nun-ka-tots fled and avoided Probert for seven years. Finally, the Indian asked the white man if he was angry with him. When Probert said no, they became friends.

Sources: *Saga of the Sanpitch*, vol. 27 (1995), 5; vol. 3 (1971), 27.

A DYING CURSE

“Millicent!” I called. I wiped a drip of sweat off of my forehead, muttering under my breath. Millie couldn't be very far away. Why wasn't she answering?

“Millicent!” I called again. I rounded a bush and caught sight of my little sister standing stock still. That certainly wasn't in her nature.

“Millie?” I said, my voice ringing with impatience. She still didn't move. What was the matter with her? Even when she slept, she moved about on her mattress with such energy that it was not unheard of for her to end up on the floor by morning. Now she stared at something I couldn't see, her hands frozen around the waist of her little cloth doll.

I moved toward her and finally saw what she was looking at. An Indian was only a quarter mile away from my little sister, moving steadily closer. He was flanked by two half-grown Indian boys.

Without even pausing, the trio of Indians marched right past the boundary rock that marked the edge of town. I was aghast. The Indians had promised that they would never venture beyond the boundary rock and into the city limits.

I dashed toward my sister. She didn't even look at me. “Millie!” I called.

“Look, Robert,” she said, pointing her little finger toward the dark-skinned visitors. “Indians.”

I scooped my sister up into my arms, and then turned and ran. It felt like miles before we reached home and burst in through the door. “Indians,” I exclaimed.

My mother clenched her hand over her heart. “Where?”

“Inside the boundary rock.”

“Go get help,” Mama said. She took Millicent from me. “Be quick.”

I dashed out the back door and ran toward the center of town. I didn't find my father, but I called out to every man I saw. “Indians! Indians in town!” Within minutes, there were a dozen men running for horses and weapons.

“Lead the way,” Clive Austin called out to me.

When we reached the boundary stone, the Indians were no longer there. I wondered if the men would think I was just crying “wolf.” I really started to worry about my reputation until someone shouted, "Over there!"

I looked to where the man pointed at the northeast hills and spotted the three Indians on the run. With a sigh of relief, I turned toward home.

A voice rose from the assembly. "Let's get 'em."

Another voice agreed. "Yeah, let's show 'em they can't get away with that!"

A couple of new men came riding up on horses. "Where are those Injuns?" one asked.

"There!"

The horsemen took off after the fleeing Indians. Even though there was no hope of matching their pace, I joined several of the other men who took to their heels and chased after the horsemen.

By the time I caught up to where the horses had stopped, the Indian man and one of the boys were on the ground. The boy, who looked to be about the same age as me, was covered with blood and lying perfectly still, his dark eyes staring up unblinking at the hot, blue sky.

The horsemen were off their horses now, standing over the Indian who clutched at a bloody wound on his chest and grimaced with crooked teeth showing white against the dark skin of his face.

The Indian's eyes turned toward the still youth lying a few yards away. "Ash-tay mik-takken," he muttered, his eyes wet with tears.

"The other one got away," Clive Austin snapped. "But not for long."

"You," the Indian said, his face hard. "We come for pannah," he gasped. "No fight."

"What's pannah?" I asked the guy standing next to me.

"Bread. Those Indians are always after our bread."

"My sons," the Indian clenched his teeth. His dark eyes flicked to the corpse of his son, and then they blazed as he looked at the white men standing above him. "We only come for bread. My sons had no weapons. We meant no harm."

"Easy for you to say now." One of the men said. Then he turned away. "Why are we standing here? I've got work to do."

"I curse you for this cruelty," the Indian said.

An eerie silence fell over the group. Even the man who was in such a hurry to get away stopped and looked back at the Indian as if he couldn't help himself. The Indian's breath came out raspy and weak, but the determination behind his soft words gave them power.

"This ground that soaks up the lifeblood of my innocent son will hold the power of life and not let it free." The Indian gasped and then grimaced. His dark eyes swept the group. "Anyone who inhabits this ground shall have no posterity."

A silence followed his pronouncement. The old Indian let out a moan that chilled my bones. His hand slid off his bloody chest and flopped to the ground, his red fingers curling up toward the sky like the claw of a dead crow that I had found out in the desert one day.

My heart squeezed with pity for the dead Indian, concern for his sons still etched on his face. Even though I feared them, this Indian had only been trying to feed his boys. There was something about him that reminded me of my own father.

Without waiting to see what anyone else was going to do, I turned away from the place of death and headed for home. I needed to find my father.

Arlea Howell told me this story and showed me the boundary stone. Her aunt and uncle owned a house on the very property in Spring City, Utah, where the Indian had died. Although her aunt and uncle had four children when they moved in, they had no more children afterward. In addition, none of their four children had any offspring, a fact that matches the curse pronounced by the dying Indian.

In the mid-1900s, the skeleton of an adolescent was found in the hills east of Spring City. Tests showed that the skeleton was male and was dated between 100 and 150 years old. Arlea speculates that it was the skeleton of the Indian boy who escaped into the mountains but didn't escape death after all.

Ash-tay-mik-taken: have peace, my son
Pannah: bread

MASSACRE

I lay in my elk skin bed, listening to Ah-peh's worried voice. "But Tin-Dup had a dream," Ah-peh said to Pee-Kage, my mother. "In it, the pony soldiers came into camp and killed all his people."

I shivered in my bed. I'd never seen a pony soldier, but I'd heard about them. They rode horses and carried long sticks called "rifles" that killed people from great distances. I hoped I would never see one in my whole life.

"But what can we do?" Pee-Kage asked. "It is the middle of winter camp. We have nowhere else to go."

"We don't know when it will come to pass, but we have been forewarned. We will watch and wait. I have checked my arrows, as have the other men in camp."

I let my breath out in relief. Ah-peh and the other warriors would keep us safe from the palefaced pony soldiers. Still, not every family had a father, and the warriors of our village had wives, children, and parents. There were more people to take care of than our warriors could defend.

"Ah-peh?" I said.

"Oh, Wy-Ve-Dah, have you been listening when you should be sleeping?" Ah-peh's voice was full of gentle reproach.

"I wasn't asleep," I said, wishing I had been. The even breathing of my older sister, Luc-Ce, beside me made me envious that she was ignorant of Tin-Dup's dream. She would sleep well all night long.

"Well, let me tell you a story about Toowats the eagle, and see if I can help you fly away to the land of good dreams." I settled down into my bed, comforted by the sound of my father's voice, and soon lost myself in sleep.

The next morning I snuggled down into my elk skin bed and squeezed my eyes shut tight. If I pretended not to be awake, then my mother wouldn't notice my eyes open and make me get up into the cold morning.

But Luc-Ce knew that I was faking. "Get up, lazy," Luc-Ce said, giving me a nudge.

"But the bed is so warm," I murmured.

"You will be warm after you get up and move around." Luc-Ce had no sympathy at all. "You need to help with chores too."

Pee-Kage gave me a nudge. "Come on, Wy-Ve-Dah, or no more stories for you at night. I've made some corn cakes for breakfast. You know you like them."

I tried to decide which I liked better, breakfast or staying in bed. Luc-Ce picked up our baby brother, Tah-Sah-Pun, and touched noses with him. Tah-Sah-Pun squealed with delight, but Luc-Ce's smile faded.

"He's wet!" she complained, holding him out away from her. Tah-Sah-Pun kicked his little legs in the air and squealed.

"There's dry moss in the deerskin bag," Pee-Kage said. "Pack some in the backboard and strap him in for me, will you?"

"You silly boy," Luc-Ce said, laying Tah-Sah-Pun down on a pile of skins so she could take up the backboard. It was easy to be delighted with Tah-Sah-Pun no matter what he did. Not only was he our father's only boy, but he had such a good nature that we couldn't ever stay cross with him.

Luc-Ce looked over at me. "Now, see, Wy-Ve-Dah? It's not one bit too cold for Tah-Sah-Pun. He's a big strong warrior, aren't you, Tah?" Luc-Ce lowered her face down close to Tah-Sah-Pun's and he grinned and grabbed one of her long, black braids.

Just then, our father stuck his head inside our shelter. "Who is going ice fishing with me?" he asked.

"I will!" I answered. I loved spending time with my Ah-peh. He was the kindest man in the whole village, and he hardly ever scolded me as I'd heard other fathers do to their daughters. He said it was because I was such a good girl—I didn't need scolding.

Ah-peh lowered his eyebrows in mock severity. "Have you eaten yet?"

"No, but I will right now."

"Then I will wait outside for you. I've got to make you a spear."

I bounced up and down with delight.

Tah-Sah-Pun was snuggled into his backboard, and Pee-Kage slid him onto her back. There was not a chance that he would get cold outside because he was bundled up so well. Neither would Pee-Kage have to change his moss all day, as it would absorb everything he could possibly do to it, and we would only change the moss that night when he was put to bed.

A frightened shout sounded from outside the tepee. Although I was used to people calling to one another throughout our village, this was different. My mind immediately recalled Ah-peh's somber face the night before, when he'd told Tin-Dup's dream to my mother. Sudden fear gripped me, and I wanted to crawl back into bed.

Pee-Kage moved to the doorway of our shelter to look out, and Tah-Sah-Pun stared at me from his place on her back, his round, black eyes solemn. I smiled at him, even though I didn't feel it inside of me, and he gave me a big grin in return.

"Luc-Ce! Wy-Ve-Dah! Come here!" my mother screamed. Since she almost never yelled at us, the sharpness of her voice made my lip quiver.

I moved with Luc-Ce to our mother's side. I turned to look in the same direction my mother had. The hillside swirled with white mist. Through the mist I saw men riding horses—men dressed all the same and wearing funny little clothes on their heads. Some of the strange riders also carried long sticks. My heart leaped up into my throat and I choked. Pony soldiers!

Pee-Kage grabbed my hand in one of hers, and Luc-Ce's hand with her other. She began to run away from the soldiers riding toward us. I threw one look back over my shoulder and saw Ah-peh running toward the enemy, his bow in his hand and his arrow pouch slung over his shoulder.

Ah-peh would protect us. Comforted by the strength of my father, I faced forward and struggled through the snow. It was awfully deep, and my legs were so much shorter than Pee-Kage's that it was hard to keep up with her. It felt as though she might pull my arm from off of my body. I dragged behind her, trying my best to make my legs move faster. Tah-Sa-Pun watched me from his place on Pee-Kage's back.

Loud sounds as sharp as a dog's bark sounded behind me. The barks came louder and more often, sounding like thunder or the growl of an angry bear.

Pee-Kage stumbled, and I nearly fell. Then I saw Luc-Ce tumble forward into the snow. Pee-Kage let out a loud cry—a frightening sound that made Tah-Sah-Pun scrunch his little face up in worry.

Pee-Kage slowed her steps and glanced back at Luc-Ce. I thought my mother would stop and help my sister up, but she didn't. Instead, she held tighter to my hand and pushed forward.

"Luc-Ce!" I called, my eyes drawn to my sister. She didn't answer, or move. She lay face down in the snow, her head and back stained bright red.

I tore my eyes away from my dead sister and let loose a cry of anguish from my aching heart. Tah-Sah-Pun let out a wail, his little face twisted up in fear and misery. Now we were all crying, and running as best we could through the deep snow—running for our lives.

We struggled along beside the river, with other people from our village who were running too. The barking was getting closer and closer. Several other people fell into the snow—fell and lay still, never to move again. I watched as some of the women leaped into the ice-edged river with baby boards on their backs, and children clutched to their chests. Even though the run through the deep snow had warmed me, I couldn't imagine how cold the river water must be. Although too swift to freeze up completely, the water had to be as cold as ice.

Then, impossibly, in mid-wail, Tah-Sah-Pun fell silent. I tore my eyes from the people who were screaming and struggling against the rushing water and glanced up at my baby brother. A bright, red ribbon of blood ran down his tiny forehead into his eyes which were open but unseeing. Little Tah-Sah-Pun with the bright smile and ready laugh was dead.

"No!" I cried, my heart twisting in pain like a snake caught in a thorn bush.

Pee-Kage stumbled forward a few more steps before her legs buckled and she went down. "Mama!" I shouted, but she lay still. Her body on both sides of the backboard was covered with bleeding wounds.

I knew I could never lift her. Terrified, I tried to run. I struggled to escape through the deep snow on my own, but without my mother to pull me along, I could hardly move.

The vibration of hoofbeats drummed through the ground, and I screamed. Then my heel exploded in a burst of hot, searing pain, and I pitched forward into snow that was stained as red as fire. Then all went dark.

A voice spoke to me in the language of white men. I opened my eyes and flailed my arms. The pony soldiers had killed my brother, my sister, and my mother. "Ah-pey!" I screamed.

A voice said something in soft, soothing tones. I looked up into the face of a lady with wrinkles by her eyes—kindly wrinkles like old Tabio in my village had worn.

I was so cold. I had no more fight in me. This white woman was not a pony soldier, so I stopped swinging my arms and let her and her man take me to their home in Franklin, Idaho. They gave me the name of Margaret Young, and I grew up among them, as the only one of my family to survive.

I am grateful to the palefaces that saved me and gave me a white man's name, but in my heart, I am always Wy-Ve-Dah.

This story was related to me by Keith Burdick, whose great-great-great-grandmother Wy-Ve-Dah (Margaret Young) was at the Bia-Ogoi (Bear River) as a little girl on January 29, 1863, when Col. Patrick Connor brought his troops down upon the Shoshone winter camp in what is now Idaho. Some of the Indians attempted to escape by jumping in the river, but they drowned or were shot. Some soldiers dashed babies against the frozen ground and ravaged the wounded Indian women. A group of Mormons from Franklin, Idaho, eventually rescued two wounded Shoshone women and five children. Wy-Ve-Dah was adopted by Brigham Young and given the name of Margaret.

LITTLE INDIAN EMISSARY

"Hey, Will, do ya want to eat with us?" Sapinay asked.

"Sure!" I said. "Will eating your mother's cooking make me as tall as you?"

Sapinay grinned. "No way! You eat too much white man's food. You'll never catch up to me."

"I notice that you don't mind eating my Mama's biscuits," I said.

"It would be worth it to be a shorty like you if I could eat them every day," Sapinay said. "Come on."

I trotted beside Sapinay through the gully that led to his family's camp. Truth is, I was tired of our winter diet of salt pork and biscuits, and nothing green had come up in the garden yet, so I was plenty eager to taste something new.

Sapinay ran into the tepee without pausing, but I stopped outside and tried to rub some of the dirt off my hands. It was a habit from home that was hard to break. I admired the fact that Sapinay and his family never bothered with the task of washing their hands before they ate.

Even though I'd been friends with Sapinay for years, I'd never eaten anything his mother had made except some dried venison he gave me while we were out playing. Now I ducked into the tepee right behind Sapinay, and his mother looked up from where she squatted by the fire. She grinned at me, showing several missing teeth.

I'd seen her use a matata, or stone bowl, to grind grain and nuts in. She would crush seeds or whatever was in there with several sharp twists of her wrist, using a smooth rock that just fit the curve of her hand. Sapinay told me that he often found grit in his food from the bits of rock that had worked loose from the grinding bowl. Perhaps his mother had a gap-toothed grin because her teeth had broken on pieces of grit. Maybe eating with Sapinay wasn't such a good idea after all. But if I left now, I might appear to be rude.

I rubbed my hands on my pant legs. Maybe I'd be all right if I just took my time and chewed carefully.

Sapinay's mother reached over and plucked a piece from a mass of black dough that sat in a woven basket on the ground at her side. She slapped the handful of dough onto her bare thigh, turning it and slapping it again and again until she'd flattened it. Then she lifted it off her leg and tossed it onto a flat rock set next to the fire. It hissed, and my stomach squeezed itself into a nervous little lump.

"Uh, Sapinay, what is that?" I asked.

Sapinay's eyes widened in anticipation. "Cricket cakes."

"Cricket?" The only crickets I knew of were the big, black bugs with stringy antennae and tiny little heads. They were definitely not something I would ever want to eat.

"Do you know what?" I said. "I'm not really all that hungry."

Sapinay cast a sideways look at me. "Well, then, how about if I follow you home and you can give me your biscuits?"

Sapinay's mother interrupted. "You two are so hard to understand," she said. "You don't speak all Indian."

Sapinay glanced at her. "Will speaks our tongue as well as I do."

She tipped her head from side to side as she spoke. "Sometimes you say words I know, and sometimes you say other words, like Will's words."

Sapinay and I grinned at each other. We hadn't even realized that we'd been mixing Indian words with English. We just used whatever language came to mind to say what we wanted to say.

Even though Mama had been after me for the past couple of years to stop hanging around with Sapinay, I hadn't paid her much mind. I knew that her complaints weren't against Sapinay himself but were based on the fact that Black Hawk had been waging war against the whites. It was hard to figure out who started it, but I'd heard that Black Hawk had been caught taking food from a storehouse and had nocked an arrow at his accusers, only to have a bucket thrown over his head. It was quite an insult to have a bucket thunked over top of you just as you were fixing to shoot someone with an arrow. Mama got more vocal whenever someone was attacked and killed, but I wasn't worried. I didn't even feel like a white boy half the time.

"Mama, it wasn't Sapinay and his bunch that did it," I'd say whenever Mama warned me to stay away.

"Well, the ones that did it used to be friendly too. You just never know when someone's going to turn on you, for reasons you don't even understand."

"Sapinay's like my brother," I said. "Nothing's going to happen to me, and I won't let anything happen to him."

I still believed my own words. My worst danger from Sapinay was death by cricket poisoning.

Still, I wished the fighting would stop. If it didn't, we all might be dead soon.

Then, one day, Sapinay told me that Black Hawk was done fighting. I told him that the whites would want a treaty. I never meant to volunteer to act as go-between, but that's how it turned out.

I was home one day when someone knocked on our door. Mama answered it, and then came to my room. "Will? There's a man here who wants you to go to a meeting with him."

"A meeting?" My heart sank like a rock in a river. I hated meetings. "Do I have to?"

"I really think you should. It sounds important."

Important meetings were the worst. Why couldn't we ever do something fun, like have a game of marbles or stick pulling and talk over business while we played?

"Do I have to wear my Sunday clothes?"

Mama smiled, and the worry lines on her forehead cleared. "No, it's not that kind of meeting. Come on."

I followed her out to the parlor and saw a man dressed in a suit coat and trousers. Although dusty, his shoes didn't show a single scuff mark. I wondered if they were brand new. I hadn't seen brand new shoes in years. I didn't usually bother to wear shoes myself, but I did like to slip on moccasins if ever I felt the need to cover my feet.

"Will Frandsen?" the man asked.

"Yes."

"Come along with me."

I looked up at Mama and she gave me a nod. "It's all right, Will," she said. "Go with the man. I'll make you some sugar cookies for when you get back."

I followed the man outside and saw a fine buggy sitting in the street in front of our house. I noticed that it made our house look poorer by comparison.

I climbed up into the buggy beside the man. I wondered if this was what kings felt like. I wished that Sapinay were with me.

The man got the buggy rolling, and in short order we drew up in front of city hall. I took my time climbing down, wondering if I'd ever get to ride in a buggy as fine as that again.

I followed the man inside. There were several other men sitting in chairs and visiting with one another. They stopped talking as soon as we walked in, and they all turned to look at me. "What?" I demanded. I felt like a bug in a jar.

One man, who wore a beard around his chin without a mustache, stood up and faced the man who'd brought me here. "Is this the boy?" he asked. It didn't sound as though he approved, so I stood up straighter and looked him in the eye.

"This is him."

The bearded man's eyebrows went up and he rubbed his chin. He glanced back at the other men. No one said anything, but all their eyes were still on me.

The man with the beard bent down and asked, "Are you Will?"

"Yes."

"Can you really speak the Indian tongue?"

I didn't like him treating me like a little kid, so I answered in my best Shoshone, "Of course I can. Can't you?"

One man in the back of the room with a scar on his nose burst into laughter. The others looked at him with their eyebrows raised.

"Good answer, boy," the man with the scar said, wiping his eyes.

The man with the beard looked at the man who had spoken. "What did he say?"

The scarred man shrugged. "He said he could speak their language, President Young." Then he winked at me. I grinned back at him.

President Young turned back to me, and now his expression seemed more friendly. "Son, do you know that Chief Black Hawk has agreed to end this war?"

"Yeah, Sapinay told me."

"We need someone to go up into the mountains and tell Black Hawk and the other war chiefs that we are here to sign the treaty. Do you know what a treaty is?"

"Yes," I answered. "I go to school, and I listen too."

By now, several of the men sitting in the room were wearing smiles. The bearded man had his hand up over his mouth. I couldn't see if he was smiling or not, but his eyes were crinkled. Maybe he was stifling a sneeze.

"Would you accept the assignment to get Black Hawk and his war chiefs to come and sign this treaty?"

"Why, yes, I would," I said. "Can I take Sapinay with me?"

The bearded man glanced over his shoulder at the others. No one objected. "Whatever you need to do in order to accomplish your mission," he said.

I narrowed my eyes at him when a sudden thought struck me. "This isn't some sort of trick, is it?"

President Young looked genuinely surprised. "What kind of trick could it be?"

"That you're going to send some army men to follow me. Men with guns."

"No, of course not."

"So it's true," the scarred man said. "He's like an Indian himself. He thinks like one."

"Why don't any of you want to do it?" I asked, my mind alive with suspicion.

"They don't know us like they know you," President Young said. "We don't know where they are, either. We need your knowledge of the Indians to contact them for us. You're our emissary."

I thought it over. "All right. I'll go, as long as Sapinay can come."

"Certainly. We'll wait here."

"No tricks?"

"No tricks. In fact, I'd like to give you a blessing before you leave."

I was genuinely surprised. "What for?"

"So you'll be safe from the Indians."

I snorted. "I'm as safe with them as I am right here."

"It would make me feel better." President Young stared at me with mild eyes.

"All right," I agreed. I sat down and folded my arms. President Young and some of the others put their hands on my head. There were so many of them, it felt as though they might push my neck down into my body. As soon as the amens were said, I stood up and headed for the door. Before leaving I turned and said, "We might not get back right away. It depends on which camp Black Hawk is using right now."

"We'll be here."

Once outside, I headed for the hills. When I found Sapinay, he agreed to go with me.

We tracked Chief Black Hawk down with no trouble at all. He was one person who wasn't bothered by our mix of English and Indian because he understood both. Black Hawk put on his best feathers and rode with us down into the valley, accompanied by his war chiefs. I was rather proud of them.

Someone must have seen us coming, because by the time we reached the city hall, there was a quite a crowd gathered. Being small for my age, I was lost among the bodies, so I didn't even get to see Chief Black Hawk write his name on the paper that the white men stuck through the window. The other chiefs made their marks.

The war was officially over. A few renegades from both sides occasionally forgot that fact and got a cactus spine stuck in their attitude from time to time, which made them stir up trouble. Still, it was good to have peace for the most part, and good to have Sapinay over for supper at my house every once in a while instead of me having to eat at his place.

In 1872, Willard Laurtiz Frandsen was sent at the tender age of nine by LDS Church President Brigham Young to invite Chief Black Hawk and the other war chiefs down from the mountains to sign the peace treaty and end the war. Will was perfectly comfortable playing with his Indian friends, and he spoke their language like a native. According to Willard's daughter, Talula, the treaty was signed through an open window with the Indians outside and the white men inside.

Source: *Saga of the Sanpitch*, vol. 17 (1985), 43.

GENERAL STORE

I stumbled on the steps that led to the front door of the general store and nearly collided with an Indian man. He was clutching a wad of red calico to his chest and quickly jerked away as if I'd brandished a hot iron in his face.

I staggered and caught my balance in time to save myself the embarrassment of falling against him. My sudden movement jarred my son, who whimpered from his place inside a fabric sling on my back.

"Shush, now, it's all right. Hush, Alan," I said, keeping my eyes on the Indian.

The Indian flinched at the sound of my voice. He made me feel uneasy. If I could believe the gossip I'd heard in the general store last week, I was face to face with a suspected spy.

It was hard to believe, because, except his obvious fear of getting too close to me, Bill seemed like any other Indian that lived in the village a few miles out of town. The bright red calico peeking out from his dark fingers looked like it was strangling in his grip. If it had a voice, I imagined it would be screaming.

Suddenly, Bill darted past me and disappeared around the corner of the store.

I sagged in relief and slid Alan off my back. "Hush, hush, hush," I said and turned him toward me. As soon as he caught sight of my face, he grinned, and grabbed for my hair. I smiled back. Alan was one of the best things that ever happened to me, right up there at the top of the list with my husband, Jim.

I carried my baby into the store. The first thing I saw was a huddle of Indian women standing at the side of the counter, their hands clutching their meager purchases and their eyes darting up to where Jilly Tanner leaned across the counter gossiping with Mrs. Constance Despain.

Last week, it was Mr. Despain behind the counter and I'd overheard him talking to Fred Harrison about Indian Bill.

"That Bill's a bad'un," Fred Harrison said. "Every time he comes to town, we get a raid on our livestock."

"Could just be coincidence," Mr. Despain said.

Fred grinned, but there was no humor in his smile. He leaned closer. "I follered 'im," he whispered. "I watched him go out of town a different way than he come in. He went a sneakin' around the back roads, lookin' into ever'body's corrals and pens. Then he hurried on out to the edge of town where his horse was waitin' for him. He was up and gone before a gopher could poke his head out of a hole to see what the noise was all about. The very next day, I tell ya, the very next day we had that raid where widow Sanders lost her buggy horse and the Fields' had most of their cattle disappear."

"He's a good customer, though," Mr. Despain said in Bill's defense. "And you have no proof that he's the culprit."

Fred snorted. "It's him, all right, and even a swaybacked horse is worth a sight more than the price of a plug of tobackee or a yard of fabric. We're gonna keep a close watch on that one from now on."

Fred twisted his head to look out the window, as if he expected to see Bill standing there listening in. "We can't abide no spies comin' in to tell his tribesmen what to steal from who. We won't stand fer it anymore, no sirree." Fred picked at one of his teeth for a moment and then said, "We hang cattle thieves, ya know."

I swallowed hard, finished my business, and left the store as quickly as I could.

Now the five waiting Indian women glanced over at me from the corners of their eyes, too shy to give me a full-faced appraisal.

Dulcie Johnson fingered some balls of wool that sat on a side counter. I said hello before I gathered up the few things that I'd come into town for. I was in a bit of a hurry, since Jim would be home for dinner at dusk, and I still had a long ride home.

I got into line behind the silent Indian women, and we waited for Jilly to finish up her business. Then Dulcie walked up to the counter right into the space between the Indians and Jilly. "I've found what I wanted," she announced. "How much for three balls of yarn? Oh, and I'd like some tooth powder too."

My eyes widened with astonishment, and I glanced down at Alan. He looked back at me, his blue eyes round with wonder at Dulcie's daring. I looked up. "Excuse me, Dulcie, but these women have been waiting in line since I got here."

Dulcie glanced over at me, then at the Indians, then back at me. "So?"

"So they should go ahead of you."

Dulcie raised her eyebrows. "They're just Indians."

"They're people," I said. "They deserve to be treated with courtesy."

Dulcie turned to stare at Constance and Jilly. "What has gotten into her?" she asked, pointing her thumb back over her shoulder toward me.

Constance twisted her mouth up in a semblance of a smile, but she didn't convince me that she meant it. "I'll just be a minute," she said. Then she moved down the counter and bared her teeth at the Indian women. It was a travesty of a smile, and she would have looked much more attractive without it.

I watched while the Indians paid for their needles and candles. Then I stepped aside to let them pass. The women darted their furtive black-eyed glances at me as they left the store.

I took my turn at the counter. "Honestly, I don't see why you're so concerned about a few Indians," Dulcie said, standing straight with her chin raised high.

"They're people, just like you and me," I said.

Dulcie snorted. "Just like us? No, you're mistaken. Just because they've taken to wearing some of our old clothes doesn't make them like us."

"I heard that Black Hawk's daughter nearly scared little Hans Nelson to death," Jilly chimed in.

I widened my eyes in mock horror. "Oh, is that the time when she was putting her generous gift of moccasins on his feet?"

"She should have known it would scare him if she touched him," Jilly sniffed.

"His parents were standing there the whole time," I said.

"That's not the only thing. Why, I saw some little Indian boys the other day wearing trousers for a change, and I thought, 'oh, thank goodness,' but when they turned around I saw that their mothers had cut the seat out of their pants so that they could do their business wherever and whenever they wanted to." Jilly wrinkled up her nose in disgust.

"Sounds rather practical to me," I said.

"Practical?" Dulcie stared at me as though I'd told her that her hair was a tangled mess of snakes. "Are you daft?"

"I just don't think you should go around judging other people," I said. "If you had lived here first and then the Indians moved in, would you have them expect you to adopt their ways?"

"Never," said Jilly.

"Well, I think they deserve consideration too, even if they act differently than we do. You don't have to like my opinion, but there it is."

"Well, in my opinion, you're carrying your child around like a savage Indian," Dulcie said.

My face reddened. “It’s very convenient. It keeps my hands free. You should try it some time.”

Dulcie laughed in derision. “Not me. I’m a white woman, through and through.”

I tucked my purchases into the baby carrier, turned, and left the store. The door shut behind me, but I could still hear muffled voices inside. It didn’t take much imagination to guess who they were gossiping about.

I swung Alan up onto my back and stalked out to where my horse waited for me. It wasn’t worth explaining to those women that my parents had some good Indian friends who were loyal enough to die for them. My parents returned the sentiment. I didn’t need to explain anything to a bunch of tight-hearted women who couldn’t even see the worth of a soul, whether it was covered with dark or light skin.

I climbed on my patient horse and headed out of town, not caring if I returned for a long while.

I was more than halfway home when a mouse darted out in front of me, followed closely by a long, green snake. The mouse jumped up in fright at the unexpected sight of my horse’s huge leg heading for him, and the snake drew back and hissed in alarm.

My startled horse reared up on his hind legs, trying to avoid the creatures, and I couldn’t stop myself from sliding off his back.

“Oh, no, dear God, please save my baby,” I prayed as I felt myself falling backwards.

I hit the ground so hard that it knocked the air out of my lungs.

Alan had no such trouble, and screamed loud enough for both of us. I was grateful that he was still alive, but I couldn’t even draw breath to call out his name or give him any soothing words of comfort.

I finally worked enough air into my shocked lungs to keep me from fainting.

“Alan,” I called. “Oh, Alan, are you all right?”

I struggled to get up, but a stab of pain shot up my leg and through my hip, making me scream. I couldn’t get up. I looked down and saw that my foot was turned at a strange angle.

No. Oh, no. My poor baby, I thought.

I tried to twist my torso so that I could get to my son and comfort him. I could only turn far enough to assure myself that Alan wasn’t being crushed by my weight, but the pain was horrendous. I couldn’t move enough to get the sling off my back, even though my arms ached to hold my son. He cried so hard that it broke my heart, but I could only talk to him and try to soothe him with my voice.

I don't know how long we lay there. I lost consciousness a time or two, and when I came back from the black depths, my little boy's voice was hoarse and strained. Even so, he kept on crying.

We were both going to die on this road before anyone found us. I was beside myself, wondering if Alan was hurt or bleeding. If only I could hold him in my arms to comfort him before we died, it would make our passing sweeter.

The tears that blurred my eyes were more for Alan's distress than my own. Another bolt of sharp pain shot up my leg, and I felt myself falling away again. Alan's cries became fainter and fainter as I faded into oblivion.

I saw a vision of color—swirling hues that shifted and moved in front of my eyes. They swayed and blended into one another, and then separated into distinct colors before blending again. There was a swishing sound like air over wings, and I wondered if it was the sound of death coming for me.

No. I couldn't leave my son. What would happen to him if he were left all alone in the road, strapped to his dead mother's back?

"No," I screamed, trying to fight off the blackness.

Voices came through the haze, speaking a language I couldn't understand. Were they angel voices?

Then I felt someone tugging Alan off my back. I grabbed the strap of my pack and screamed. These couldn't be angels, because angels would never steal my son.

My eyes opened wide, forcing my awareness up from the haze that shadowed the edges of my mind. I stared up into the face of an Indian woman. There were others behind her, and some behind me, and they were stealing Alan. No! They couldn't have my son.

"Get away!" I screamed, and fought the hands that held me back. Stabs of agonizing pain spurred me on to fight like a wounded wildcat for her kitten. The voices that weren't angels spoke soft, soothing words that maintained kindness in the face of my outburst. It frustrated me that I couldn't understand them.

Suddenly, Alan stopped crying.

I whipped my head around, twisting my body until my leg screamed in protest and I gasped with the pain, the blood draining from my face. Through the gray haze that crowded in on all sides, I saw an Indian woman cuddling my son against her breast, shushing him. When she caught my eye, she smiled at me.

"What's going on?" My husband's shout filled me with joy, and I was free to fall back into the welcoming darkness. I was safe. Alan was safe. And angels looked strangely like Indians.

I woke up in my own bed while the doctor was wrapping a splint tightly against my leg.

"Where's Alan?" I asked.

The doctor looked over at me, his eyebrows raised. "Your son is fine. He's in the other room."

"I want to see him," I said.

The doctor stepped over to the door and called for Alan to be brought in. Jim was there in an instant, with Alan held against his broad chest. I reached out and took Alan into my arms. The instant I held him, my heart nearly burst with relief, and tears coursed down my cheeks.

Jim had his hand on my head, smoothing my hair over and over, his eyes blinking to fight back tears.

"Is he all right?" I asked.

"Perfectly fine," Jim answered. "Thanks to those Indians."

"Indians?" My brow furrowed in thought as I rested my chin on Alan's head, my arms wrapped securely around my son. "I thought I saw angels."

Jim laughed. "You probably did." He dropped a kiss onto my forehead. "They looked like angels to me when I came searching for you and found you lying on the road."

The next day, the five Indian women from the general store came to visit, bearing flat bread singed nearly black and baskets full of berries and a comb of honey.

"Thank you," I said, my eyes filling with tears of gratitude at their kindness.

They examined my splinted leg with admiring eyes, talking back and forth between themselves. They took turns holding Alan. They made me tea and laid wet cloths on my forehead. I hadn't been delirious—angels did look like Indians.

A few days later, my neighbor Ellie came over with a cake.

"Did you hear about that Indian, Bill?" she asked.

"No."

"He's been to town for the last time," she said. "Harrison and several others escorted him out of the city limits and into the foothills. They came back without him, so we've seen the last of him, for sure."

My heart ached for the frightened Indian whom I'd last seen clutching a wad of red calico as though his life depended on it. In all the time it took my leg to heal, there were no more livestock raids, and we never saw Bill again.

In 1870 a family was moving out of Fort Gunnison. The major hostilities of the Black Hawk War had ceased. When they encountered some Indians in their travels, Black Hawk's daughter scared little Hans when she picked him up, but she only wanted to put a little pair of moccasins on his feet.

At around the same time, a young mother helped some Indian women get their turn at the store, even though it wasn't the popular thing to do. On the way home, her horse was startled and she fell off. She was hurt so badly that she couldn't reach her little son, who was strapped to her back. The Indian women from the store found her and helped her.

Bill was an Indian who came into town fairly regularly. A day or two after each one of his visits, there would be an Indian raid and the townspeople's livestock would be stolen. One day, a few of the townsmen escorted Bill out into the foothills and came back without him. The raids on the animals stopped. Bill was never seen again.

Source: *Saga of the Sanpitch*, vol. 3 (1971), 6, 15.

BED AND BREAKFAST

"Dagnabbit, where's that apple I left here yesterday," I mumbled to myself. I cast a suspicious glance at my two oxen. "Did you root it out, Bawl?" At the sound of his name, the ox turned his big brown eyes toward me. He was clearly puzzled, so I turned to fix my other ox, Bill, with a stern gaze. "Was it you?" Bill snorted and shook a fly off his head, totally unconcerned with my accusation.

Since it was obvious that I wasn't going to get anywhere with this line of questioning, I gave up and went back to work.

By the time the light was gone, I still hadn't finished tilling the ground for my spring planting. Whichever ox had stolen the apple that I'd hidden yesterday sure hadn't made very good use of the extra energy.

I led my oxen into the pen at the edge of the field where I'd left them last night. I didn't like leaving them there because there was always a risk that they'd be taken by Indians. Still, it was five miles back to town, and they'd slow me down. I already had precious few hours to sleep before I had to get up and come back early tomorrow. I wanted to get this field tilled so I could plant it.

"You guys stay here and behave yourselves," I said. I cut some long grass from the side of the road and threw it into the manger. "There's your breakfast. Eat up before I get here tomorrow, or you'll be mighty hungry while pullin' the plow."

I got on my horse and headed for home.

The next morning I rode up to the pen where my oxen stood staring at me over the fence. "You ready for work?" I asked. I swung off my horse and turned him into the pen. Then I moved toward Bill and Bawl and glanced into the manger. Instead of the scrambled bits of hay that I expected to see after two hungry bovines rummaged through their breakfast, there was an indentation in the center of the manger grass that was about the length and width of a human body.

"What've you two been up to?" I asked, staring at the hay in confusion. Neither one of them confessed.

Another few days of hard work got the field plowed and planted. I didn't spare the time to wonder much about the odd mornings when I found indents in the manger hay. I did wonder what kind of thieving critter was stealing my lunch, though. It only happened on days I worked straight through noon, not stopping to fetch my tin pail from where I'd tucked it inside the manger. I trusted that my horse would leave it be, since he had no talent for taking lids off of tin pails, as far as I knew. On a couple of those evenings, I was so tired that I forgot and left my lunch pail there. When I came back the next morning, it would be right where I'd left it. I'd pick it up, pull off the lid, and stare down into an empty pail. How in the world any critter could get the lid off in the first place baffled me, but to have the ability to stick it back on again was downright spooky. Even Bill and Bawl wouldn't be able to pull off that kind of shenanigan.

On Monday I left the oxen at the field again. Come Tuesday, I got to work early, ready to irrigate my newly planted field. From the road, I spied a dark shape in the manger. I moved close enough to recognize a person lying there—an Indian, Chief Arropeen, to be exact.

Well, well. I wondered what brought him down to these parts. Had he had an argument with his wife and chosen to spend time with my oxen instead? Or maybe his wives had all ganged up against him, since every chief had more than one.

Well, the reason he was sleeping here was his own business, and I wasn't going to bother him none. If Bill and Bawl didn't care, then it was no concern of mine, except maybe for the food that the chief had taken from my lunch pail. On second thought, I counted myself fortunate that he'd at least left me the pail.

I backed off and went around to where Bill and Bawl stared at me over the fence. "I don't need you guys today," I said. "Just let the old chief sleep, okay?"

I was halfway down the first row, coaxing the water along the proper channel, when I saw Chief Arropeen roll out of the manger and give himself a good scratching. He dug around the edges of the hay for a bit before heading for the hills. I wondered if it was the chief who'd found that missing apple after all. I decided that I'd take Bill and Bawl home tonight and leave a little something from my lunch in the manger for the chief.

Once my crop was up, the deer found out that they liked it—a lot. I figured I'd better get me a fence up right away and try to save some crops for harvesting. I gathered a load of fence posts from the mountains and set to work digging holes. Before I even got all the poles set, I could see that I didn't have enough to go all the way around, but by then it was time for first cutting. The deer hadn't managed to eat everything.

When half my harvest was in, I looked up toward the mountain one afternoon and noticed a trail of dark-skinned people wearing skirts walking down the mountain. They all carried long, dark objects crossways in their arms. When they got closer, I could see that the Indian women bore straight, wooden poles—poles that were perfect for fence posts. Without a word, the Indians deposited the poles at the end of the unfinished fence line. Then they turned and walked back up into the mountains.

I stood and watched them go. Although I hadn't recognized any of them, I'd bet my next foal that they were Chief Arropeen's wives and daughters. I thought that enough poles to finish my fence was mighty generous payback for providing the chief a rudimentary bed and a little breakfast.

Peter Mickel Munk homesteaded sixty-two acres west of Arropeen Valley, which was named for old Chief Arropeen. Some nights when he got done working late, he didn't want to bother herding his oxen, Bill and Bawl, the five miles back to town, so he'd fill the manger with hay and leave them there. Some mornings, he'd find an indentation in the hay roughly the size and shape of a body. When he stashed food at the farm, intent on eating it later, it would disappear.

One morning he arrived early and found Chief Arropeen sleeping in the manger. Later, when Ike had a big fence-building project, Arropeen's wives carried fence posts down from the mountain for Ike to use.

Source: *Saga of the Sanpitch*, vol. 5 (1973), 7.

ABANDONED

“What is this?” Captain Emmett’s icy voice chilled me like a blast from a January storm. I whirled to face the steel-eyed captain, whose mouth was pulled down in a familiar frown. In one hand Captain Emmett held a portion of honeycomb no bigger than his thumb. His other hand rested on the pistol butt at his side.

“It’s nothing,” I said, my heart sinking even as I spoke. “It’s only a scrap of honeycomb.”

Captain Emmett did not move his eyes off my face.

“Where did you get it?”

I held the captain’s gaze. “I came across it when I was out hunting.”

“And you didn’t bother to add it to the provisions for the entire company to draw from?”

It wasn’t a question. It was an accusation.

“There wasn’t much,” I said.

“No?” the captain clearly did not believe me.

“No. I gave it to my wife.”

“And why is she more important than any other person in this company?”

“Well, she is with child.”

“She is not the only one,” Captain Emmett roared. “There are many in camp who have excuses to be dealt out extra food, but you choose to ignore them and cater to your own wife. Is that very Christ-like of you?” The captain did not wait for an answer but growled, “You will not get away with this, John Winn. You will be punished.”

Captain Emmett strode away, leaving my soul stinging with pain composed of shame and anger. Of course I would look out for my wife before any other person, but I hadn’t meant to hurt anyone else. I knew that others in the company were suffering too, but hadn’t I given up one of my oxen as soon as Captain Emmett told me there was a family who needed it more?

We were well beyond the Missouri River now, deep in the wilds of the South Dakota Territory. It had been so long since I had seen the inside of four walls that I almost couldn’t remember what it was like to live in a proper house.

The trek had been hard on us all, but it seemed to have had an especially bad effect on Captain Emmett. The further we traveled, the more heavy-handed he became. His demands were stringent, made in a harsh voice that stung my ears like a whip. When he reduced our rations to two measures of corn per day, saying that the provisions in the wagons were reserved for harder times ahead, I could no longer bear to see my wife suffer. When we made camp to let the worn-out animals rest for a couple of days, I took it upon myself to go hunting. Not only did I shoot a grouse, but I had the good fortune to come upon a stash of wild honey. I carried it home in my tightly woven game bag, and took it straight to my own wagon. My satisfaction at seeing Julia's eyes light up as she tasted the rare treat was enough to fill my soul with sufficient sweetness that I didn't need any honey for myself. Julia pressed it upon me, however, and said that she couldn't bear it if my cousin Jim and his wife Nancy didn't have some too.

I contributed the grouse to the community larder, even though I knew that Captain Emmett and his favored friends would be the only ones to taste the fresh meat. But the honey was for my Julia.

Now Moses Emmett, the captain's pimply faced son, strode up to our wagon to fetch me for trial. He tried to act tough but couldn't pull it off. He was just a skinny sapling of a boy, not even full-grown, although he tried to act like he was. I stared him down until he dropped his eyes to the ground and said, "Come with me."

Captain Emmett paced before a group of men seated on the ground. As soon as he saw me, he stopped and pointed a thick finger at me. "This man is a thief."

Upon hearing this brusque accusation, several of the assembled men sat up straighter and turned their gaunt faces from the captain to me and back again.

Captain Emmett continued, "He admitted to me that he gave his wife food that he gathered while supposedly out hunting for the whole company." Captain Emmett held up the piece of honeycomb, and several of the men leaned forward and squinted at it.

"I found this on the ground beside his wagon," Captain Emmett said. "He confessed that this honeycomb was given to his wife, with none to spare for the likes of us."

"I'm sorry," I said. "I just thought that . . ."

"Quiet! You have admitted your guilt and your callousness, and for your cold-hearted efforts to kill us all, you are condemned to die!"

A sudden intake of breath from the onlookers punctuated the sudden burst of fear that shot through me.

Then the reasonable voice of Max Baker spoke up. "Now, wait a minute." Brother Baker stood up from his seat on the ground. "Maybe John did something he oughtn't to have done, but to kill him for it just isn't right."

Several other men murmured and nodded their heads. Captain Emmett turned his fierce gaze on Brother Baker. "He tried to starve us to death. Do you hear me? To death! When a man tries to take another's life, then he shall forfeit his own. It is God's law! Do you have aught to say against God?"

Max Baker sat down again.

"Now, those of you who are scheduled for the next guard watch shall load up your weapons and dispatch this thief before we retire for the night."

No one moved. Several of the men shook their heads, and I heard one of them say, "Murder." It didn't surprise me too much that no one championed my cause. For one thing, there wasn't much fight in a starving man. And while none of them seemed to agree with what Captain Emmett was doing, he pretty well had his thumb on us all. He claimed that he'd been called by the church leaders to head up our company, but in truth he had taken it upon himself to convince us that we were called to settle in the North Dakota Territory. Clearly, it was up to me to defend myself.

"Look," I said, "I didn't mean . . ."

"Quiet!" Captain Emmett said, drawing his pistol and aiming it straight at my face.

"Moses!" he called.

The gangly Moses shuffled over to his father's side. The captain pressed the pistol into his son's hand and helped him point it at me. "He must die," Captain Emmett hissed.

I stared at the barrel of the pistol. At this range, it would be hard to miss. The crazed eyes of Captain Emmett pierced me with blazing hatred.

Moses blinked at me several times over the pistol sights, and the gun barrel wavered. My heart hammered so hard that I was certain it was visible to all, making a perfect target.

We stood like that for a lifetime. I held as still as I could, not even daring to draw breath while I faced the men who held my life in their hands.

"Shall I shoot him, Father?" Moses' voice quavered and nearly cracked.

Captain Emmett's eyes narrowed, and he darted a look at his son. His features softened. "Do as you please, son," he said.

Then something snapped inside me. The thought of my Julia as a widow, standing next to my grave while carrying our child, made me so angry at this despot who threatened me with death that I pulled back my shoulders and stood erect. I grabbed the front of my shirt and pulled, popping the buttons off in a spatter of bright orbs sailing through the air and landing with soft plops in the dirt.

"Shoot, you cowardly rats. I dare you to," I bellowed, shifting my gaze from the gun barrel to the captain. There was no compassion in his eyes, but a sudden look of fear flitted across his face.

Moses lowered the gun and handed it to his father.

"This has gone far enough," Max Baker said, rising from the ground. "What John did is no killing offense."

"Brother Baker is right," Jeb Carter said, struggling to his feet. Several other men pushed themselves up from the ground and stared at Captain Emmett.

The captain turned his back on them and holstered his gun. "You will not be shot," he said. "But you will not eat from our stores. You will get your own food." Then he stalked toward his wagon with his son trotting along behind, leaving me standing before my peers.

I turned toward the hungry faces staring at me. "I'm sorry," I said. "I didn't mean to steal from anyone. When I found the honey, all I could think of was Julia and our unborn baby."

Several heads nodded, and Max Baker said, "I would have done the same myself."

I put my hands out toward my fellow travelers. "Besides, there is plenty in the wagons for us to eat. I don't understand why the captain isn't more generous with our rations."

"Perhaps he knows something that we don't," Max Baker said. "We shouldn't question our leader but must follow his advice if we are to survive."

I had my doubts, for what good would it do for us to reach our homesteads in North Dakota if half of us died from hunger?

The next morning, Captain Emmett strode toward our wagon, his cold granite gaze fixed on me.

"Get behind me!" I said, stepping in front of my wife.

"What is it?" Julia asked.

I didn't have time to answer before the captain bellowed, "John

Winn, for your crimes against this company, you are to be left behind, to care for yourself and your wife however you see fit."

"No!" I said, thoughts of slow starvation and watching Julia die in agony creating a far worse fear in me than being shot. "You can't do that!"

"I am the leader of this company, and I do what is best for all. Leaving you behind is best."

"John?" Julia's voice cut through the heavy silence that followed Captain Emmett's pronouncement. My wife's fearful question cut me to the very quick of my soul.

"It's all right," I murmured, even though I didn't believe my own words.

"Now we leave you," the captain said.

"No!" Julia wailed. "You can't do this! My baby!"

"We'll just get our things," I said, moving toward the wagon. I desperately searched my mind for everything I could grab in the precious few minutes I had that would best help us survive.

"No!" the captain bellowed. "You have no things. You are as you are. Make your way as best you can, just like you did before."

I stared the captain in the face. "This is murder," I said.

The captain grinned—an evil twist of his lips that set my hair on edge.

"You will stay behind," the captain said. "Now—move."

I didn't move until the captain drew his gun and shot a bullet into the ground at my feet. Then I leapt back, dragging my wife by the arm.

"No!" Julia screamed. "I need my things!" She jerked her arm out of my grasp and stumbled toward the wagon.

Another shot rang out from Captain Emmett's other pistol. Julia staggered back.

"Julia!" I screamed, and ran to my wife's side, slipping my arm around her waist and holding her close. I couldn't see any blood.

Julia turned to the captain. "You are a beast! A heartless monster! What am I to do when my baby is born? I need the flannels and clothes and blankets I've made with my own hands." Julia lifted her hands toward Captain Emmett in entreaty. "I need my own clothes. How are we to survive with nothing?"

"Now you'll see how the rest of us felt while you enjoyed your sweet treat of wild honey," the captain sneered. "Now you are the ones who will have to do without, so see how you like it."

"No matter my crime, if you truly believe me guilty of anything, my baby is innocent. I need my baby's clothes," Julia said. She pulled herself up and stared the captain in the eye. "I will not leave without them."

"You will not have them," the captain said.

Just then, Nancy appeared from the behind the wagon with two satchels in her hands. She made straight for Julia, not even bothering to glance Captain Emmett's way.

"Here you go, Julia, for you and your baby," Nancy said.

"Oh, thank you, thank you!" Julia cried, reaching for the cases. I put my hand out and grasped one of them, hoping that Nancy might have thought to put a gun and some ammunition in it.

"So, you wish to join them?" Captain Emmett asked, his voice as hard as flint.

"What?" Nancy's eyes darted up, and she stared at the captain.

"Nancy!" Jim called, hurrying over to us. "I was down at the river and heard gunshots. What's the trouble?"

"No trouble," Captain Emmett said. "Sister Wilson has decided that you will stay behind with Brother and Sister Winn while the rest of us move out."

"What?" Jim's eyes went wide with disbelief.

It took some explaining, and more arguing, before Jim and Nancy finally found themselves standing beside us, watching the wagon train pull out. There were many faces pointed our way, watching us recede into the distance, but no one challenged Captain Emmett in his decision. They were too weak and depressed from hunger and fatigue to put up a fight. I didn't believe that anyone besides the captain thought that we deserved this punishment for my indiscretion.

I turned away before the wagon train disappeared. I couldn't bear to see our lifeline go over the rise and disappear from sight.

"Come on," I said, picking up Julia's satchel as well as the one I held. "We'll probably be just as well off on our own as we were with that despot."

Julia sobbed. She didn't believe my words any more than I did.

Nancy hadn't thought to put anything in the satchels besides clothes. She was sorry for it too, but there was nothing to be done about it now.

More than once over the next few days, I suggested that we leave the satchels behind, as they were doing us no good.

"No!" Julia said. "They're for our baby." She threatened to carry them herself if I did not, so I kept carrying them, with Jim to spell me off.

We tried prying roots out of the ground with sticks, but it was a long and tedious process, and we didn't get much. We had no way to cook any of the roots we dug, so we ate them raw. Some of them cramped us up inside, either because they weren't good for us or because our stomachs were so crazed with hunger that they ached when we put food in them.

We didn't have the good fortune to come across any more honey, nor did we find any berry patches with ripe fruit. As we trudged along beside the river, I longed for a simple fishing line. Every fish that jumped out of the water mocked our hunger. Whenever I caught sight of a bird on the wing, my hands itched to hold a loaded gun.

After a few days, I could hardly pick up my feet. Julia was a walking ghost of herself. Nancy and Jim were in bad shape too. The two measures of corn that we'd been allotted in the wagon train seemed generous beyond belief.

I dragged my feet forward with my eyes on the ground, when Jim suddenly cried, "Look!"

I raised my head and saw a cloud of dust in the distance. I made out riders on horses. Squinting my eyes brought lances into focus—their points bristling the air, their ends fluttering with what looked like feathers.

"Indians!" Nancy squeaked.

"No!" Julia said, her voice tight with fear.

"Hide!" Jim said, pulling his wife by the arm toward a screen of brush that was near at hand.

"Wait!" I said. "Perhaps we can ask them for help."

Jim's eyes widened in disbelief. "Ask Indians for help? Are you daft?"

"Look, Jim, we are in a bad way. We need food. At least it's a chance."

"I don't like it."

"Neither do I!" I exploded. "I don't like any of this! I didn't ask to be stranded."

"John," Julia said. "Jim is not our enemy."

"I'm sorry," I said. "But don't you see that they're our only hope? We've got to ask them for help."

"First say a prayer," Julia said.

I stared down at my wife. Her cheekbones jutted out beneath her calm blue eyes.

"Yes, Julia, all right," I said.

We bowed our heads and offered up a prayer from the very center of our hearts and souls. Then I looked at the ladies. "Stay hidden," I said.

"Don't come out for anything, unless you hear me or Jim call to you. Do you understand?"

Nancy and Julia nodded from where they crouched side by side, holding on to one another.

Jim and I headed for the band of Indians. It looked like they were passing us by, moving away at an angle, riding their horses faster than we could walk.

"Run!" I said to Jim, now desperate to make contact with these native people who hadn't always proved merciful to whites.

But we were dying anyway. If we had to die, perhaps it would be better to go swiftly at the hands of the Indians than to waste away from hunger.

I pulled my hat off my head and waved it in the air. "Hey!" I called. "Hey!" My legs wobbled beneath me when I tried to run.

Jim called out. "Over here! Wait for us!"

I ran harder than I'd ever run in my life, weaving from side to side as my undernourished body struggled to meet the demands I made of it. I felt light-headed, and for a moment it felt as though I was outrunning myself, my spirit soaring ahead of my emaciated body to turn the heads of the Indians so that they could see us stumbling toward them, our hats raised and our arms reached out in supplication.

The Indians pulled to a stop. Their horses milled about and stamped with impatience.

My heart surged with relief. As we drew closer, the braves on horseback readied their bows and raised their rifles, their wary eyes upon us.

Two braves slid down off their horses and walked toward us, their rifles aimed at our hearts.

"We need help," I called.

"You give guns, give knives," one of the Indians said. Furry strips of animal skin were woven into his braids, and a band of what looked like bear claws circled his neck.

I held both of my hands out. "We don't have any guns or knives," I said.

"We see."

Bear Claw turned to his companion and said something in Indian. Then he held his rifle steady on us while the other Indian came closer and searched us for weapons.

"We were left with nothing," I said as the Indian felt in Jim's pockets. I hoped that my admission was not a mistake. They could easily take advantage of a couple of unarmed whites, but what did it matter what I told them? They were bound to find out our true state of affairs sooner or later.

"Where go from?" Bear Claw asked.

"We were with a wagon train, and they left us behind."

"Sick?" Bear Claw took a step back from us, his eyes narrowing in suspicion. His companion joined him, his rifle raised toward us as well.

"No, no, we're not sick," Jim said. "We're hungry." He opened his mouth and pointed to it.

"Come," Bear Claw said, motioning with his rifle.

He led us over to a middle-aged Indian man, who stood on the ground beside his horse, glaring at us from under dark brows, his arms folded across his chest and his hair bristling with feathers. I was fairly certain that this was the chief.

The chief spoke to Bear Claw in Indian, and Bear Claw said to us, "Who sent you?"

With Bear Claw interpreting, we tried our best to convince the chief that we were left alone by our fellow whites, and had no intent to harm them, but the chief kept a suspicious eye on me.

"Please," I said. "Our wives are starving. We just need some food. Then we'll trouble you no more."

Bear Claw's eyes widened. "Wives?"

"Women," I said, putting my arm out to include Jim. "Our women."

Bear Claw turned and spoke rapidly to the chief. The chief gave a start and glared at Jim and me before he called out an order and three braves appeared at his side.

"You shouldn't have said that," Jim said.

My heart sank as Bear Claw grabbed Jim by the arm. "You stay," he said to me.

"No! Wait!" I cried, but a rifle barrel jabbed into my stomach silenced me.

Bear Claw pulled Jim back the way we had come, with two other braves trailing along behind.

I wanted to rip my own tongue out. How could I have betrayed our wives like that? I couldn't bear the thought of what these savage Indians might do to them. Even though they hadn't hurt us yet, their guns, spears, and arrows had been constantly at the ready, poised to kill us at a single command from their chief.

I risked a look at the chief's face, hoping to find any hope of mercy there. His features were so impassive that they could have been made of wood. My heart quailed within me, and I turned again to watch Jim's stumbling progress.

All too soon, the three Indians were heading back with Jim, Nancy, and Julia. One of the braves even held Julia's arm. My fists tightened at my sides, and I pulled myself up erect.

"Do not harm them," I said.

The chief glanced over at me but didn't say anything.

When Julia was close enough, I reached out to her and she came into my arms. I held her close until I caught the chief watching us. When we broke apart, his gaze traveled down to my wife's distended belly. He said something to Bear Claw.

Bear Claw looked at Julia and pointed at her stomach. "You child?"

Julia cupped a hand protectively around her middle. "Yes."

The chief nodded, and gestured toward a spot where the Indian women had begun setting up camp. I hadn't noticed their activity, since my attention had been on my companions.

We walked over to the wickiups that were rising quickly from the prairie floor. I kept my arm around Julia, and Jim helped Nancy. The sight of our starving wives must have touched the old chief's heart.

We were each taken apart from the others and questioned separately, with Bear Claw acting as an interpreter for the chief. Ultimately, he seemed satisfied that we were all telling the same story.

The chief called out a command, and the braves gathered around him. They spoke among themselves briefly before the young braves broke off and scurried like rabbits, putting on war paint and feathers, shouldering their weapons, and leading their horses to assemble around the chief.

Jim and I both jumped up from where we had collapsed onto the ground. "What are you doing?" I asked Bear Claw.

"Where's everyone going?" Jim asked at the same time.

"We go, kill all who leave you," he said. Then he gave us a nod and started away.

"No! You can't!" I yelled.

Bear Claw looked back over his shoulder, surprise evident on his face.

"They're good people," Jim said. "Only the captain is at fault."

"No good people," Bear Claw said. "Better dead." He strode away from us.

"What are we going to do?" Jim asked.

"Stop them, John," Julia said, pushing herself up from the ground with some difficulty.

"I'll try," I said. I followed Bear Claw with Jim at my heels. By the time we caught up to him, he was talking to the chief.

"Please don't do this," I said. "Those people are our friends."

Bear Claw said something to the chief, who looked at us with disdain. He spoke a single word.

Bear Claw turned back to us. "No. You not right. We kill."

"No, please, you don't understand," I said. "It's not all of them who did this."

"They're good people," Jim added.

"No good leave you," Bear Claw scoffed.

No matter how hard we protested, the Indians were determined to carry through on their plan to massacre the entire wagon train. The chief called out another command, and all of the Indian warriors leapt up onto their horses and turned them in the direction we had come from.

I was at my wit's end. Our friends were already suffering enough under the leadership of the tyrant Captain Emmett. They didn't need any more trouble heaped upon them.

The chief's cold eyes shifted to something behind me, and I turned to see my Julia stumbling toward us. Her eyes, brimming with tears, were fixed on the chief.

In spite of her hollow cheeks and cracked lips, Julia had never looked more beautiful to me. My wife walked up to the chief and sank down onto her knees at his feet. Her face upturned, her hands clasped in front of her, she looked up at the Indian chief and said, "Please, don't kill them. Please, don't kill them." Tears coursed down her cheeks, making silvery trails that slid down her throat and disappeared into the neckline of her dusty dress. Then Julia bowed her head and sobbed.

The chief looked down on Julia's head, his dark eyes inscrutable. I had to blink the tears from my own eyes before I saw the chief raise his eyes to his mounted warriors. He called out a command, and the braves dismounted.

I stared at the warriors as they walked their horses back to the wickiups.

"You stopped the attack!" I cried to the chief. "Thank you! Oh, thank you!"

The grim-faced chief raised his hand, palm toward me, and turned and walked away.

Then Julia collapsed, toppling forward from her knees until she lay on the ground as still as death.

"Julia!" I cried, bending over my wife. Before I could lift her up, I was pushed aside by several Indian women. They carried her into a wickiup and laid her on a bed of buffalo robes.

I tried to follow my wife, but I couldn't get close because of all the Indian women who were seeing to her needs. Jim and Nancy joined me, and we were soon fed a simple meal of jerky, parched corn, and broth. I'd never been so hungry in my life, and the simple food tasted better than anything I'd ever eaten before.

Julia soon fell asleep. We rapidly followed suit, exhausted and finally free from sharp hunger chewing out our insides.

It was early light when I awoke. For a moment, I wondered where I was. The Indian camp was strangely silent. I stuck my head out of the wickiup and looked for our rescuers. They were gone.

I pulled myself outside and looked around. No one was in sight, but on the ground was a buffalo robe folded over itself. I lifted the top fold and stared at what lay inside. A generous supply of jerky, parched corn, a few potatoes, and a couple of cooking pots were nestled in the folds of the robe. My eyes blurred as I stared at this bounty.

Then I heard a horse blow out of its nostrils, and whipped my head around. Jim crawled out of the wickiup, his eyes wide with surprise. Then, as one, we moved around the shelter and found three ponies tethered to a log at the back of our camp. Beside them was an American pack saddle.

I was astounded at the generosity of the Indians who had left three of their precious horses behind for us to make our escape. When I compared the hearts of the savages to the one that beat in Captain Emmett's chest, I knew who the true savage was.

We wasted no time in saddling one of the horses and packing our new belongings onto him. Jim struck the small wickiup, and tied it onto the saddle while I rolled up the buffalo robes we'd been sleeping on. When I lifted the last robe, I was utterly astonished to discover a cap and ball rifle, a generous supply of ammunition, and a hunting knife.

Overcome with gratitude, I fell to my knees and buried my face in my hands.

"John?" Jim called out. "Are you all right?"

I pointed at the ground. "Look what they left for us," I choked out. "They gave us a rifle, Jim. They gave us one of their own rifles."

"Praise be!" Jim called out.

"Jim," I said, wiping my eyes. "I need you to witness my vow. From this day on, I will help and aid the Indian race at every opportunity."

Jim nodded, unable to speak.

We gathered up our precious rifle and ammunition, secured our packhorse, and helped our wives up onto the other two horses. Then, with light hearts and sure steps, Jim and I grabbed the lead ropes and headed toward the morning sunrise.

In 1845, John Winn and his pregnant wife, Julia Anne (or Mary Jane) Akes, joined a wagon company headed by Captain James Emmett. Emmett claimed to have been called by Church authorities to take a band of settlers to North Dakota after the Mormon prophet, Joseph Smith, died. His claims later proved false.

The tyrannical Captain Emmett abandoned the Winns on the trail for the crime of supplementing their meager rations with wild honey. John's cousin Jim Wilson and his wife, Nancy, were left behind too.

A band of Indians, probably Sioux, took them in. Winn's party had to convince the Indians not to massacre the wagon train in order to avenge them. The Indians fed the wanderers and let them sleep in a wickiup.

The next day, the Indians were gone but had left provisions behind. Before they headed back to their families and safety in Nauvoo, John vowed to help and befriend Indians at every opportunity. By the time they arrived back in town, Julia had given birth to a baby boy named Minor.

Captain James Emmett was last seen heading for California in the company of two Indian women.

This story was taken from two separate accounts that differ on a few points, though the events were markedly similar.

Source: David Scott submitted this fascinating story from his family's history.

TWO FOR TWO

I wasn't there when the Indian cursed the school. Heck, I wasn't even born yet. Dad was just a boy when it happened, but the event made such an impression on him, and he told it often enough, that I might as well have been right there on the spot.

"Danny-boy, don't blame old Chief Washakorie," Dad would say. "He gave us fair warning."

That may be, but what good's a warning if no one listens?

The trouble really began in 1893, when they started construction of the new Spring City school. I don't know exactly how the old chief caught wind of the building project, but he showed up at the place just as a couple of men were putting their shovels in the ground to hollow out the basement.

"Don't dig here," Washakorie said, his lined face and hard, black eyes as unyielding as a balky mule. His black braids were shot through with the silver of old age, but he was far from feeble as he confronted the white men, his back straight and his arms folded across his chest.

"But, Chief, we've got to. This is where the new school's going," Stanley Hodge said.

"Not here," Washakorie insisted, his voice rolling out in warning like the ominous rumble of boulders crashing down a mountainside. "This is sacred burial ground."

Stan Hodge glanced over at Jack Bawden, who grinned, shook his head, punched his shovel into the ground with his foot, and pried out another plug of dirt.

Stan looked back at the old chief. "Now, now, it'll be fine," he said. "If there really are any of your tribe here, we'll cart 'em on up to Indianola and put 'em to rest beside your other ancestors."

"No!" Washakorie said.

During this exchange, Jack Bawden kept on shoveling, paying no mind to the argument. Washakorie folded his arms in disapproval and watched with hawk eyes as the two men continued digging. Stanley wished mightily that the Indian would just move along, but Washakorie didn't act like he had anything better to do.

Not even a full hour into the digging, Jack Bawden's shovel came up full of dirt mixed with bones—human bones.

Washakorie stalked over to the dig and glared down at the pieces of skeleton. Then he pinned Jack with his fierce, black eyes. Washakorie pulled himself up straight and tall, looking for all the world like an Indian warrior in his prime instead of an aging man. "Now stop," he said.

Stan looked up and wiped his brow. If he were being honest with himself, he was as unnerved by the authority in Washakorie's voice as he was at the sight of the bones. He'd been sure that Washakorie's claim to an ancient Indian burial ground was just an old man rambling.

"Put them back," Washakorie said, jabbing his finger at the scarred earth.

The two diggers looked at each other. Stanley nodded. He was all for filling in the holes, and he couldn't even tell you why. It was like a chill wind blew over the bald spot on top of his head, even though he was wearing his old felt hat. He was shivery clear down to the soles of his boots.

This time it was Jack that turned toward the Indian. "We can't stop. We've got a school to build."

"Not here," Washakorie said, his black eyes staring holes into Jack.

"Look, we'll get these bones out nice and easy, treat 'em with all the respect in the world. Then we'll re-bury them."

Washakorie shook his head once with enough force to kick his braids into a brief and macabre dance around his shoulders. "You desecrate sacred ground."

"We can't hold up the entire construction project for a couple of old skeletons." Jack's impatience was obvious. "We'll just move 'em to the graveyard."

Washakorie's eyes hardened into two points of flint. "No," he said. "Leave them."

Well, that Indian made a real nuisance of himself. Jack went for reinforcements, and Stanley followed, unwilling to stay alone with Washakorie. There was something different about the old Indian—something Stan had never seen before. It was almost like he was someone else, as though the spirits of those dead Indians stood on either side of him with weapons brandished and murder in their eyes.

The two men soon returned, their courage bolstered in the company of several other men. A couple of them took hold of Washakorie's arms, but the Indian pulled free. He turned and strode away, but before he was out of earshot, he turned to face the white men.

"You'll be sorry," he said before he turned and left. He didn't shout, only spoke just loud enough for all of them to hear, but his words paralyzed the group as surely as if he'd smacked them with a shovel. They stared after him, and it was only when he was out of sight that they got back to digging.

The dedication of the new school took place in 1896, the very same year that Utah joined the union of The United States. Dad said it was quite a celebration. There was a band, banners, flags everywhere, and people dressed in their Sunday best, on a weekday, no less. The horses wore polished tack, and normally dusty carriages shone. Some were decorated with garlands, and some with ribbons woven through the wheel spokes.

No one worked in the fields that day. All the households contributed to a community picnic, putting their rolls, deviled eggs, and fried chicken on big tables set up on the new school grounds.

Before the new school bell sounded to signal the start of food and games, the mayor stood up at the podium. All the kids groaned. They wanted potato salad and pie, not long-winded speeches.

"We have gathered here today on this most momentous occasion," the mayor began. "How fitting that in this historic year of statehood, we also witness the dedication of our new school." He stretched his hand toward the three-story edifice behind him, and there was a smattering of applause. Some of the kids clapped too, but that was because they hoped that he was done speaking so they could help themselves to the food table.

Before Mayor Christensen could resume his speech, a tall figure with long, black braids shot with silver walked up toward the front of the crowd.

A voice called, "Get back."

Someone else said, "The mayor's talking up there." A general murmur arose, but the Indian ignored it all. He reached the front of the assembly, spun on his heel, and faced the audience. Every eye was on Washakorie.

"I curse this place," he said, his loud voice carrying in the sudden stillness. "You disturbed the spirits of my people. In return, they will occupy this building for a hundred years." A couple of men stood and advanced on Washakorie. He ignored them and swept his gaze around the crowd, pointing a finger at the school. "For the two Indians whose bones you broke with your shovels, two white men's lives are demanded!"

The men grabbed Washakorie, but he broke free.

"I'll go," Washakorie said. He strode off a few paces, and then turned and shouted, "Two for two!"

Then the Indian took off down the road, not running, but moving out in that peculiar gait that takes the Indians for miles and miles without breaking stride.

The men watched him long enough to satisfy themselves that he was really gone. Then one turned to another and shook his head. "Crazy Indian."

The mayor straightened his lapels, cleared his throat, and started up where he left off, much to the dismay of the hungry boys in the crowd. Their hope, that Washakorie's speech would replace what the mayor had to say, was in vain.

By the time I started school in the 1930s, Washakorie was dead and buried, but he left his curse behind. It didn't occur to me until later how unfair it was that we had no part in digging up those bones, but we had to bear the brunt of the curse. Yet, on that first day of school, none of this worried me. I was simply excited to be there.

It's true that I'd heard the stories about the haunted school piano from the older kids. But I knew from personal experience that they lied about things like what's poison oak and what isn't, so I wouldn't admit to believing their spooky stories.

Even though I doubted their word, I was relieved to discover that the piano wasn't in my classroom. Instead, it sat alone in its own room across the hall. Even though the school bell summoned us to line up at the school doors every morning, it was nice old Mrs. Wintch's job to sit at that piano and play a catchy marching tune when it was time for us to come inside, go home for lunch, and come back in for afternoon classes. Whenever I passed the piano room, I'd peek inside and see Mrs. Wintch pounding the keys with gusto. It always surprised me to see such an old lady playing such lively tunes. The cheery melodies that rolled off her fingers made you want to swing your arms and tap your toes.

One day in the fall, the school sat solemnly under a gray sky, leaves outside fading from brilliant red and gold to rusty iron and moldy wheat. It wasn't a very cheery day, to be sure, but Mrs. Wintch's come-inside melody helped lift my mood some.

I remember that my class was busy practicing writing our alphabet letters, because I was concentrating on the intricacies of the capital

"B" with my tongue sticking out, and I almost bit it off when the first unexpected piano chord sounded. I pulled my tongue in and lifted my head along with everyone else in the classroom. Our eyes turned in unison toward the door.

Somber, ominous notes floated through the doorway and sent a shiver down my back. I knew I was supposed to stand, but I didn't. The last thing I wanted to do was line up and march out into that hall. Cold prickles raised up along the back of my neck, but I didn't dare to reach my hand back and rub them down. I didn't dare move at all. I was flooded with a sudden fear that if I so much as blinked, something awful would see me, and some terrible thing would happen to me. What, I didn't know, but I didn't want to find out, either.

"Whatever in the world?" our teacher, Miss Jenkins, said. "Stay where you are, class." I obeyed, frozen to the edge of my chair with my hands gripping the seat. Miss Jenkins disappeared through the doorway.

I was scared for her—I really was. I didn't have any idea why Mrs. Wintch had changed her tune. I hoped that Miss Jenkins would tell her to stop scaring us.

Suddenly, another thought struck me. What if it wasn't Mrs. Wintch playing the piano? What if the principal had hired a new teacher?

The music stopped. Miss Jenkins appeared in the doorway, her hand pressed over her heart like when we said the Pledge of Allegiance. Her face was as white as the chalk on the blackboard ledge.

Alice Kinsey raised her hand. "Who was it?" she asked, not even waiting to get called on.

Miss Jenkins seemed to have difficulty focusing her eyes on Alice. "No one," she said. She moved toward her desk. "It was no one."

Then Miss Jenkins grabbed a book as though it was the last stick of wood in a winter camp, and opened it up. "Let's read a story together, shall we?" she asked, her face smiling but her voice unnaturally high and tense. We put our writing practice papers away and folded our hands on our desks to listen.

This wasn't the last time I heard that death march music, and it wasn't the last time it sent cold prickles squirming down my back.

One of the best things about school were fire drills, especially after I moved to the older grades on the top floors. The fire escape was a curved slide, slanted down from the third-floor windows and turning the corner of the building at the second story level to allow students from that floor to climb out their window and escape the pretend fire. The third floor was best, because you got the longest ride.

At the sound of the school bell, the little kids on the first floor had to line up and march out the door with their teacher. This was a good arrangement, because some of them were too scared to slide down. Even some of the second floor students would scream and cover their faces when told to get on the slide. When this happened, their teachers led them down the stairs. They didn't know what they were missing.

Us lucky students in the high school classrooms on the third floor scrambled for the designated fire escape window as soon as we heard the signal. We'd shift our feet and whisper and nudge each other until the teacher said, "All right, single file, be courteous. Now, go!" Then we'd whoop and holler and scramble out the window onto the metal chute.

Sometimes when we passed other windows, kids would try to cut in and hop on the slide ahead of us. It was quite a scramble, as we could get zipping along pretty good from the top floor. It was great.

We older boys were instructed to wait at the bottom of the slide and catch the younger kids when they came flying down. Some of them weren't coordinated enough to land on their feet but would instead go sailing off the edge with their legs out straight and end up with a rude bump to their behinds.

It was no trouble for us to catch the little kids, especially when the girls from our grade stood around to watch us. I imagined Polly with her eyes pinned on me as I stretched my muscular arms out to catch the children. I hoped she was impressed.

I'll never forget the spring day when the bell rang loud and insistent, signaling a fire drill. My little sister Ginny had graduated to a second floor class, and even though I sometimes let on to my friends that she was a pain, inside myself I really wanted to make sure that she got down the slide safe and sound.

Before the first clang of the bell had faded away, I was up and standing in front of the window. It helped that my desk was right next to it. Jay hustled into line and bumped into me. "Be careful!" I exclaimed.

"Shush," said our teacher, Mr. Walters. "You should set an example for the younger students. If this were an actual crisis, they would need you to show them the way."

"Set an example," Jay whispered. I could hardly keep from laughing out loud. I let my chin drop but kept my lips together, pulling my face into a long and haughty expression.

Jay snorted and said, "If the teachers are gonna stand around and talk our ears off while we burn up, at least we'll die with dignity." Then Jay copied my expression.

Mr. Walters swept a glance around the room to make sure there were no stragglers. Then he gave me a nod. "All right, you may proceed."

The window was up and I was out. I slid down on the seat of my pants and sprang up with a flourish as soon as my feet touched dirt. Jay was right behind me. I turned and waited for the rest of my class to get down. I watched Polly, Rebecca Ann, and Melinda from my class swoosh toward me and Jay, holding their skirts tight against their legs and blushing when they caught my eye. I didn't smile back, though. I wanted to show them that I was a real man in any crisis, and not one to take escaping from a fake fire lightly.

When the girls neared the bottom, Jay jumped in front of them. He screamed and put up his hands as though afraid that they were going to knock him over. The girls shrieked, and Jay jumped aside at the last minute, grinning from ear to ear. He was so childish.

The smaller kids started trickling down the slide, and I bumped Jay out of the way so I could be at the bottom for Ginny. I was well aware that the girls from my class were still milling around, watching me.

Ginny's friend Ted came into view, his feet looking half a size too big in his older brother's cast-off shoes. He started down the slide, raised his eyes, and caught sight of me. Instead of grinning, as I had expected him to do, his eyes went round as eggs, and his mouth opened up and let out a scream. He twisted over, his fingers scraping the smooth metal surface of the slide as though trying to climb back up.

"Ted!" I called. "What's the matter?"

"Get away!" he screamed in a voice of abject terror. "Mommy!"

I reached for him. Unbelievably, he screamed even louder. I managed to get hold of him and set him on his feet. He took off, running blindly, until Polly caught him. She bent down to talk to him, and his arms wrapped around her neck as tight as a cocklebur on a sheep's hide.

I looked at Jay and spread my hands. "What did I do?"

Jay shrugged. "I dunno."

I looked up the slide just in time to see my little sister's face peer out of the window. She looked down at me, so I waved to her. "Come on, Ginny. I'll catch you."

Ginny's eyes sprang wide open, and she shook her head with such violence that I was worried it might come off. I could see her teacher lean out to speak to her, and after a moment, Ginny disappeared from view. What was going on?

Jay took my place at the bottom of the slide. Even though I'd been told to stay with my class during every fire drill, my concern for Ginny was stronger than the school rules. I walked around to the door where the first floor kids were trickling outside. I didn't go against the tide but waited and watched until Ginny appeared, clutching her teacher's hand.

I walked over and looked down at Ginny's tear-stained face. "Why didn't you slide down?" I asked. "I would have caught you."

Ginny let go of her teacher's hand and grabbed me around my waist. "Daniel, where were you?"

Was she blind? She'd looked right at me. "I was at the bottom of the slide. I told you to come down."

Ginny shook her head against my shirt. "That wasn't you. I heard you calling, but I couldn't see you anywhere."

I pushed Ginny away and stared down at her. "Then who was standing at the bottom of the slide, I'd like to know?"

Ginny's eyes went wide, and fresh tears welled up and spilled over her cheeks. "It was a scary old Indian with a mean face and long, black hair."

It felt like my heart stopped beating, and I had the awful sensation of spiders crawling down my neck. Was Ginny seeing things, or had something happened to me that I didn't even know about?

I pulled Ginny into a hug and held her until we both quit shaking.

Still, that wasn't the worst of it. The worst day was a stormy one, with the dark clouds hanging around after a night of thunder and lightning that kept waking me up. So it was with bleary eyes and dragging step that I made my way to school that morning.

I should have stayed home.

The inside of the school felt as cold and damp as the air outside, and even the marching music failed to lift my spirits. Maybe there was something wrong with me. Maybe I was coming down with a fever. I reached out and touched a finger to the radiator in the upstairs hallway. It was stone cold. Why hadn't the heat been turned on?

We found our seats in our classroom. Then Principal Erickson stuck his head in our door. "Boys and girls, I'm going downstairs to see what's taking Mr. Fjeldsted so long to get the heat going. Keep your coats on. We'll soon have the problem set to rights." Then he was gone.

That was the last time I ever saw him.

I shivered in my jacket and tried to follow what my teacher, Mr. Walters, was saying at the front of the room. I watched him scratch the chalk across the black surface of the board and I wrote down the spelling words five times each.

It seemed as though time had almost stopped, and that the day would never end. I felt as though I were trapped in a sticky fog that wouldn't let me move freely. Something was dragging at my heart and slowing down my whole world.

I was sure that enough time had passed that the school day should have been over when the door to our classroom banged open. We all looked up to see who would dare burst in without knocking first. I couldn't believe it when I saw Miss Jenkins standing inside the doorway, her face alive with panic. "There's a situation, Mister Walters. Please, will you come?"

I think that she was trying to be discreet, but her cryptic message only served to whet the appetite of our class. We looked at each other with wide eyes. Some of the girls looked worried and scared.

"Sit quietly and wait for further instructions," Mr. Walters barked. Then he was out the door at a run.

If he really thought we'd sit quietly, he didn't know us very well. Some of us crowded to the windows to see if we could see anything. Others peered out the door, shushing the rest of us in the hope that they might hear something that would give them a clue as to what was going on.

My earlier fatigue was replaced by a terrible anxiety. It was not an improvement.

It seemed to be another long day before Mr. Walters came back, his face creased with emotion. "Boys and girls," he said. "You are dismissed. Everyone go home."

He was met with shocked silence. This had never happened before—ever.

"Class, stand up," Mr. Walters said, his voice patient, as though speaking to a group of first graders.

We stood. I shivered inside my jacket, the cold of the room taking on a sharp edge that cut through to my heart as sure as a north breeze could cut through my shirt in the dead of winter.

"Dismissed," Mr. Walters said. "Go straight home." Then Mr.

Walters disappeared through the doorway without even waiting to make sure we followed orders.

We murmured among ourselves as we made our way to the door, leaving behind our books and papers and filing out into the hallway, boys on one side and girls on the other, heading for the exit.

My concern for Ginny overrode my training. I risked breaking ranks in order to detour to my sister's classroom and pick her up. I knew deep inside that something was terribly wrong, and I wasn't leaving my sister's safety to chance.

I found Ginny lining up with her class, her eyes wide with worry. I reached toward her, hoping that she would recognize me and not mistake me for some old, grizzled Indian. Ginny smiled up at me and took my hand. Her teacher was still shooing students from the corners of the classroom toward the line. When I lifted my hand, Ginny's teacher saw me. I pointed to Ginny and then to myself. The teacher nodded, and I took my sister with me.

Our exit from the school took us down the hall that held the stairway to the cellar. The cellar door was open, and Mrs. Wintch stood at the top of the stairs looking down, tears coursing down her cheeks and her mouth all twisted as though she were trying to hold in a scream.

I slowed my steps and looked over my shoulder. No one else was around. "Are you all right?" I asked.

Mrs. Wintch looked at me, but I don't think she really knew who I was, or else she wouldn't have said what she did. She may have mistaken me for someone older since I was tall for my age and was holding Ginny by the hand.

"Oh, they're dead! They're both dead!" she cried.

Her words struck me with a pain as sure as if she'd slapped my face. "Who?" I asked. I wasn't sure I really wanted to know. The question just popped out without me thinking about it.

"Mr. Fjeldsted and Principal Erickson! They're both dead!" Mrs. Wintch wrung her hands and stared down the stairs, not even trying to wipe off the tears that rolled down her cheeks.

Mrs. Wintch was old. Surely she was confused. I had seen the principal alive not more than an hour ago. He couldn't be dead. She must be mistaken. But I didn't say any more. I just took Ginny home.

Later that day, Dad came in, his face as saggy as a half-full bag of potatoes. He gathered us together and told us that, as near as they could figure, Mr. Fjeldsted had gone down into the basement to check on the furnace and saw that the floor was underneath a couple of inches of water. He must have tried the light switch, but it didn't work. It seems that he waded through the water and turned on the light bulb with the pull cord that hung down beside it. Something was wrong with the wiring, and electricity coursed through him, killing him on the spot.

When the principal went down to check on Mr. Fjeldsted and saw him lying in the water, he'd rushed to help him. He must have tried the light too, because he was electrocuted as well.

When Miss Jenkins had gone looking for the principal, she spotted the two bodies in the dim light coming in from the basement windows. Miss Jenkins never left the safety of the stairs but ran back up and called on Mr. Walters for help. Mr. Walters knew enough to call the city electrician, who turned off the power before anyone went in to retrieve the bodies.

I never could walk down that hallway again. I always went around the long way. Even seeing that door from a distance sent a cold snake of fear sliding down my back.

The legend of old Washakorie's curse flared up. It was all the kids talked about, even after the school re-opened, which didn't happen until after the funerals.

"It's just like he said," Jay told me, his voice tight with excitement. "He said there'd be two dead men for the two skeletons that were dug up. It's just like he said."

I didn't answer him. There was nothing else to say.

The school bell was the pride of the whole community. Besides being used to summon us to school and for fire drills, it was rung for any and every important occasion. The Fourth of July was brought in with its clear tones ringing against the mountainsides and rolling back down into the valley. It was rung through the cold air of Christmas Eve and the bright morning of New Year's day. It sounded on election days and Founding Father's Day. The ring of the bell would herald every celebration in town.

After the deaths of Mr. Fjeldsted and Principal Erickson, that all changed.

The day after the funeral for the school custodian and principal, I woke up in the middle of the night with my heart pounding in fear. Then, with my eyes wide, and scared in the darkness of my room, I heard the unmistakable toll of the school bell ringing in the midnight air. The sound set my teeth on edge. Who was ringing that bell? There was no town meeting in the middle of the night, and it wasn't any holiday that I knew of. Could it be that someone's house was on fire?

I hopped out of bed and went to the window. I looked out and saw nothing but stars.

Suddenly feeling like a scared little boy, I hurried out into the hall and down the stairs to my parent's room. Their door opened before I even reached it, and my father stepped out.

"Daniel?" he said. "What's going on?"

"I don't know," I said, my voice squeaking on the last note, but I was too scared to feel embarrassed.

"I'll go see what it is," Dad said. "You stay here."

He didn't have to tell me twice.

Mama came out in her dressing gown. She sat me at the kitchen table and fixed me some homemade bread spread with a generous layer of plum jam. Normally I love plum jam, and my mother is hard pressed to keep it in the house. But tonight I could only nibble the edges of the bread. The ominous sound of the bell filled my ears and took away my appetite.

I gave up and set my bread and jam down on my plate. "Where's Ginny?"

"She must be asleep."

"How can she be?" I asked, getting up from my chair and heading for Ginny's room. I imagined her cowering in a corner of her room, her hands tight over her ears to try and shut out the gong of the night bell.

Mama followed me. I pulled open Ginny's door. Her still form made a hump under her blanket, and her golden head rested quietly on her pillow.

"See?" Mama said.

"I've got to check," I answered, moving into the room.

"Don't you dare wake her up," Mama warned.

"I won't," I whispered. I couldn't tell Mama that my heart was worried sick that Ginny wasn't sleeping at all but was really lying there dead.

I bent over Ginny and saw the slight rise and fall of the covers over her chest. The flood of relief that coursed through me was hot enough to bring tears to my eyes.

I backed out of the room and pulled the door shut. "How can she do that?" I asked as we headed back to the kitchen.

Mom shrugged. "I don't know. Maybe she's dreaming of bells."

As soon as I sat down at the table, the bell stopped. The silence that followed was as ominous as the ringing had been.

Dad came in a little while later. Mom and I both looked up at him. He shook his head. "No one was at the school."

Mom spoke up. "But who rang the bell?"

Dad spread his hands. "No one was there. I met Ed Winters and Theodore Southby at the door. Ed opened the school with his keys, and we all headed for the bell room. The rope was swinging up and down all right, but no one was in there." Dad dropped his hands and shook his head. "It was the darnedest thing. As we watched, the rope went limp and the bell quit ringing. We checked the whole building. It was empty."

There was silence. I looked from one parent to another. Neither one of them seemed to know what to say.

Finally, Mom broke the silence. Her quiet voice made me jump. "Lock the door, Harold. Let's all go back to bed."

I headed for my room but I didn't go in. When I heard my parent's door click shut, I went back to Ginny's room. I grabbed the extra blanket that Mom kept folded at the foot of her bed and curled up on the rug on her floor. I lay there and shivered for a long time until I fell into an uneasy slumber.

After that night, the bell would sometimes ring of its own accord. We couldn't figure out why until we made the connection that someone in town always died when the bell rang.

That wasn't even the worst of it. When World War II broke out and Donny Simms went out to fight in the war with some other fellows, the bell rang itself again. The odd thing was, no one in town turned up dead.

For a couple of days, it seemed as if the spirits that cursed the school were way off track. Then Donny's mom got a telegram telling her that Donny had been killed in battle two days earlier.

I got to hate that sound of the ringing bell. It sounded for a couple of other dead soldiers until the end of the war silenced it. I had a hard time going to school under the cold, metal eye of that haunted bell. It seemed to be watching me like a vulture, waiting for the day when it could ring itself over my cold, dead corpse.

One good thing that happened at school was the arrival of our new film projector. We were awfully proud of it, even though it only showed black and white films instead of the new colored movies that were in theaters.

Unfortunately, we didn't get to see any wild west films, but what did we expect for free? We were treated to the life cycles of bugs, forest fires, and cultures from other countries.

The projector was kept under lock and key by Mr. Madsen, who served as our school librarian. He was the only one qualified to operate it, and was ultimately responsible for its safety.

Usually on film days we couldn't keep quiet. We'd only seen a couple of them when we were informed one day that we'd be watching a film on East Africa. I was excited to see it, as I didn't imagine that I'd ever get to Africa in my lifetime. Mr. Madsen threaded the film through the projector and switched it on.

"All right, everybody, quiet down now," he called. I couldn't really see much point in that, since the films were silent.

"Turn off the lights," Mr. Madsen called. Someone flicked off the light, and the black and white images burst into life on the screen. After a few minutes, we were all silent, mesmerized by the unfolding scenes of life in Africa.

Then something odd happened. A reddish tinge spread from behind a grass hut on the right side of the screen. It crept out toward the black natives dancing up and down with their spears held aloft. The film image switched to a row of giant bugs skewered on a long stick held over a fire. The reddish stain was there too. After a few seconds, the redness crept back into the corner of the screen and disappeared.

I glanced back at Mr. Madsen, who was fiddling with the controls. He looked back up at the screen and gave a quick nod.

I leaned over to Jay, who was sitting beside me. "Did you see that?"

"Yeah. Creepy."

From the other whispers going around the room, I knew that everyone had seen the red stain.

That wasn't the last time. From then on, a reddish tinge would creep across the different films we watched every once in a while, and not always from the same place. The day I really started dreading films was when shadowy, indistinct faces superimposed themselves over the images on the film.

One day, Mr. Madsen asked me to carry a stack of paper supplies for him. I said I would. I filled my arms with paper and followed him up to his supply room. I watched him put his key in the lock. I heard it click when the bolt disengaged, and I followed him in. There was the unmistakable whir of machinery, and I fixed my eyes on the film projector. It was turning its little wheels in a race to nowhere. The film posts were empty.

I shot a sideways look at Mr. Madsen, wondering if he was embarrassed to be caught in his carelessness of leaving the projector on.

Mr. Madsen turned to stare at me. "Do you see that?"

It seemed to be a pointless question, but I answered, "Um, yes, sir."

"I did not leave that running. I know I didn't. Who else could have a key to this room?"

I didn't answer. Mr. Madsen didn't really expect me to. He was just talking to himself. I set the paper down on the counter and got out of there as fast as I could.

The next film we saw was on the Grand Canyon. A kid named Arlo Anderson was goofing off at the front of the room, braying like a donkey when a string of pack mules appeared on the screen. Mr. Madsen's warnings to be quiet didn't have much effect, since the girls were giggling in delight at Arlo's antics.

At last Mr. Madsen abandoned his post beside the projector and headed toward the front of the room. I expected to see Mr. Madsen grab Arlo by the ear and pull him out into the hall. Then Arlo would be braying for real.

Before Mr. Madsen reached Arlo, the projector clicked, then clunked, then whirred. A hush fell over the room when the film began running backwards. My eyes were drawn from Arlo back to the screen. Donkeys scurried up the Grand Canyon trail backwards as fast as they could go, their tails uphill of their heads.

"Mr. Madsen," I said, my voice sounding small in the darkened room. I raised my hand as though waiting to be called on, even though Mr. Madsen wasn't looking at me. I could see from the flickering light bouncing off the white screen that Mr. Madsen's eyes were fixed on the projector. I turned and looked too. No one was even within arm's reach of the machine that busily churned the film backward as though it had a mind of its own.

From then on, I always sat at the back of the room, on whichever chair was closest to the door. I would avert my eyes when the red tinges appeared and disappeared. I fought down panic when strange and shadowy images popped up on the screen that had nothing to do with the film subject. Before long, Mr. Madsen returned the projector to the manufacturer as defective.

As one of the upperclassmen, I was privileged to claim membership in the fearless group called "Ledge Monkeys." It was our good fortune that the school was built with six-inch wide ledges all the way around, just underneath the windows. In spite of the fact that they were out of reach from the ground, we found a way to overcome that obstacle. Jay was the first one to dare climbing up the fire escape slide in order to gain access to the ledges that circled the ground floor windows. He was an insufferable braggart after he completed his circuit without falling to the ground. Of course, we other fellows couldn't let him get away with a solo victory, so we all followed suit. When we were caught, we were scolded and told not to walk the ledges anymore.

In spite of the warning, it was only a matter of time before we set our sights on the more challenging second story ledge. Because we'd been warned by school authorities to keep off, we made our second story attempt under cover of dusk. This took more courage. Still, I was willing. After all, I was nearing eighteen and almost ready to graduate. I had to leave some sort of legacy behind.

We climbed up the fire escape, pulling with our hands and pressing our bare feet into the bottom corners at either side of the smooth, metal slide. When we reached the second story, we climbed out onto the six-inch ledge, our hands gripping the rock that lined the window openings so hard that the grit dug into our fingers. It was a harrowing journey, much higher than it appeared to be when looking up from ground level. Making the trip at dusk added an element of danger, and I almost wished I'd stayed home. Almost.

When we completed our circuit, I felt like a king. I whooped and let go of my death grip on the building, sliding my way down the fire escape to the ground. I was invincible.

It seemed to me that we'd achieved the ultimate accomplishment, since a fall from the second story would almost assuredly result in a broken limb or two. But the next thing we knew, Arlo had his sights set on the third story window ledge. When the rest of us expressed our doubts, Arlo called us a bunch of broody hens.

"But what if you fall?" Jay said. "At that height you risk more than a broken bone. Death is more like it."

"That's why I'm gonna do it," Arlo bragged.

"We wouldn't be much help to you if we were all standing up on that ledge." Jay looked around at us other guys. "We'll follow along underneath to catch you."

Arlo was silent for a moment. "Ha!" he said. "What makes you think

I'll fall?" But it was all bluster on his part, and he agreed to Jay's plan.

Arlo looked very small in the moonlight, perched up there at the top of the fire escape, twenty-six feet in the air. I could only imagine how he felt when he looked down at us.

Arlo reached out from the fire escape and grabbed the edge of the window frame in slow motion. He positioned his feet on the ledge. I stared up at his heels hanging out over the ledge. Only his toes held him on. One slip, and we'd have to catch him or watch him die.

I glanced around at the other fellows gripping the edges of a blanket that we intended to use to catch Arlo if he did happen to fall. I hoped that we'd all head in the same direction if worse came to worse, instead of pulling each other off balance. I shivered at the thought of the ghostly bell-ringer pulling the rope for Arlo.

Arlo began shuffling around the window ledge. We followed along underneath him, keeping our hands tight on the blanket and our faces pointed upward. The other fellows were washed pale with moonlight. It made them look like a gathering of ghosts staring up into eternity. I wondered if they were as scared as I was.

Arlo rounded the first corner. Now that the fire escape was out of sight, he moved with more caution along the second wall. His progress was painfully slow. When he neared the end, I noticed that I was getting a crick in my neck, but I didn't dare look away. We were Arlo's only hope if things went wrong.

Arlo rounded the second corner and I relaxed my grip a little. It looked like he was going to make it. His face was pressed pretty close to the windows as he passed his hands from one window frame to another, his feet shuffling along in increments of inches. He neared the third corner and pulled himself over to the next to last window. He froze. I could see his back go rigid. Then a scream of sheer terror ripped from his throat, the most frightening scream I'd ever heard come out of a human being. My disbelief turned to horror as I watched him let go. He tipped backward, and I stood staring with my mouth gaping open. A tug on the blanket nearly pulled me over.

"Move it!" Jay yelled. I blinked and stared in dismay at the obstacle before us. We'd never be able to save Arlo's life now. A big, blue spruce tree grew right where we needed to stand in order to catch him. Panic seized me and I screamed.

Arlo hit the spruce branches and crashed on through. Since his single, awful scream, he'd made no sound. I wondered if he was dead. Could the curse have claimed a third victim?

The other fellows yanked on the blanket, and I followed them to the edge of the spruce. With no help from me, they managed to get the blanket stretched tight just as Arlo rolled out of the bottom branches. By some miracle, he landed on our makeshift trampoline, but we weren't prepared for his weight. We all grunted and tumbled to the ground, ending up in a tangle of arms and legs.

My voice quavered. "Is he dead?

The only answer was the wild scrabbling of Arlo's arms and legs. As soon as his two feet touched earth, he was gone, racing across the lawn faster than I'd ever seen a person run before. If he was bleeding, I didn't see it. If he had a broken bone or two, they weren't slowing him down any.

We all scrambled to our feet and hurried across the grass after him, figures running in the moonlight. We found him huddled in a ditch.

"Arlo?" I asked, afraid that the fall had somehow damaged his brain. "Are you all right?" Maybe he'd hit his head and didn't know us anymore.

Arlo's eyes were as big and white as two moons, looking past me toward the upper story of the school. "Horrible," he muttered. "Watching me." He shuddered and covered his face with his hands. "Something's up there."

We helped Arlo home, casting glances over our shoulders at the dark building watching us go. The school windows glowed an eerie silver in the moonlight. When I had to part company with the fellows and head for my own house, I admit that I ran all the way.

The next day, we discovered that someone had pushed the dressmaking class's full-length mirror up against the corner window, right at the spot where Arlo had been so spooked that he took a dive off a third-story window ledge. It was no comfort. For all we knew, the Indian ghosts pushed it there after we left the school.

Eventually, I graduated and moved away. It was several years later when I heard that the school was being torn down. My curiosity got the better of me, and I made the trip to my old hometown. I almost didn't recognize the place. Part of the grand old building was reduced to a pile of rubble. I noticed that several people were picking up bricks and carrying them off as souvenirs. As soon as I wondered if I should take one, I decided not to. There were still ten years left of the Indian's curse.

This story is based on reports that Chief Washakorie warned the settlers of Spring City in the late 1800s that they shouldn't build a school on top of a Indian burial ground. They built the school anyway, and an angry Washakorie cursed the school.

Several decades later, two men were electrocuted in the basement of the school after flooding rains. There were also reports of students seeing the faces of old Indians on the upperclassmen who were stationed at the bottom of the fire escape slides, haunting music sounding from a piano where no one sat, and strange images and reddish tinges coming and going on the screen where a projector showed various educational films. One student walking the third-floor ledge screamed in panic and fell through the branches of an evergreen tree. He told his friends that he'd seen an old, spooky Indian face looking out at him from the upper window. The next day, the boys discovered a full-length mirror pushed up against the glass at the point where the boy had fallen.

Sources: *Book of Mt. Pleasant 1938* and *Hansen Family History 1976*.

SO SCARED

"Bringing in the sheaves, bringing in the sheaves," I sang along with the other kids as I bent to grab another handful of wheat stalks. I knew all the words of the old hymn by heart, and it was fun to belt them out as I worked. Mary Ann Hyde always made our work go faster when she had us sing as we gathered up the loose stems of grain that had escaped harvesting.

I pretended that I sang only because Sister Hyde asked me to, but truth be told, sometimes I'd sing when I was out herding the cattle, after looking around to make sure that no one was within earshot. I didn't always mind having anyone hear me sing, but lately my voice would catch me off guard, warbling up to a squeak before it dropped back down to where it belonged in its new, lower range. Since I had a couple of older brothers, I knew that being thirteen would do that to a guy, but no one said I had to like it.

I carried my armload of wheat over to the wagon and saw my mother headed toward it with a small bundle of wheat stalks gripped in her hands. She wasn't looking at me, though. Her head swiveled from side to side, her brow wearing a familiar crease of worry that had been there for so long that she even looked worried in her sleep.

I knew that Ma was scared spitless of the Indians. Even if she hadn't told me over and over again, I would have seen it in her eyes. She was like a mouse in constant fear of meeting up with a cat. Her graying hair was even the color of a mouse's fur.

I glanced over at Sister Hyde, who was laughing at something Iona Clay had just said. Even though Sister Hyde was about the same age as Mama, her brow was smooth, and the lines on her face were laugh lines. Even though she'd lost every single baby she'd ever had, she still found joy in life.

Why couldn't Mama be like that? Why couldn't she stop being afraid? The mountains were dotted with cheerful spots of autumn red and yellow, and the bugs were less voracious since the cold nights were nipping them to death and the days were only warm enough for a few lazy flies to bumble along through the air. There was a lot to be happy about.

When I dropped my wheat in the back of the wagon, I caught

a whiff of the fried chicken and corn bread that sat under the fabric covering the lunch basket. Dared I snitch a mouthful? No one would need to know. I could chew and swallow pretty fast. It was almost time to eat lunch anyway. I rationalized that I'd just take less food when it was finally passed around.

I glanced up to see if anyone was watching. Mama's eyes connected with mine, and the opportunity was lost. I gave her an innocent smile. She tried to smile back, but her eyes didn't look the least bit happy. Sister Hyde had somehow talked Mama into coming along to help glean the fields today, even though Mama preferred to stay in the cabin with the latch solidly in place, carding wool and spinning and baking. She wouldn't generally open the door for anyone unless Pa was there. She had been told, along with everyone else, to give food to the Indians when they came asking for it, but Mama didn't like to. She trembled at the very thought, and if she was alone, she'd usually pretend she wasn't home.

Ever since she'd started on the trek across the plains, Mama had been deathly afraid of being killed by Indians. She was still afraid, even though we'd lived in Spring City for several years. Poor Mama. There was more to life than being afraid.

I turned away from the wagon. Strains of "Johnny's So Long At the Fair" drifted along the staggered row of children moving down the field together, bending and picking up wheat stalks as they went.

A movement caught my eye, and I turned to see three riders approaching. I gave a sudden start and stared hard, not wanting to believe my eyes. Indians were coming.

My first thought was to find my mother. I looked for her where I'd last seen her, but she wasn't there. If she saw the Indians, she'd be in a terrible state. In near panic, I glanced all around me but didn't see her anywhere. "Mama?"

The sound of muffled sobs reached my ears. I bent over and saw my mother huddled under the wagon, her head bent down and her hands covering her ears. She'd already seen the Indians. I decided that she was in the best place she could be.

I hurried down the row of gleaners. "Sister Hyde," I said. "Indians."

The children close enough to hear me stopped singing and whirled around to see for themselves. Sister Hyde turned to look too, her blue eyes watching the Indians approach. They were close enough that I could see a tomahawk in the lead rider's hand. Their heads bristled with feathers, making them look like birds of prey swooping down to pluck up some small animals for their bloody supper.

"Keep singing, children," Sister Hyde said.

If I didn't sing, I might scream. "He promised to bring me a bunch of blue ribbons," I sang, too scared to be embarrassed when my voice cracked on the word "blue."

"Orson," Sister Hyde said, putting her hand on my shoulder. "Go over to the wagon and get the food basket."

I suddenly remembered when Charles Christensen told me about the time he was just ten years old and his grandma filled a cloth sack with cookies for him and his little brother Fred, to eat on their way home. They headed off across the hills instead of sticking to the road. Charles insisted on rationing their sweet treat to make it last.

But Charles completely lost his appetite as soon as he heard the thud of horses' hooves. His worst fears were realized when a couple of Indians rode up to the brothers on their horses, shaking their fists and calling out things he couldn't understand. The Indians looked at each other and laughed, and then shook their bows and knives at the boys. Charles knew they were done for.

One of the Indians pointed to the sack that Charles clutched in his hand. Charles was so afraid that he couldn't even move, but Fred wasn't. He grabbed the sack away from his older brother and thrust it up at the Indian. The Indian slid down from off his horse. Charles was so scared that he almost peed his pants, but Fred stood his ground. Charles was sure that he would be forced to watch the Indian grab Fred and ride off with him.

Instead, the Indian grabbed the bag, opened it up, and looked inside. Then he gave a mighty whoop and leapt up onto his horse. He took off at a gallop, and his partner sheathed his knife and wheeled his horse in hot pursuit.

Charles wasted no time in grabbing Fred's hand and hightailing it home. After that, he always stuck to the road.

I turned away from Sister Hyde and made a dash for the wagon, passing the row of gleaners whose eyes were fastened on the Indians who would soon be within scalping distance. Sister Hyde's voice rang out over the field with the words to "Johnny's So Long At the Fair:"

"Oh, dear, what can the matter be? Oh, dear . . ."

The other children gradually began singing along with Sister Hyde as I sprinted toward our lunch. I heard Mama whimpering underneath the wagon when I grabbed the basket. "Stay quiet," I said. Then I turned and headed back. No Indian would get my Mama today if I had anything to do about it. They'd have to kill me first.

Sister Hyde walked toward the Indians, who brandished their weapons and bared their teeth. They could strike her down as easily as not, yet she didn't hesitate. She walked straight and tall, though she was no taller than me, and raised her hand, palm out flat, in a gesture of peace.

My feet slowed. I knew I needed to take the food to Sister Hyde, but she was just too darn close to the Indians for my liking. Yet I had to do whatever I could to help the others, especially Mama.

I set my jaw and headed for Sister Hyde, singing, "Johnny's so long at the fair." The food in my arms didn't even tempt me any more. My stomach was too twisted in knots. If I had snitched a bite earlier, it would have been wasted because I knew the fear in my belly would have thrown it up by now.

The three Indians turned their eyes on me—eyes so black that I felt as if I were staring into a well that had no bottom. "He promised to bring me a bunch of blue ribbons," I sang, my voice cracking on "ribbons."

One of the Indians grinned wickedly. He turned and said something to the others before he sang a quavering note in a falsetto voice that sounded eerie and wild. They all burst into laughter. My face burned with embarrassment, but I kept on singing. The Indian with the tomahawk pointed to the basket that I held.

Sister Hyde gestured from the basket to the riders and spread her arms out with her palms facing backward. She glanced over her shoulder at the children and shook her head, and then stared at the Indians. "If I give you food, you leave." She pointed in the direction the Indians had come from.

I moved beside Sister Hyde, still warbling about Johnny at the fair. The children's voices were so soft I felt as though I was singing a solo. Still, I sang, my voice off-key and cracking. If we were lucky, my awful singing would give those Indians a bad headache.

"Thank you, Orson." Sister Hyde lifted the basket. The Indian with the tomahawk leaned down and grabbed it in his large hand, the muscles on his biceps bulging as he raised the basket up to his lap. He lifted the lid, and his face split into a grin. With a quick shout, he wheeled his horse and rode away. His two companions took off after him, yelling and whooping.

Then my legs gave out and I sank to the ground. I didn't mean to, but it just happened.

"Orson? Are you all right?"

"Yeah. My legs just stopped working." I pushed myself back up onto my feet. "I've got to see to Mama."

"Why don't you take her home, Orson?"

"She won't go."

"Why not?"

"Because the Indians are out there." I felt a quiver in my stomach even as I spoke the words. I was scared too.

"Well, without something to eat, we really can't do much more today," Sister Hyde said. "Let's all go home."

She rounded up the children and I walked over to the wagon and bent down to see my mother curled up, rocking and crying softly.

"Mama, they're gone," I said, putting my arm around her as best I could. "The Indians have gone."

Mama kept her hands over her face. "I'm so scared," she said. "I don't want to be killed by Indians, I don't! Someday they're going to get me, I just know it."

"They're gone," I said again. "You're okay."

Mama wouldn't come out until Sister Hyde led the children over. "Everyone put your gleanings in the wagon," she said, her voice lilting and cheerful. "My, but we got a lot done this morning. Come on, everyone, back to town, and we'll see if we can't find some bread and honey for our lunch."

The sound of Sister Hyde's voice gave Mama the courage to crawl out from under the wagon. She crept close beside it all the way home, shooting frequent glances at the mountains through her red-rimmed eyes.

Mama would never go gleaning after that.

It was only a couple of weeks later when I went out herding cows so they could forage one last time before we'd have to shelter them for the winter and feed them on stored hay. Papa was away working at the shingle mill. The shingle cutter that he'd brought over from England made the work go much faster, and the shingles he made with it were more uniform than the ones made using the old method. He always had more than enough work to do. Papa's skills were in high demand with all the people moving into the valley, and he wasn't home very often. Mama had never liked being left alone, but she liked it even less now. Even though my older brothers were all moved out and on their own, and I was the last one living at home, I couldn't stay with Mama. I had to see to the cows.

"Look, Mama, if any Indians come around, they'll only be wanting a little food."

Mama gripped her hands together and looked as though she might start crying right there on the spot.

"Okay, Mama, I'll keep in sight of the house. I'll hurry down if I see anyone coming, all right?"

Mama nodded her head. "I'm sorry I'm so scared," she said, biting her bottom lip.

"It's okay, Mama. Sometimes I get scared too."

Mama sank into her rocking chair and took up some mending with trembling hands. I cut myself a thick slice of the bread that Mama had baked several days earlier. It was dry and hard—really only good for bread and milk. Even though John had moved out months ago, Mama still baked as though all my brothers were still home.

I hurried outside, welcoming the freedom of being outdoors. I soon had the cows moving up into the little draw above our homestead.

The sun was lowering in the sky when I noticed a horse headed for the house. At first I thought Pa was home early from work. When I looked closer, I saw that it wasn't Pa at all but an Indian brave. I knew that I would never get to the house in time to intercept him, but I took off running anyway. I saw the Indian dismount and disappear around the corner that hid the front door.

I'd raced a few hundred yards when Mama's scream brought me up short. Her wail of terror sliced through the air and cut deep into my heart.

I stared at the house as my heart fought to escape my chest. What should I do? I knew in an instant that I couldn't handle this alone. I had to get help.

I turned and ran for the sawmill and Pa. When I got there, it felt like my lungs were ready to explode. I grabbed at the stitch in my side that had me bent sideways. "Pa," I gasped. "An Indian . . . Ma."

Pa didn't wait to hear any more. He ran out to his horse, jumped on, and helped me scramble up behind him. I hung onto Pa's waist as we raced for home.

The Indian's horse was gone. We dropped to the ground and dashed inside.

Ma was curled up on the floor, retching; the floor beneath her head was stained with blood. "Emmeline!" Pa gasped. He bent down and touched Ma's hair. The blood was oozing out of Ma's mouth, and she had her arms folded tight around her middle.

"Orson, go fetch the doctor, and if you can't find the doctor, get Sister Hyde."

I spun around and dashed out to the horse, my eyes blurred with tears. Why had I been such a coward? Why didn't I keep running to the house to save Mama from the Indian? The sight of Ma curled up in pain spurred me to ride faster than I'd ever ridden before. I got the doctor and, for good measure, Sister Hyde too. But I was too late. Mama died anyway.

"It's not your fault, son," Pa said, blinking back tears.

"I didn't keep going to help her after I heard her scream," I said. "I got scared. I should have kept going, but I was too scared."

Pa was shaking his head. "It's not your fault. I don't know how the Indian got inside in the first place. Maybe she forgot to latch the door."

The doctor said it looked as if she got hit in the stomach once, hard enough to break something up inside. Pa clamped his jaw shut and wiped his eyes. "With that bread we found on the floor, we can only guess that the Indian didn't like the old, dry bread your mother gave him. In his anger, he must have kicked her to do so much damage, and she was hurt too badly for the doc to do anything. And if the doc couldn't do anything, neither could you. She would have gone anyway, son, so none of this is your fault."

In spite of Pa's reassurance, it was still hard to convince myself.

While digging Ma's grave at the edge of the cemetery, we struck a solid rock ledge, so we shifted the hole over to one side. Pa said we wouldn't mark the grave until after the Indian unrest died down.

When I was an old man, they built a wall around the cemetery, using the rock ledge we'd uncovered while digging Ma's grave as a foundation. Ma's grave was on the outside of the wall, so my poor mother, scared to be alone for so much of her life, was consigned to a solitary resting place in death.

Orson Hyde and his wife Mary Ann Price Hyde never had any surviving babies of their own, but Mary Ann enjoyed children and took them with her to glean the fields around Spring City, Utah. They would sing as they picked up the stalks of grain that had escaped harvesting.

One day in the 1860s, three warriors carrying tomahawks and bristling with feathers rode up to them. Mary Ann told the children to keep singing. She gave the Indians all their food. Appeased, the warriors left the group unmolested.

Source: *Saga of the Sanpitch*, vol. 6 (1974), 17.

Glenn and Terri Morris told me the story of Glenn's great-great-grandmother Emmeline Arundale, who married John Lee in 1829 in England. When they immigrated to Utah, Emmeline could not shake her fear of being attacked by Indians. In 1866 thirteen-year-old Orson Pratt Lee saw an Indian enter their cabin and heard his mother scream. When Orson fetched his father, they found Emmeline on the floor, coughing up blood. After she died from her injuries, they buried her in an inconspicuous grave beside a submerged rock ledge. When the cemetery walls were erected in 1925, they enclosed the opposite side of the ledge, missing Emmeline's grave entirely. The pioneer lady who was so consumed by fear in her mortal life now rests in a lonely grave, alone outside the cemetery wall.

Around 1871, Charles John Christensen and his brother Fred were sharing a bag of cookies from their grandmother as they walked home from her house. Suddenly, some Indians swooped down on horseback, taunting the boys and laughing. The brothers finally surrendered their sack of cookies, and the Indians rode back into the hills, leaving them alone.

Sources: *Saga of the Sanpitch*, vol. 6 (1974), 17; vol. 21 (1989), 45.

GUESS AGAIN

I folded a dish towel four times over before opening the oven door. A wave of hot air hit me and forced me to turn my head. I grabbed the bread pans and plunked them onto the sideboard. Then I closed the oven and fanned my face.

Even though the kitchen door was open, it was still awfully hot. The open door let the bugs in, but having a few of them flying around was better than melting into the floorboards. I didn't want to melt. I wanted to go riding. Even though I'd done a full day's work, I was never too tired to ride.

I glanced around the house. The dishes were done, even though the grease from the family's breakfast of side pork had been awfully hard to clean from the plates. I'd already refilled the hot water reservoir on the back of the stove. It was hissing and sputtering in its metal confines, but it would quiet when the fire died down.

After the Seely family had left for town this morning, I'd fed and watered the calves and hogs, scattered grain for the chickens, mixed the dough, baked the bread, swept the floor, washed up the dishes, and finished the mending and darning.

Now I grabbed the hard bar of homemade soap and shaved some into the pan that sat on the back of the stove. In no time, the soap shavings would be softened and ready for the next batch of dishes or laundry or for scrubbing the outhouse seat.

I hurried out the open door and scooped up an armload of firewood, noticing that it would be time to split more soon. I had to fetch another armload to fill the box right up to the top. I chipped a corner off the salt block and dropped it into a bowl of water. I'd use the salted water for the family's morning mush. Now all that remained was the afternoon milking of the cow.

I really liked working for the Seely's. They paid me a generous thirty-five cents a week plus my room and board. The best thing about working for them was the privilege of riding their horses after my chores were finished.

I grabbed the milk bucket and headed for the barn, glad that I had refused the Seely's offer of a ride into town with them. If I'd gone, I would have had to catch up on my work when we got back, and there wouldn't be any time for riding. But now, I could get in a good, long ride before dark.

As I squeezed the milk into the bucket, I imagined galloping across the fields, my hair loose and streaming out behind me. I loved riding; I loved the freedom and the sense that I was flying across the fields. The only bad thing about it was when the Indian boys spotted me, they'd come galloping up behind, whooping and hollering until they caught up to me. They'd ride along beside me, calling out things that I didn't usually understand, but it was easy to guess that they were teasing me. I did my best to ignore them, but still, I hoped that they wouldn't see me today.

I finished with the milking and headed back to the house—one arm out to the side to balance while my other arm hung down heavy with the full milk bucket. I carried the milk down into the cooling cellar and strained it through a cloth. I skimmed the cream from the morning milk pans and poured it into the butter churn. Then I put the morning's milk into a pitcher. Next I carried the milk pans upstairs, washed them, and took them back down so I could pour the newly strained milk into them. I set the bucket at the bottom of the steps.

I looked at the butter churn out of the corner of my eye. I knew it was full enough to churn a batch of butter, but I wanted to ride. But what if the Seely's came home before I got back? I couldn't bear to think of them being disappointed in me.

I sighed and walked over to the churn. I worked the cream until the butter formed. The basement no longer felt cool; I was warm from the effort of churning the butter.

I scooped the butter out of the thick buttermilk and slapped it into the butter molds. I should strain the rest of the buttermilk, and pour it into a pitcher, but daylight was burning. I was hot, I was impatient, and I figured that I could save one chore for when I got back from riding.

I picked up the dirty milk bucket and made my way upstairs. As hot as the cooling cellar had felt, the kitchen was still hotter. I longed all the more for the breeze that would cool my face when I rode the horse out across the fields in the early evening air.

I used a ladle full of water from the soft, soapy pan at the stove's back to scrub the milk from the bucket. I knew from experience that it was easier to clean when the milk was fresh then after it had time to dry. I carried the bucket into the yard and rinsed it with clean water from the pump until it shone. Then I carried it back in the house and turned it upside down on the drain board.

Finally. I was ready.

A long shadow stretched across the floor and slanted across my feet. Alarmed, I whirled around. An Indian man stood in the doorway. The gnarled, old fist of one hand grasped a bent and battered bucket. His other hand clutched a heavy walking stick. He stared at me with one scarred eye, puckered up in a dark face crisscrossed by deep age lines. I sucked in my breath and stared at him with growing horror. I knew this Indian, and I was scared to death to be alone with him.

I'd seen this man walking along the back roads, supporting himself on his heavy walking stick. Brother Seely had warned me that this particular Indian wasn't quite right in the head. I believed him. More than once, I'd watched him swing that very same stick at young Indian girls who surrounded him and teased him. With his face twisted in fury, he would swing the hammer-like knob on top of his stick at the girls' heads. They would squeal and dance out of the way. I knew in my heart that he would not hesitate to smack one of them with the full force of his strength if he got the chance.

"Bizhi nehwe." I jumped at the sound of the Indian's voice. His mouth barely moved, and his eyebrows were pulled down. My stomach turned over. What had he said? I was fairly certain that if I didn't figure it out, there would be dire consequences.

The Indian raised the bucket in his hand and held it out toward me. The last thing I wanted to do was to get any closer to him, but if I didn't take the bucket, it might be the end of me. I took a few steps and stretched out my hand to grab the bucket handle. He let go.

I glanced into the bucket. It was in much worse shape up close. Someone must have thrown it out. Dirt clung to the dents that riddled the sides, and bits of grass and insect parts rattled around the bottom.

I wrinkled up my nose. Then I noticed that the Indian was staring at me. What did he want? Was I supposed to clean out his bucket? He could have rinsed it himself in the stream, but maybe he considered it women's work. I grabbed a cloth and wiped the inside clean. Then I turned it upside down over the floor. I would worry about sweeping up the dirt and bugs later.

I looked up at the Indian. He twisted his head slightly so that he could see me better out of his puckered eye, but he didn't make a move to take the bucket from me. A shiver ran down my back.

He must be looking for food. Bread was the most obvious choice, since I'd just baked some, and the smell was heavy in the air. I plucked a loaf from off of the drain-board and dropped it into the bucket. Then I held it out toward him.

The Indian didn't touch the bucket but reached inside and pulled out the bread. He tucked it under one arm. He gestured to the bucket and said, "Bizhi nehwe."

My heart sank. "Bizhi nehwe" obviously did not mean "bread." What else could it be? Then I had an idea. Since he'd gone to the trouble to bring me a bucket, it must be something liquid that he was after. He could have scooped all the water he wanted out of the stream, so he must want milk.

My heart lifted. There was plenty of milk in the cooling cellar. Once I fetched him some, he would surely leave.

"Just a minute," I said, holding up my index finger as though that single gesture would make him understand my words. I turned and made my way across the floor to the cellar door. Then I walked down the narrow stairs. I set the bucket on the floor and poured some of the morning's milk into it. I picked up the bucket and turned to go. As soon as I saw the Indian standing at the bottom of the steps, blocking my only exit, the room shrank in around me and I gasped. He had descended on his moccasined feet so quietly that I hadn't known he was there.

I gathered my wits in time to keep from dropping the milk, but I couldn't keep my hand from shaking when I held the bucket out toward him.

He clamped his walking stick under one arm along with his bread, and took the bucket in both hands. Instead of turning around and climbing out of the cellar to set me free, he tipped the bucket up to his mouth. When he tasted the milk, he lowered the bucket so fast that milk splashed over the sides.

"Dechende!" He up-ended the bucket and spilled the milk out onto the dirt floor.

I was outraged. That milk had taken a lot of my precious time to get, and he was wasting it.

"Stop that!" I demanded, my hands on my hips. I glared at the Indian.

He thrust the battered bucket toward me again. "Bizhi nehwe." His puckered eye glittered, and he pulled his walking stick out from under his arm and clutched it in his gnarled hand.

I decided not to argue any further. I snatched the bucket out of his hand and turned to survey the cellar. What else could he possibly want?

My eyes landed on the cream that had risen to the top of the milk pans. That must be it. I pulled my ladle across the pans several times over and dumped the cream into the Indian's bucket. Then I whirled around and shoved the bucket at him.

His good eye narrowed with suspicion before he lifted the bucket and tasted what was in it. He yanked the bucket away from his mouth and glared at me.

"Bizhi nehwe!" he shouted. Little flecks of cream spewed from his lips. He tossed the cream onto the ground and threw the bucket at me. I flung my arm up just in time to deflect it. It clattered to the floor, and the Indian gripped the head of his walking stick. He stared at me with his jaw thrust forward and his brows pulled down.

I stared back at him, breathing heavily. What else could he want? We had no whisky—no firewater. The flutterings of panic pushed away my anger, and I bent to retrieve the bucket. I had to get out of here. Maybe I could tell him that "bizhi nehwe" was upstairs, and then when I got there, I could run out of the house and escape.

I turned away from the Indian again, my mind working desperately. The back of my neck tingled with cold chills when I realized that if he got angry enough to take a swing at me with his stick, I wouldn't have anywhere to run.

My eyes flitted from the milk pans to the cream bowl to the milk pitcher to the butter molds. What could he be after?

Then my desperate eyes landed on the butter churn where the buttermilk waited patiently to be strained. Buttermilk! It was my last hope.

I dropped the bucket onto the ground, grabbed the butter churn, and tipped it over the bucket. The lumpy buttermilk splashed inside. I snatched the battered bucket and pushed it at the Indian. He wasted no time in tipping it up to his mouth.

There was nothing else for me to offer him. My eyes darted to the stairs. Could I push my way past him as he tasted this final offering and make my dash for freedom? With fear nipping at my heels, I didn't worry that I could outrun him, but would he be quick enough to grab me if I tried to squeeze past? Or would he hit me with his stick before I could get out of reach?

The Indian lowered the bucket and raised his hand to wipe the buttermilk from his lip. It was too late to run. He grunted. Then he turned and mounted the stairs on silent feet.

I nearly collapsed with relief. I'd finally guessed right.

I made myself wait until the stairwell was clear before I finally put a foot on the bottom step. When I reached the top, I slowed and peered around the doorjamb to see if the Indian was still lurking in the house. He was nowhere in sight.

I hurried to the door and looked out. The Indian was moving away, tipping the bucket up to his mouth every so often to take a swig of buttermilk.

I slammed the door and lowered the bar across it. Then I let myself shiver and shake a bit before I washed out the butter churn.

I wouldn't be riding today, or the next time the Seely's went into town, either. The next time they went shopping, I'd be going too.

In 1882, the Indians were less threatening to settlers than during the Black Hawk War but could still dish out a world of hurt if angered. Bothilda Hansen was a girl of sixteen, working at the Moroni "Rone" Seely house in Indianola when she was visited by an Indian man who was known for his strange ways. Bothilda had seen him threaten Indian girls who teased him by swinging his heavy walking stick at them. The Indian carried a bucket to Bothilda but spoke no English, so Bothilda had to guess what he wanted until she got it right.

Sources: *Saga of the Sanpitch*, vol. 6 (1974), 48; vol. 12 (1980), 105; vol. 17 (1985), 98.

Bizhe newhe: butter milk
Deschende: not good

INDIAN COURT

"But, Chief, you said that we should bring our problems to you and you'd take care of them," Little Dog said, turning his head so that he was looking at me from the sides of his eyes. I knew this evasive gesture. As sheriff, I'd dealt with Indians for quite some time.

It had been fifty years since Black Hawk signed the peace treaty, and the Indians and whites were pretty well used to each other by now. We'd had enough time to condition the Indians to our way of justice—the white man's method of holding a trial and using a jury to decide a person's guilt or innocence. The Indians' tradition was one of swift justice. If someone did wrong to you, then you did the same to them, or worse, as soon as possible.

"Little Dog, I've got to have evidence before I can take it to court."

"Isn't my dead brother enough evidence for you?" Little Dog said in a voice so soft that I could barely make out his words.

"I'm sorry," I said, and I meant it. "Your brother was a good man. It's just that I have to have some evidence of who killed him."

"It was Alchesay," Little Dog said, speaking the name of a tribesman who'd had brushes with the law before. "He's been jealous of Bear ever since he bought his own flock."

Bear had been a diligent sheep man, learning the trade while working as a herder for white men over the course of several years. Bear was an ambitious fellow, with a proud bearing and a quick mind. He saw that the new sheep industry was bringing in good returns for his white neighbors, so he worked and saved and bought himself a few sheep that he soon built into a small, yet prosperous flock.

Bear had been the one to dub his brother Little Dog, since he'd followed the older Bear around like a puppy. Little Dog had been known as Little Dog for so long that I don't think he even remembered his real name. I sure didn't.

Bear was known by some Indians and whites alike as Joe Standing Bear, but to Little Dog he was always Bear.

"When I find the evidence, I'll put Alchesay in jail," I said.

Little Dog gave me another sideways look before he turned and walked out of the door. I felt sorry for him, but there was nothing else I could do, so I went back to my paperwork.

The next day I was called out to Martin Begley's farm to look into some vandalism that had been done to his tractor. I spent some time questioning Martin before his wife called him into the house. I poked around looking for clues until Martin's son Henry came back from town.

"What'cha doing sheriff?"

"Someone came in the night and dented your dad's tractor. I'm checking into who might have done it. Did you hear anything last night?"

Henry Begley's ears turned red, and he ducked his head.

"Well, Sheriff, I'm afraid that it was me."

"You?"

"Yes, sir. I was going to tell Pa, I just didn't find the right time yet."

"Why didn't he know about this when it happened?"

Even though he wasn't quite a man, Henry stood as tall as me. "Well, maybe that's because I came out after he was gone to bed."

"What were you doing working in the dark?"

"Well, you know this is a new tractor, and Pa's been doing all the driving. I wanted to take it for a turn around the field myself. I figured that I'd get to drive it lots sooner if I just helped myself instead of waiting for him to say I could."

I raised my eyebrows at Henry, but it was he who spoke. "Yeah, I know. I'll probably never get to drive it now."

With the problem resolved, I headed back to my office. I was only about a mile out of the Begley's place, riding easy, when I spotted Alchesay on the side of the road, a cloth sack hanging heavy from one of his hands. When he looked up and saw me, he gave a guilty start. He clutched the sack to his chest, turned away, climbed a fence, and trotted off through a field.

"Alchesay!" He didn't look back but picked up his pace. I knew he'd heard me, and wondered if I should chase him down. I decided not to, but I'd be sure to talk to him about this later.

The next day I rode out past the Indian village and saw about a dozen men sitting in a circle. Little Dog was one of them. I got off my horse and walked over to them. All conversation ceased, and most of them ducked their heads to stare at their hands in their laps.

"Hey, how ya doing?"

No one answered me.

"You having a powwow?"

"Just talking," Little Dog said.

"About what?"

"Indian business."

I looked around at all the bowed heads. "Anything I can help with?" I asked.

"No," Little Dog said.

Something felt wrong here. I looked around at the gathering again, but no one would meet my eyes. There wasn't anything I could do about it. They weren't breaking any laws, as far as I could see.

"Anyone know where I might find Alchesay?" I asked.

A couple of heads turned to look at the others, but it was Little Dog who answered me. "No."

I waited a few more minutes. No one said anything, so I cleared my throat. "Well, call me if you need me," I said.

"Okay."

Silence.

I turned and walked back to my horse. It wasn't until I mounted and headed out that I glanced back and saw several of the Indians raise their heads to watch me leave.

Later that day, I spotted Alchesay crossing the street in front of the tobacco store.

"Hey, Alchesay," I called. He darted a look at me and he tensed, as though he might start running.

"Alchesay," I shouted again. "I need to talk to you."

His shoulders slumped, and I knew he'd stay put. When I got close to him, I smelled whiskey. If he'd been drinking, I may not get much information. On the other hand, the alcohol might loosen his tongue. I figured it was worth a try.

"Alchesay, I called out to you yesterday and you ran away from me."

"I didn't hear," he mumbled.

"I think you did."

Alchesay was silent.

"What was in the bag you carried?" I asked.

Alchesay shuffled his feet. I wasn't sure he was going to answer me, but I was determined to wait. At length, he said, "Feathers."

I was taken aback. "Feathers?"

Alchesay nodded.

"What did you want feathers for?"

Alchesay did not raise his head. "Fletching arrows."

It was a reasonable answer, since the Indians fastened feathers on their arrows in order to balance their flight through the air. Still,

Alchesay was being evasive. I knew it, but without evidence that he was guilty of anything besides carrying around a sack full of feathers, I couldn't arrest him.

"Next time you hear me calling, you stop. Understand?"

Alchesay nodded.

"If you don't, I'll put you in jail," I said.

Alchesay nodded again.

I turned and walked away. When I glanced behind me, Alchesay was gone.

It was later that same day that I got a report from Jeb Thomson that widow Marks was missing some hens. She'd been home alone and hadn't been able to get word out until Jeb rode by to check on her. He brought the report straight to me.

"She doesn't think it was a fox," Jeb said. "It looked like someone lifted the latch and snuck off with them."

Alchesay, I thought. He'd been moving away from Widow Marks' place when I saw him with the bag. It could just be a coincidence, but my gut instinct told me otherwise. Feathers. Ha. Feathers with chickens still attached was more like it.

"Okay, Jeb, thanks. I've got an idea of who to talk to about this."

Well, even if Alchesay might be getting away with murder, at least I could catch him for stealing chickens.

I stood up and got ready to go out to Alchesay's place when Mr. McCreedy came in pulling young Clem Fife by the arm, hollering about his broken window. Clem's mother was right behind them, crying her eyes out.

I couldn't just leave them like that, so we worked out the problem. Clem agreed to help Mr. McCreedy with some of his chores in order to pay for the broken glass.

By then it was supper time, and I went home to eat. There'd be time to deal with Alchesay in the morning.

The next day, I swung up on my horse and headed for the Indian village. I stopped the first Indian I saw and addressed him from the saddle of my horse. "Where's Alchesay?"

He shook his head but didn't speak. I rode a little further and saw two Indian women sitting in front of a house. "Have you seen Alchesay?" One woman looked at me with wide eyes full of shocked surprise. The other answered, "No," and tugged at the silent woman's skirt.

"You sure?" I asked.

"Yes." The women bent their heads over the buckskin they held spread across their laps.

Something was awfully strange. I slid down from my horse and walked him to the next yard. A familiar figure ducked around a corner of the house. "Little Dog?" I called. "Is that you?"

Little Dog came back into view with his back straight, but his eyes fixed on my horse instead of me.

"It's me."

"Have you seen Alchesay?"

Little Dog's eyes shifted up to my face and then darted away. "No," he said.

Something was wrong here, but I couldn't figure out what it was. I knew from experience that asking more questions at this point would get me nowhere. Alchesay was a flighty character, no question about that, but still, where else would he be if not here? Well, no matter. He was bound to show up sometime.

"If you see him, let me know. I need to ask him some questions."

Little Dog gave me a single nod. He flashed a glance up at me, and I caught a glimmer of knowing in his eyes. He knew something that he wasn't telling me. Even if I were to haul him in and lock him up—even if I were to resort to primitive torture—I sensed that he would never tell me his secret.

I headed back to my office, my mind puzzling over the look in Little Dog's eyes. I tried to make sense of it, and played over the past few days in my mind. He'd come to me looking for justice for his brother. I'd said it could take some time to get evidence, if there was even any to get, and it was plain that he'd been disappointed.

Then there was that meeting I'd interrupted a couple of days back, the meeting of a dozen braves sitting on the ground in a circle, with other Indians looking on. Why weren't all of them in the circle? That was the natural order of things, unless they were having a powwow inside a tepee. Then they would only include those who needed to be there.

A dozen. There was something significant in that, I was sure of it, but the meaning escaped me.

I thought back to Alchesay running with a sack full of feathers, which must have been stolen chickens or I'd swallow my own boot. I'd seen Alchesay just the day before. He couldn't have gone far.

I reached the sheriff's office and took care of my horse, before stepping inside. Jeb Thompson was waiting for me.

"Sheriff, I got that list of men you wanted, the ones for the jury."

I stopped, my heart pounding hard against my ribs. I suddenly remembered why the number twelve was so significant. There were twelve men on a jury.

I never saw Alchesay again.

An Indian was murdered by another Indian in the early 1900s. Since the white men did nothing about it, an Indian council convened and voted on who they believed the guilty man to be. A few days later, the man named as guilty disappeared and was never heard of again.

Source: *Saga of the Sanpitch*, vol. 28 (1996), 41.

FROM LITTLE THINGS

Christine pulled another paper off the stack at her elbow and centered it on the table in front of her. She tried to decipher the blotchy scrawls that wormed across the page, but she was too tired to make any sense of it. She pushed the paper aside and stood up, placing her hands upside down on the small of her back to stretch out the kinks.

There was no better job in the world than that of schoolmistress, but sometimes it was hard. When she had students who struggled with their work, she felt their frustration. She imagined that for some of the younger children, learning the alphabet was like her trying to learn the Indian language. She'd never been able to make sense of their syllables, and wondered if she ever would.

There was time enough for papers later. Right now she just wanted to go to bed.

Before she reached the bedroom where her husband was already sleeping, Christine heard a knock on her door. It startled her, but she wasn't surprised. She often had callers at odd hours, because she had done some doctoring in the settlement and was said to have "the touch."

Now her interest in who was here and what the problem was chased her fatigue away. She moved to the door and pulled it open. She gasped at what she saw and took a step back.

The huge Indian brave at her door followed her in, seeming to take her retreat as an invitation to enter. Christine stared at the man, hoping he wasn't to be her patient. Then she noticed a small bundle clasped in the giant's arms. The little Indian baby was such a small thing, and it was so quiet. Its little mouth was open and it struggled to breathe. From the sheen of sweat on its small forehead, Christine guessed that the child was suffering from fever.

Without a second thought, Christine held her hands out toward the sick baby. The Indian handed him to her, and said something in his own tongue that Christine could not understand.

"Yes, he's got a fever," she said, even though she doubted that the Indian understood her.

Christine took the baby and pulled a tablecloth off the shelf. She tossed the tablecloth on the table without unfolding it and laid the baby on it. She looked inside the little mouth, and felt the baby's head. "Oh, you are so sick," she crooned to the infant, who lay silently sweating and staring up with big, black eyes. His innocence and obvious misery tugged at Christine's heart.

"Him sick. Make well," the Indian said.

Christine guessed that the boy had been suffering for some time, since he seemed to have lost his will to even cry. He merely lay there, struggling for air, waiting for the end to come with a patience that was far beyond his years.

Christine turned to the stove and slid some wood inside, checking the teakettle to make sure that it had water in it. Steam could help the baby breathe easier, but she needed to do something for his fever. She tried an alcohol rub, which made the little boy gasp and the whites of his eyes show all around the dark irises. He trembled and shook. Christine wrapped him up again and held him close, carrying him over to the now steaming teakettle. She lifted the kettle off of the stove and carried it back to the table.

"Bring me a bowl," she said, pointing to the cupboard. The Indian strode over to the cupboard, picked up a bowl, and brought it back to Christine. Then he folded his arms and watched as Christine poured hot water into the bowl and made a makeshift tent with another tablecloth. As she worked, she spoke to the baby in soft tones, murmuring reassurances that he would be fine, that he shouldn't worry, and that she would do her best to take care of him.

Christine grabbed a handful of dried poplar bark and dropped it into the bowl of boiling hot water.

In spite of the steam tent, the baby's breathing became shallower.

"No, little one, hang on," Christine said.

The baby closed his big, dark eyes.

Christine turned to the big Indian and looked up at him through eyes wet with tears. "Your baby is very sick. I am afraid that he will die."

Christine tensed as the Indian stared at the child, and then back at her. He looked again at the baby, and lifted his chin toward his son, as though telling her to get back to work.

"Him sick," he said.

Christine wished that she had some beef kidney; even if she did, she sensed that there wasn't time to heat it and tie it to the boy's feet in order to draw the fever out. It was simply too late.

Christine dipped a cloth in cool water, squeezed it out, and wiped the baby's sweating brow with it. The boy sighed, and was still.

Christine stared down at the dark little body. Tears escaped her eyes and slid down her cheeks. She hadn't even known this boy two hours ago, yet the time she'd just spent trying to make him well had nestled him into her heart. Now her chest squeezed with pain at the loss of this little spirit.

A brown arm reached past Christine and scooped up the boy as though he were a rag doll. Christine whipped around, her eyes blazing through her tears. "You treat him with respect."

The Indian stared at her through his dark inscrutable eyes but didn't answer. He turned and carried his son out the door and disappeared into the darkness.

Only after they were gone did Christine have the sense to realize that she should have been scared. Yet the Indian had not taken his frustration at the death of his son out on her. At least, he hadn't yet. He might come back later to settle the score.

But Christine didn't think so.

Weary in spirit and body, Christine crawled into bed beside her husband.

Two weeks later, the news of an Indian killed several miles south reached the settlement. It was rumored that the Indians were on the warpath and out for revenge. Even though Christine hadn't seen the Indian father since he'd left her house, she wondered if he, too, held revenge in his heart. She listened with growing trepidation to the reports of the whites who were killed. After several battles that took lives from both sides, the whites and Indians settled into an uneasy truce.

One evening when she was home alone, Christine heard a knock on her door. "Who's there?" she asked.

"Open door." The deep command could only have come from an Indian.

Christine shrank back. "What do you want?"

The Indian spoke again, but through the solid wooden door, his words made no sense to Christine. Then there was a heavy silence. At last, the voice said, "Him sick, make well."

Christine's heart all but stopped. Was the baby's father back for revenge?

The Indian spoke again. "Open door."

There was something so compelling in the voice that Christine moved toward the door. She stared at it, her heart tripping over a little burst of fear. The latchstring was out.

She realized that the Indian could have pulled on the latchstring and let himself in at any time. This small detail reassured her, and Christine pulled the door open.

The big Indian stood there, much as he had on their first meeting, but she almost didn't recognize him. His face was painted and he carried a bow in one hand. Her heart faltered.

"We come," the Indian said, walking his fingers through the air. "You no fear. You no sick." He formed his arms in a protective circle in front of his body, and shifted the quiver of arrows on his shoulder. Christine flinched. The Indian shook his bow at her. "I watch, you stay well," he said.

Christine was confused. The Indian must have seen it on her face, because he said again, slowly and distinctly, "You well."

He turned and left. Christine shut the door and pulled the latchstring inside. Then she sat and stared at the door, waiting for her husband to get home.

It wasn't until the next day that Christine learned that there had been a raid on the settlement. Livestock were stolen, and some of the men who'd gone out intent on saving the animals had been shot. Lee Johnson's barn was burned to the ground, and the Dunbars lost all their poultry after the Indians killed their dog.

Christine hurried out to help the wounded. When she applied a poultice to Stan Severne's wounded leg, her brow creased with worry, hoping against hope that the treatment could save the leg from amputation.

Stan looked up at her and said, "Who's your Injun friend?"

Christine's startled eyes flew to Stan's face. "What?"

"Yer Injun friend. After I took that arrow, I laid there on the ground for the longest time, pretending I was dead so they wouldn't kill me for real. I saw him standing in front of yer house, bow and arrow ready, waving his fellows on past yer place if they got too close. How'd you get your own Injun guard?"

Christine didn't tell him. Her heart swelled so big with gratitude that it was difficult to speak. The Indian knew that she'd tried to help his baby, not kill him. She was glad that he had understood her intentions, and she felt relief in knowing that she had a big, strong Indian ally.

Mrs. John McAllister tells this story based on her grandmother's life. Around the 1850s, Christine did her best to save the life of an Indian baby but wasn't able to. The baby's father took the baby away from her house without a word.

Later, when the Indians attacked the settlement, the baby's father stood guard over Christine's house and wouldn't let any harm come to her.

Source: *Saga of the Sanpitch*, vol. 2 (1970), 35.

ABOUT THE AUTHOR

Shirley Bahlmann grew up among different ethnic groups in New Jersey, but she didn't have any experience with Native Americans until she was named honorary "Princess Roan Eagle" of the Sioux tribe. After her family moved, she was fascinated to find Native American placement students in her new school, and she even struck up a friendship with Loretta Nez, who taught her a few Navajo words.

Shirley prefers the country smells of horse and cow manure to the city aromas of gas fumes and fast food. She lives in rural Utah with her husband, Bob. They are the parents of six sons—Andy, Jeff, Scott, Zackary, Brian, and Michael. And she's delighted to have daughters-in-law and grandchildren.

Check out what Shirley is up to at www.shirleybahlmann.com.

0 26575 12340 1